AD ASTRA

THE 50TH ANNIVERSARY SFWA COOKBOOK

EDITED BY
CAT RAMBO AND FRAN WILDE

AD ASTRA: THE 50TH ANNIVERSARY SFWA COOKBOOK

Edited by Cat Rambo and Fran Wilde.
© 2015 Science Fiction and Fantasy Writers of America, Inc.

Cover design by Sherin Nicole.
Cover art by Kirsty Pargeter.

Print ISBN: 978-0-9828467-1-1
Ebook ISBN: 978-0-9828467-2-8

SFWA, INC.
P.O. Box 3238
Enfield, CT 06083-3238

ACKNOWLEDGEMENTS

With thanks to:

Progenitors: Greg and Astrid Bear

Testers: Beth Cato, Cynthia Felice, Lee Hallison, Megan Hutchins,
Steven H Silver, Alexis Latner, Rachel Kleinsorge, Christian Klaver

Above and Beyond: Sean Wallace and Paula Guran

Proofreading: Jennifer Melchert

DEDICATION

To:
Anne McCaffrey
Jeanne Gomoll
James Tiptree, Jr.
Greg & Astrid Bear
and all the cooks

In memoriam:
Jay Lake
Eugie Foster
Ann Crispin

CONTENTS

Sweet Snacks and Desserts

Beverages

Brunches

Potluck Dishes

Extras

About the Contributors
199

*Badger Artwork throughout by Ursula Vernon
and M.C.A. Hogarth*

FOREWORD

Within the science fiction and fantasy community, writers work wherever they can find a table, often among friends, virtual and face to face. It's a blend of friendship and business, of celebration and craft. It's messy sometimes. It's beautiful.

In celebration of fifty years of the Science Fiction and Fantasy Writers of America, *Ad Astra: The 50th Anniversary SFWA Cookbook* has collected recipes old and new from writers across the span of its membership. But this is more than just a cookbook. What you hold in your hands is a historical document. You'll find a history of SF/F entertaining that goes back more than fifty years. Some of it is funny; some (like the bash cake/Mars colony cake), is itself a historical document; some of it is conversations between multiple writers. Some of it is written in fanciful, or . . . colorful language.

Here be Dragons.

Not everyone we wished to include are within these pages. But many are. We hope many more are to come in future cookbooks.

We are happy to have been part of the long tradition of science fiction and fantasy cookbooks. All proceeds from *Ad Astra: The 50th Anniversary SFWA Cookbook* will go towards the SFWA Legal Fund, supporting writers in need for many years.

EDITORS' NOTES

You hold in your hand something very special: *Ad Astra: The 50th Anniversary SFWA Cookbook*. It holds a wealth of recipes from our community, including some who are, sadly, gone but certainly not forgotten. It is a diverse range, but all of them have something in common: they have been contributed as much from a love for SFWA as any love of cooking (or eating).

Our loose theme is "Party!"; it was a natural choice for a 50th anniversary cookbook, but it also seemed appropriate because of something else I know well: writers know how to party. They know how to celebrate, how to take a threadbare moment and make it a splendid occasion, how to cobble together a party from a pan of brownies and a candle. They know that a party isn't just props—it's an attitude as well.

And our members provided their favorite party dishes for this cookbook— whether the party is for one or for a horde: divided into sweet snacks and savory, drinks of all kinds, brunch food (for the morning after the party), potluck dishes, and more.

Some are economical, some not so much.* Some are easy to make, others a bit more complicated, but many are favorites of their contributors—and they may well become favorites of yours as well.

Some of the recipes were collected by Astrid and Greg Bear as part of an earlier cookbook that never made it to the printer; I'm happy to see them presented here for the first time. And the cookbook itself, of course, is an homage to the two cookbooks edited by Anne McCaffrey in earlier years, *Serve It Forth* and *Cooking Out of This World*.

In all of this effort, I had a fabulous co-conspirator, Fran Wilde. This cookbook, which wouldn't be here without her, is our invitation to you—celebrate SFWA with us this year, and in years to come. Good appetites to you all.

Cat Rambo, Seattle, 2015

*All recipes are certified fairy-free.

—

Putting a cookbook together is a bit like throwing a party: you plan, you try to stay organized, and you look forward to seeing old friends and meeting new ones. Sometimes things go off-plan, sometimes you find a piece of cake or a spare guest pressed between the sofa cushions a few days after.

Similarly, working with someone else on a party or a cookbook makes everything more fun. Many thanks to my co-editor Cat Rambo for all the late-night, cross-country conversations it took to pull this cookbook together.

One thing I've learned from three years of hosting the interview series *Cooking the Books* (franwilde.wordpress.com/cooking-the-books/) is that the unexpected adds spice—both in food and in conversation. You'll find within these pages both the familiar and the unexpected. Several of the recipes within come from *Cooking the Books*, and I want to thank those authors for agreeing to share their thoughts again here. Thanks as well, and in no little part, to everyone who sent in a recipe, offered to help in the kitchen, and to you, who are taking the time to use the book. We hope you find it delicious.

Fran Wilde, Philadelphia, 2015

—

CHARLES BROWN'S ADVICE ON COOKING
via Connie Willis

The most valuable cooking advice I ever got was from Charles N. Brown, the editor of *Locus*, who said you can be a great cook by starting with a very simple recipe or something you eat in a restaurant, figuring out why you like it, and then adding more of that.

We were eating some of his terrific asparagus at the time, which he made by microwaving it, then drizzling a little sesame seed oil and some soy sauce over it. Best asparagus ever!

I took his advice to heart, and use it on everything from spaghetti sauce (take a jar of Blue Parrot sauce, add crumbled fried Italian sausage and fresh garlic) to salsa (take a jar of grocery store salsa and add fresh cilantro, chopped tomatoes, and chopped green onions) to my favorite guacamole (mash up a bunch of avocados and squeeze the juice of an orange into it). I'm not kidding. Best guacamole ever, and my *Primeval*-watching buddies agree with me. (NOTE: Did you honestly think I'd get through this without a reference to my favorite TV series ever? BBC's *Primeval*, starring Andrew-Lee Potts and Ben Miller. Dinosaurs in modern-day London. Oh, and since all this great food advice came from Charles Brown, I guess I should plug *his* favorite TV series ever: *Buffy the Vampire Slayer*, though *Primeval* is better. But only because the show has such a great ending!)

Anyway, Charles's food advice was terrific, just like all the advice he gave me on writing and writing careers and life in general, though you'd expect him to be especially good on the subject of food. He loved to eat and loved food! *Bon appétit!*

COCKTAIL LABORATORY
Carrie Vaughn

We're living in something of an alcohol golden age—dozens of varieties of wine are available from all over the world, the craft beer movement has matured and expanded, and craft distilleries are on the rise, making small-batch and vintage liquors. Vintage cocktails like the Aviation are coming back into vogue, and infused alcohols are expanding what's possible in the world of mixed drinks. What's a budding connoisseur to do, especially when the only drink you've ever ordered is a gin and tonic?

The answer is: Cocktail Laboratory.

This isn't about drinking for the sake of drinking, this isn't about drinking to get drunk: this is realizing that there's a lot more to liquor than rum and Cokes. For almost all of human history, people have fermented or distilled just about anything that was possible to ferment and distill, and the resulting possibilities in flavors and effects are pretty much endless. In a word, this is all about SCIENCE. And fun parties. But mostly science. (That's my story and I'm sticking to it.)

> *"The difference between screwing around and science is writing it down."*—Adam Savage

How to Conduct Cocktail Laboratory

• The experiments: Make a list of drink recipes you want to try. This will determine your shopping list of base liquors, mixers, and garnishes. Go shopping.

• The lab bench: Clear counter space near a sink. A big bucket of clean ice for drinking should be handy. There should also be a place to dispose of juiced lemons and limes and other detritus.

• Good tools to have on hand: shakers, jiggers, measuring cups, stirrer, juicer, ice tongs, a grater for garnishes like nutmeg, and a towel to dry up messes. The tools don't have to be fancy, they just have to work. Bowler hat and curly mustache are optional.

• IMPORTANT: Plastic shot/taster cups. I first encountered these at a distillery tasting—little disposable taster cups. They're available at many large liquor stores. By limiting portions, you can limit alcohol intake and prevent overindulging when you really do only want a taste. Mix one serving of a drink, split it out among five or six taster cups, and imbibe a fraction of the alcohol you would otherwise. And when you've mixed a drink that everyone ends up despising, you haven't wasted a bunch of ingredients making that drink several times over.

• It's best to have just one or two people involved in the actual mixing—it keeps things neater and reduces the chaos.

• Write each recipe on an index card. On the back of each card, everyone who tries that recipe notes their opinion. This is very important, because this is the whole point of the experiment: what do people like? What do they not like? Which recipes should you throw out, and which should become part of your repertoire, to memorize and take to other parties and impress people during games of stump the bartender? At our first Cocktail Laboratory, we were saved from disaster several times when we flipped over an index card and realized that not only had we already made that drink—everyone hated it. And remember, writing it down means SCIENCE.

• Taking notes also makes this a social activity—participants discuss what they've been drinking, clarify their opinions, argue (politely), and discover that the reason there are dozens of different liquors and thousands of different drink combinations is because there are about that many different palates and tastes. (And if someone doesn't like gin, there is absolutely nothing you can do to it to make them like it. Trust me, I've tried.)

• As always, drink responsibly. Have a designated driver.

VARIATIONS

• Focus on one kind of liquor. Do side-by-side tastings of different labels of rum, gin, vodka, scotch, or absinthe, for example. Choose one cocktail—gin and tonics, vodka martinis, brandy Alexanders—and make the drink with different brands of liquor. You might be amazed at how different the same ingredients can taste when the formulation of the base alcohol is just a little different.

• Choose a theme. Pirate rum punches. 1920s Speakeasy with Prohibition-era cocktails (this is when the cocktail really came into its own—they had to make that bathtub gin palatable somehow). Tiki bar drinks. Cocktails of the future. Have everyone mix their own version of the Pan Galactic Gargle Blaster.

• Non-alcoholic alternatives: Those among us who don't drink alcohol can still have fun, because the varieties of possible non-alcoholic mixed drinks are also endless. Use every kind of fruit juice imaginable, including more exotic varieties like pomegranate juice, guava, and so on. Mix with tonic, club soda, other kinds of soda. With a blender and frozen fruit, you can add smoothies to the repertoire. Discover the joys of ginger syrup, or floral syrups like rose and lavender. Mix ginger syrup with a little club soda and lemonade, over ice, and you've discovered something a character in a fantasy novel might drink. Mix and match, and always take notes so you can replicate your results. Remember, this is SCIENCE.

A FEW RECIPES

Aviation

The story goes this drink got its name from its pale sky-blue color. It was popular in the days of Lindberg and Earhart, when airplanes started getting really sexy. Every one of these I've made has been more lavender colored than blue, but it's still a great, zingy gin drink, an alternative to the standard martini.

- 1 1/2 oz gin
- 1/2 oz crème de violette
- 1/4 oz maraschino liquor
- Juice of 1/2 lemon

Place ingredients over ice in a cocktail shaker. Shake well, strain into glass.

Brandy Alexander

A decadent parlor drink, perfect for conversing around the fire in the dead of winter.

- 1/2 oz crème de cacao
- 1/2 oz brandy
- 1/2 oz heavy cream

Shake with ice, pour into glass. Garnish with freshly-grated nutmeg.

Jack Rose

This has become one of my favorite kick-back-at-the-end-of-the-day indulgent drinks. It's tangy, fruity, and packs a bit of a punch.

- 2 1/2 oz applejack
- 3/4 oz lemon juice
- dash of grenadine

Shake with ice.

Green Russian

I'm not a fan of straight absinthe, but the possibility of making mixed drinks with absinthe was a revelation to me. It turns standard cocktails into something weird and intriguing.

- 3 oz heavy cream
- 1 1/2 oz vodka
- 1 tsp absinthe
- 1 tsp sugar

Mix gently in a highball glass, add ice, and garnish with mint leaves.

Ginger Syrup (non-alcoholic)

I love this recipe, because it tells you how to make any kind of syrup. Add a few teaspoons of ginger syrup to a glass of club soda to make your own ginger ale. Even better, coat the ginger slices you strain out with sugar to make candied ginger for garnish.

- 3/4 cup peeled and thinly sliced fresh ginger
- 1 cup sugar
- 1 cup water

Add ingredients to a saucepan, then bring to a simmer over medium to low heat, stirring frequently, until sugar is dissolved. Simmer, uncovered, for thirty minutes. Strain out ginger. Let syrup cool. Store syrup in a glass container and refrigerate. (To make simple syrup, a common drink ingredient, just boil the sugar and water.)

IRISH COFFEE
(AKA: How to create an Irish Coffee Bar)
LARRY NIVEN

You wouldn't think it would take much effort would you? Irish coffee has only four ingredients! Serving only Irish coffee is work for an idiot, if others are doing all the work except pouring.

The first Irish coffee bar opened on Sunday night of the 1985 LosCon. I offered because I thought it might be fun. Emotionally I was prepared for failure. Nobody had tried this before. Subsequent LosCons have featured an Irish coffee bar on Saturday night. Oddly enough, it changes nothing.

In a pinch you can always go to hotel coffee. We almost did. I brought my Bunn coffeemaker, and remembered to bring all the other stuff: filters and filter cones and pots and all that (though not plates and spoons.) Then I cut the cord on the coffeemaker by slamming it in the lid of my trunk! Committee member Bob Null repaired it on the spot.

Quantities were guesswork. I poured by hand, and tasted often, trying to get the proportions right. Hic. Excuse me. I've had to do that every time, because the Committee keeps changing the size of the cups on me.

I learned of another problem the first time I tried this outside LosCon. Is the kid old enough to drink? Did I offer to bartend in order to tell a reader and fan what he can't have? I did not. The woman who helped me out in Dallas and Houston was tough enough to do that part of the job for me. In Los Angeles I've had to refuse two or three customers; but we had to insult scores of them in Texas. Then again, those were comic conventions ...

What follows is my recipe for Elsewhere-Cons. If I can drive, I have another list; I can bring some of my own equipment. You should consider doing the same.

The proportions were developed by experiment, after I realized that I can mix bigger quantities in a nice stable measuring cup and then pour into whatever cups the committee have brought me. Proportions are a matter of taste. Feel free to fiddle.

I like stable cups that don't tip over when I pour. I never get them, but that's what I want. The whipped cream should not be too stiff to flow; you want it to melt a little on the coffee. Brandy or rum work as alternatives to Irish, but use less sugar. Don't add sugar if you're using liqueurs instead of Irish, and resign yourself to not using very much until the Irish runs out or the line thins, because you have to keep explaining what it's for.

The two most important rules are these:

1) You should run out of booze first. You'd feel like an idiot running out of whipped cream or ground coffee or sugar or cups when there's two bottles of whiskey left. (Once or twice the Committee has had to search a darkened city for whipped cream or cups.)

2) The booze should run out before the bartender collapses. Rather than staggering off to bed after spilling too many drinks in a row, you should be forced to quit while there's still time to join a party or a filking group.

Why bother? Put it this way. You've worked your tale off to become a well-known author. If you came to a convention, you came to be admired, like the rest of us. It gives you back your motivation. You'll work better afterward.

But they make you scintillate wherever you go. They stop you for autographs and pop quizzes on your work, in the halls and at parties and even in the restaurant! Anyone who ever stood in an autograph line thinks you should remember his name. Enough of that can wipe the smile off your face and make you forget how to string words together . . . and they still expect you to be witty.

What can you do at a convention, in public, that will take you off the hook for a while?

This was one of the brightest ideas I ever had. Nobody expects me to scintillate. They expect me to pour; nothing else. When the Irish runs out, then I'm ready to scintillate again.

Irish Coffee Requirements for Elsewhere-Cons

Proportions
- 1/4 c Irish whiskey
- 3/4 c strong coffee
- 1 heaping T sugar

First time: stir like hell, then taste, then adjust. Keep it sweet. Pour cups half-full or better then add a glob of whipping cream. If it tastes too strong, you may want to use less booze; but try making the coffee stronger first!

Filling the cup may be a mistake. If it's big and tall, it may topple over.

Tools

To serve 200 cups I will need:

- 8 bottles Irish whiskey (Jamesons or Bushmills)
- 1 bottle Sambuca or Gran Marnier or almost any liqueur that isn't fruity (interesting variants).
- 4 lb Mocha Java coffee, ground fine for the Bunn coffeemaker
- 5 qt heavy cream
- 4 lb brown sugar (or Demerara or white sugar; but white is your last choice.)
- A refrigerator for the cream, or just a container of ice; no big deal here.
- *Working room!* A stretch of counter, or a big table. The more room I have to work in, the better, up to a point.
- Three hundred or more cups. (Yes, I said I'd make 200. I could be wrong. Running out of cups has nothing to recommend it.) Use foam plastic. Better: there are plastic cups with handles, and they look more elegant than the foam cups, and they're stable. Don't buy thin plastic that will burn a customer's fingers if there's hot stuff in it!
- A sink is nice. Otherwise someone has to keep going for water for the coffee.
- A garbage can or wastebasket. It takes either a big one, or many, or one that gets emptied frequently (not by the bartender).
- *Help!* The LosCon event was a dead dog party that started at 8:00 p.m. I looked up at a line like the autograph line at a Worldcon! I needed a permanent volunteer to make the coffee and whip the cream, continually, and things still didn't slow down until 20 minutes before the Irish ran out.
- Mixing bowl and mixer for the cream.
- A bowl for sugar. (Digging into the box slows me down.)
- Bunn coffeemaker, with all accessories: plastic cone and many paper filters. OR anything that makes coffee.
- Containers for coffee: 3 glass carafes and 1 thermos worked out fine.
- At least 2 large spoons (tablespoons or thereabouts).
- At least 2 plates to put them on.
- Measuring spoons for coffee. Use large ones.
- A jigger.

NOTES: I WILL BRING MY OWN MUG or buy one at the Convention. (I'm entitled to a perk and that's it. Also I'm likely to lose track of which drink is mine.)

CLEANING UP IS SOMEBODY ELSE'S JOB.

JENNIFER & RICH'S SPRING PIG ROAST
Jennifer Stevenson

Every spring we throw a pig roast. The first time, we did it for our 25th wedding anniversary. I heavily researched pig roasts and found several ways to roast a pig, but only one that was practicable for us.

The ones that wouldn't work, briefly:

Cuban style, in the ground. Dig a hole four or five feet deep. Line the bottom with stones heated on a grill. Fill the pig with fruit, sew it shut, then wrap it in banana leaves and then burlap. Lower the pig onto the hot stones. Cover with dirt. In 24 hours, dig it up. Makes an incredibly tender roast pig. Usually used with "suckling pigs" or young pigs, about 40 pounds.

Mississippi style, above ground. Also doable if you live in Florida and can't dig a hole because, 12 inches down, you hit the Atlantic Ocean. Build a rectangular enclosure two cinderblocks high on level ground. The drippings will attract animals, so don't do this near your house. Bolt together an H-shaped frame out of heavy angle-iron. The ends of the H should overlap the cinderblock by a foot. Lay a sheet of chain link fencing over this and U-bolt it securely to the frame. Now it's ready for the pig. Get the butcher to butterfly an adult pig, 300+ pounds. You want a mature, fattier pig because this is a dry cooking method. Spread it open and wire it to your frame in many places. (Once it starts cooking, bits will try to drop off.) Cook it surrounded by but not over coals, covered with a plywood tent, for 24 hours or more. Have lots of booze handy for the minders. It always takes longer than you expect.

Because we don't have room for a cinderblock enclosure and you can't dig a foot down anywhere in our yard without hitting tree roots, we use a smoker.

My husband built a smoker out of two steel 55-gallon drums. He sliced the drums lengthwise, then welded the ends of each half together to make two 70-inch half-cylinders. He put the completed cylinder together with hinges. He built a table-height steel frame, with wheels, and set the cylinder into the frame so the top opens like a clamshell. Holes went into the top half of the cylinder for vents, with covers to help tweak the temperature inside, and for a metal meat thermometer.

Inside the cylinder he mounted a 60-inch steel spit made of heavy pipe with holes drilled through it at one-foot intervals. He rigged the spit to a motor that makes one revolution per minute. This is a nice, slow, even rate that exposes the pig to heat without burning it.

I order my pig two or three days in advance. I keep the feet and head on, although you can order yours without these lifelike appendages. After long practice I stick to 40-45 pounds. I pick it up the day before and ice it overnight.

I also say a little prayer over it because, although I'm not a vegetarian, I'm aware that this specific pig was killed just for me at my order, and I want it to know that every bit of it will be deeply appreciated and it will be the star of the party, the object of everyone's admiration and enjoyment.

The morning of the pig roast, I wash the pig inside and out and salt it. Rich and I hook the spit through the pig, in at the butthole and out the jaws. (Usually I have to pry the jaws open a bit.) Rich drills through the pig's back, then runs threaded steel dowel down through the pig, through the holes in the spit, and out the open underside of the pig. He affixes nuts to the dowel to keep it in place. He then belts the pig to the spit with steel wire and uses wire to anchor the dowel. This is important, because as the pig cooks it will soften, and cooked bits will start to fall off. He trusses the front feet reaching forward and the back feet flying back so that the pig is stretched out long. This keeps its toes out of the fire.

Next, I fill the cavity with spears of red Jamaican papaya. If I feel rich I add pineapple. Then I sew the cavity shut using stout fiber dental floss (NOT plastic!), a leathermaker's needle, rubber gloves, and a pair of pliers to push and pull the needle through the thick skin.

Now the pig is clean, salted, spitted, stuffed, and sewn up. Because a 40-pounder is only about four feet long, there's room on the spit for a few ducks, which I wash, salt, prick all over, and spit. These also are wired on with dowel. They will cook quickly and can be removed and eaten at the point when everything smells wonderful but pork is several hours away.

Bonus: I put empty foil trays under the ducks to collect duck drippings.

Carefully we mount the spit in the smoker, which has been preheated with very few hot coals. Rich rearranges the coals along the sides, not under the pig, maybe adds a few coals, and closes the clamshell. The pig is now in an L5-shaped vessel headed for a lot of stomachs. For eight hours Rich checks the temperature frequently to keep the interior of the smoker at 200°-225°F, adding coals a handful at a time, ensuring the pig isn't slipping, burning, or otherwise misbehaving. This method uses about 50 pounds of charcoal briquets. Toward the end he inserts meat thermometers in the shoulder and the hip, which cook slowest where meat and bone are thickest. Also, he now raises the heat to 250°-300°F.

After about eight hours, we remove the spit from the smoker and lay it on a long narrow table (plywood on saw-horses) covered with heavy plastic sheeting. The spit is removed. The stitches are snipped on the pig's cavity, the fruit removed to a platter, and then the skin is removed, not without swearing because it's piping hot. Someone calls dibs on the skin and sets it aside to take home for chicharrones. Someone calls dibs on the head and feet to take home for head cheese.

If we had the patience, we would let the pig cool, but we haven't. Wearing thick rubber gloves, we pull the meat off the carcass in strips. Pulled meat is juicier than sliced. And then the locusts descend.

HOSTING A PRANCING PONY PARTY
Ken Schneyer & Janice Okoomian

Most years since 2007, on a date as close to September 29th as we can manage, Janice and I host a party to commemorate Frodo's arrival in Bree. About an hour before sunset, we take our guests on a hike through the nearby woods. When we return, with the light fading and a nip in the air, the house has been transformed into an inn, with three or four separate tables lit by candles. We then serve a meal designed to simulate the supper the hobbits ate at the Prancing Pony:

> *They were washed and in the middle of good deep mugs of beer when Mr. Butterbur and Nob came in again. In a twinkling the table was laid. There was hot soup, cold meats, a blackberry tart, new loaves, slabs of butter, and half a ripe cheese: good plain food, as good as the Shire could show, and homelike enough to dispel the last of Sam's misgivings (already much relieved by the excellence of the beer).*

We usually read that passage aloud (starting somewhat earlier in the chapter). We put the food in a central location, buffet style. There is much singing and merriment.

As for the food and drink—

Good Deep Mugs of Beer

Usually there are two beers, an ale and a stout, and we pour these into pitchers the moment we get back from the hike. We also have a pitcher of cider for the kids and teetotallers. We use whatever mugs or tankards we have in the house, although in a pinch we'll use glasses.

Hot Soup (Ken's Onion Soup)

Make in mid-afternoon, the day of the party.
- 8-10 large onions, ideally red and yellow onions mixed
- 3 T olive oil
- 48 oz broth (I prefer beef broth, but vegetable broth works too.)
- 1 T flour
- 4 oz vermouth
- Salt and pepper to taste

Cut the onions into rounds or thin wedges.

Heat the olive oil in a large pot (12 quarts or bigger). Add the onions and cook at a medium-high heat, stirring frequently, until they begin to brown. (This will take a long time.)

Add the flour and stir until it is well mixed.

Add the broth and vermouth, and bring to a boil.

Lower the heat, cover, and simmer for at least 30 minutes, preferably longer, stirring occasionally.

If the soup appears to need it, you can add some more broth or hot water.

Salt and pepper to taste.

Keep the soup warm on the stove during the hike.

Cold Meats

We usually get three different meats from a local deli. Or, you can roast and chill them yourself. For atmosphere, we present the meats whole on the board so that guests can slice them themselves. Usually we serve roast beef, ham, and turkey breast. We've also used pepperoni and salami.

Barliman Butterbur's Blackberry Tart (Janice's Recipe)

This recipe makes two tarts. I used one tart pan and one cheesecake pan (the latter having a smaller diameter, so the crust and filling were deeper). Start the day before the party (or earlier).

Crust: Pâté Sucrée (*The New James Beard*, p. 510)

- 2 c flour
- 1 egg yolk
- 6 T frozen butter, cut in 1 T pieces
- 1 T cold water
- 1/8 t salt
- 2 T sugar

Put all ingredients into food processor. Turn machine on and off rapidly several times. Then continue processing for a couple of minutes, until a ball of dough forms.

Divide into two balls and chill overnight.

Preheat oven to 450°F.

Roll out one ball of pastry and put it into a tart pan. Prick the bottom of one shell, then line it with foil and weight in down with raw rice or beans.

Bake 14-16 minutes until the bottom is set and the edges lightly browned.

After the initial baking, remove the shell from the oven, remove the lining, and return to the oven for about 2 minutes, which will seal the bottom and prevent a soggy crust. Remove to a wire rack to cool.

Roll out and bake the second crust as above, using the same foil and rice.

Filling (adapted from *The New James Beard*, p. 510 and *Sundays at Moosewood*, p. 560)

- About 9 c blackberries (9 small boxes)
- About 3/4 c water
- 2 T black currant liqueur

- 2 c sugar
- About 3 T cornstarch, dissolved in 2 T water

Put aside one box of berries.

Put the other eight boxes of berries, the water, sugar, and liqueur in a saucepan, bring to a boil, and simmer.

When the berries have become soft and have started to come apart, add the cornstarch-water mixture. Stir, and simmer for about ten more minutes, until the mixture is thickened.

Divide mixture into half and pour into tart crusts. Take the last box of blackberries, cut them in half if they are excessively large, and press the fresh halves into the filling in each crust.

Chill for several hours. Can be served at room temperature.

New Loaves (Ken's Recipe)

Partially adapted from Beard on Bread, *p. 101. Start the morning of the party, or the day before.* Makes 2-4 loaves.

- 2 packages active dry yeast (I prefer quick-rise varieties)
- 2 t granulated sugar (honey works too)
- 2 1/2 c warm water (100°F to 115°F)
- 4 T butter
- 1/4 c molasses
- 2 T salt
- 7 c white flour
- 1 1/2 c whole wheat flour
- 1 1/2 c rye flour
- If using a baking stone and pizza peel: cornmeal to cover them.

Dissolve the yeast and sugar in 1/2 cup warm water in a large bowl and let proof for five minutes. Five minutes should be enough, but wait for large bubbles or foam to appear at the top.

Combine the remaining water, molasses, and salt in a saucepan, and heat to lukewarm. (Not above 115°F) Stir into the yeast mixture.

Add white flour, one cup at a time, and beat vigorously. Add whole wheat and rye flour, also one cup at a time, and continue to beat.

The dough will be sticky and difficult to handle. Turn it out onto a lightly floured board and fold the dough over to incorporate the flour. Repeat this process until you can knead with your hands, using only enough additional flour to make a smooth dough that is springy to the touch. (I prefer to add one of the whole-grain flours for this purpose.) The stickiness will not be completely eliminated.

Shape into a ball, put in a buttered bowl, and turn to coat the surface with the fat. Cover and let rise in a warm, draft-free place until doubled in bulk. (This can take a few hours.)

Punch the dough down. Shape into either two or four loaves. For this event I prefer either round loaves or braided loaves, but oblong works too.

If using baking sheets, set the loaves directly on the sheets. If using a pizza peel and stone, then coat the peel with cornmeal and set the loaves there. (Probably not all the loaves will fit on the peel. You can set the others aside on a board that's been coated with cornmeal.)

Cover the loaves and let them rise until doubled in bulk again. (Again, this may take an hour or two, although it will probably take less time than the first rising.)

Preheat oven to 425°F. Put loaves in the oven for ten minutes, then lower the temperature to 350°F and bake for about 35 more minutes, or until the loaves sound hollow when tapped with the knuckles on top and bottom. Remove and cool on racks. (Again, with a recipe of this size, you may have to do this in shifts, baking half the loaves and then the other half. If you do, don't forget to turn the oven back up to 425°F. before you start the second batch.)

Slabs of Butter

Soften one stick of butter for each four-to-six guests. We use salted butter.

Scrape each softened stick into the center of a small plate. Using one or two spreading or pastry knives, mold each lump of butter into a flat, square slab.

Put each plate of butter on a different table. If the table has more than six guests, put two.

Half a Ripe Cheese

We usually use three or four different cheeses. "Half a cheese" is often a huge quantity, so we will have somewhat smaller hunks, but we try to have at least one kind that comes in a wheel shape. Our instinct has been to favor northern European cheeses. In the past we've used Brie, sharp Cheddar, Cotswold, Jarlsberg, Chevre, and Bleu.

A PHILOSOPHY OF CAKE
Esther Friesner

"Dost thou think, because thou art virtuous, there shall be no more cakes and ale?" That's from Shakespeare, as if you didn't know. Ah, Shakespeare, a fine writer and a great American who knew his way around a flagon, a tankard, a stoup, and a stein, but more important, a man who recognized the vital importance of cake in the life of any writer worth his/her salt/chocolate frosting.

Cakes have been a part of celebrating happy human events for millennia. Indeed, certain occasions demand cakes. The cake is not a lie, it is a festive obligation, and a mighty delectable one at that. Birthdays and weddings are the better for the inclusion of this glorious embodiment of kitchen chemistry gone fabulously right.

Cakes can be all things to all people. They are a platform for creativity and improvisation. Their mind-boggling and constantly growing variety of form and flavor are inspirational to the artistic spirit. They simultaneously embody the wicked allure of the Forbidden ("Cake? No, really, I shouldn't, bathing suit season is . . . Well, maybe just a sliver."), the sparkle of enchantment (Remember Alice and the magical EAT ME cake?), the March of Memorable-Albeit-Not-Accurate History ("Let them eat cake!"), and the dark and dire specter of cruel Revenge ("A fruitcake? She sent me another holiday fruitcake? What did I ever do to her?!").

Most of all, cakes are a practical, polite, and socially-acceptable device for conveying mass quantities of frosting into your gaping maw, er, dainty mouth, even when everyone's watching.

And so let us now join in solemn appreciation of our most cherished example of patisserie. Where would we be without cake?

Probably trying to blow out the candles on our birthday codfish.

Pass the cake.

CELEBRATIONS FOR ONE: WRITER'S BREAK-TIME SWEETS IN A MUG
Ricia Mainhardt

You have written for hours and you want a sweet snack but you don't want to go to the store or bake a full batch of brownies, cookies or a cake. What can you do? Bake in a mug. You get a serving of what you want without a batch of sweets to tempt you to go back and eat more. You can make the sweet before you begin writing so it is there when you take a break or when you complete your writing goal, whether it is a number of pages or a number of scenes. Maybe you just need a break. Make it then.

All cooking times are approximates, depending on your microwave and your preferences. (I found the cooking time of 2 minutes for brownies too long, I cook the brownie for 90 seconds instead of 2 minutes. Also I found the cooking time for cheesecake made a cake-like texture. I reduced the cooking time to 70 to 75 seconds instead of 90. The last 30 seconds I use 15 to 20 seconds. It depends on how generously I add cream cheese and sour cream. This makes a smooth creamy texture.) Amounts of ingredients don't have to be exact. I am very liberal with cinnamon, vanilla, cream cheese, and sour cream.

Carrot Cake

- 1/4 c flour
- 1/2 t cinnamon
- 1/8 t pumpkin pie spice (or a pinch of mace and pinch of nutmeg)
- 1/4 t baking powder
- 1/8 t baking soda
- 1/8 t salt
- 1/2 "egg" of choice (I used egg beaters.) You can crack an egg, mix the yolk and white and pour in about half. Use the rest for scrambled eggs.
- 1 1/2 T brown sugar
- 1 T sugar
- 1/3 c canned carrots, drained (or steamed carrots, peeled) (for a variation, sub with 1/4 c pureed pumpkin)
- 1 T milk
- 1 T oil or more milk
- 1/4 t pure vanilla extract

In a small bowl, mix dry ingredients (not carrots). If you have a blender, mix all wet ingredients and blend. (Option for those without a blender: simply fork-mash the carrots very well before combining with the other wet ingredients.) Then mix dry into wet and stir. Do not over-mix. Pour into greased mug. Cook for 1 minute and 20 seconds.

Chocolate Brownie

- 2 T butter
- 2 T sugar
- 1 T firmly-packed brown sugar
- 1/4 t vanilla
- Pinch salt
- 1 egg yolk or scant 1/8 cup egg beaters
- 4 T flour (I use whole wheat)
- 1 T cocoa

Melt butter for about ten seconds in the microwave. Stir in sugars. Stir in egg yolk. Add flour and cocoa, stir well. Bake 45 seconds in the microwave.

Cinnamon Roll

- 2 T applesauce
- 1 T oil
- 1 T buttermilk (you can mix half yogurt and half milk)
- 1/4 t vanilla

- 1/4 c plus 1 T flour
- 2 1/2 T firmly-packed brown sugar
- 1 t cinnamon
- 1 dash nutmeg
- 1/4 t baking powder
- 1/8 scant t salt

Combine wet ingredients. Add sugar and stir well. Add flour, baking powder, and salt. Stir well. Add cinnamon and nutmeg and stir until swirled into batter. Bake 1 minute in microwave.

Cheesecake

- 2 oz cream cheese, softened for ten to 20 seconds in microwave
- 1 t lemon juice
- 1/2 t vanilla
- 4 T sugar

(*This is my favorite. I love cheese cake.*) Stir cream cheese and sugar until well combined. Add rest of ingredients and stir well until smooth and no lumps. You cannot over-stir. Cook 90 seconds, stirring every 30 seconds. Cool in refrigerator while you write.

Cream Cheese Icing

- 1 T cream cheese, softened for ten to 15 seconds in microwave
- 2 T powdered sugar
- 1 t milk

Soften cream cheese in microwave for about ten seconds in microwave. Mix butter with sugar. Stir wet ingredients. Mix all ingredients together well. Spread on warm or hot cinnamon roll.

Oatmeal Raisin Cookie

- 2 T rolled quick cooking oats (not instant)
- 1 1/2 T flour
- 1 1/2 T firmly-packed brown sugar
- 1 t egg whites (use egg whites left over from brownie)
- 3/4 c cinnamon
- 1 dash nutmeg
- 1/4 t baking powder
- 1/8 scant tsp salt
- 1 T raisins

*This is my favorite. I love cheese cake.*Mix wet ingredients with sugar. Mix in dry ingredients. Mix in raisins. Cook in microwave 2 minutes on 60% power.

Coconut Blonde Brownie

- 1 1/2 T butter, melted for about ten seconds in the microwave
- 1/4 c brown sugar
- 1 t egg powder
- 1 t vanilla
- 1 T egg (can use leftover egg white from brownie, egg beaters or from scrambled egg mixture)
- 1 T water
- 1/4 c flour
- 1/8 t baking powder
- 1 1/2 c coconut

Mix butter and sugar. Add wet ingredients, mix well. Add dry ingredients until just mixed. Stir in coconut. Bake 2 minutes at 60% power in microwave.

Chocolate Chip Cookies

Makes two cookies—cook the two mugs separately. If you cook all ingredients in one mug you will get a mess as the dough will run over the top of the mug.

- 3 T flour
- 1 t baking powder
- 1/8 t baking soda
- 1 egg
- 1 1/2 T brown sugar
- 1 T sugar
- 1/4 tsp vanilla
- 3 T flour
- 1 t baking powder
- 1/8 t baking soda
- Pinch of salt

Melt butter in microwave. In a small bowl, mix wet ingredients with sugar until well blended. Add 1 1/2 T water. Add dry ingredients, stir well. Pour equal amounts into two mugs. Bake each mug at 60% power for 2 minutes.

Fruit Cobbler

- 1/2 T butter
- 1/4 t sugar
- 1 T brown rice syrup or agave nectar
- 2 T oil
- 3 drops milk

- 1/4 c flour
- 1/4 t baking powder
- Pinch salt
- 1 T blueberries (can use other berries in season)

Strudel topping
- 1/2 T butter, softened
- 1 T brown sugar
- 1/4 t cinnamon

Stir butter, sugar, and syrup till smooth. Stir in flour and cinnamon until just blended and still lumpy. Pour strudel topping over dough in mug. Bake in microwave 75 seconds until just set. Don't over-bake.

Banana Cake

- 1 egg yolk
- 1/4 c sugar
- 1 T buttermilk
- 1/4 t vanilla
- 1/8 t cinnamon
- 1 T oil
- 1 T applesauce
- 1/3 c flour
- 1/4 c baking powder
- Pinch salt
- 1/2 banana, mashed

Combine wet ingredients till well mixed. Whisk dry ingredients and stir till just mixed. Some lumps should be left. (*It is okay if some dry ingredients are not totally mixed into the wet. Be careful to not over over-mix or the texture will be rubbery. True for all the cakes and breads.*) Mix in banana. Bake in microwave 2 1/2 to 3 minutes.

Frosting
For the frosting I keep the powdered sugar the same but add an extra half ounce of cream cheese. I found this is much better as it is a little less sweet and makes more icing. My husband thinks the extra icing is perfect. This same icing is good on carrot cake.

- 1 1/2 T cream cheese softened
- 4 T powered sugar

Mix well. Frost cake at room temperature.

Rice Krispie Treats

- 3/4 T butter
- 4 large marshmallows
- 1 c Rice Krispies

Soften butter. Add marshmallows. Microwave 20 seconds. Marshmallows will fluff up. Don't let them drip over the top of mug. Stir butter and marshmallows. Mix in Rice Krispies until well blended.

Sugar Cookie

- 1 T butter
- 2 T sugar
- 1/4 t vanilla
- Pinch salt
- 1 egg yolk
- 3 T flour
- Colored (or white granulated) sugar for sprinkles

Melt butter. Add sugar, vanilla, and salt. Stir well. Add egg yolk, stir. Add flour, stir. Sprinkle with colored sugar. Microwave for 45 seconds. Check for doneness at 40 seconds.

Snickerdoodles

- 1 T butter
- 1 T sugar
- 1 heaping T firmly-packed brown sugar
- Pinch cream of tartar
- Pinch salt
- 1/8 t vanilla
- 1 egg yolk
- 3 T flour
- Cinnamon

Melt butter for ten to 15 seconds in the microwave. Use fork to stir butter and sugars. Add cream of tartar, salt, vanilla, two dashes of cinnamon and stir. Stir in yolk. Add flour and stir. Top with cinnamon. Cook in microwave 45 to 60 seconds.

THE BIG PLASTIC BUCKET: HOMEBREWING FOR WRITERS
Michael J. Martinez

You've done it a million times—you're heading to dinner at a friend's house, or some sort of party, and you make a quick stop at the liquor store for a bottle of wine. Faced with rows upon rows of classy-looking labels, you grab one that's inexpensive, but not ungodly cheap, and hope for the best. Or maybe, depending on the party, it's a six-pack of some kind of beer. It has a pretty label, so whatever.

You can do better. And you can do it in your kitchen with a big plastic bucket. Welcome to the joys of brewing your own beer.

Now, this isn't going to be your typical six-pack of mass-produced American fizz. This is real beer, with flavor and a nice kick. I've brewed stouts, IPAs, Belgians, and English bitter at home—all of which were far better than Budweiser, and on par with decent craft brews. And invariably, it's one of the first bottles opened at the party, because people are intensely curious. "You made this?" they ask. "What, do you have a brewery in the basement?"

Nope. I got a big pot for the stove and a five-gallon plastic bucket. And the best part? Once you make the initial (relatively inexpensive) investment in equipment, you can make two cases of homebrew for the cost of four six-packs of good craft beer. We're writers—we like cheap.

What *Is* Beer?

Beer is basically water, barley, hops, and yeast. The main ingredient is malted barley, which is roasted to varying degrees prior to brewing; the darkness of the roast correlates to the color of your beer, and the amount you use will give your beer its sweetness, or lack thereof. Darker roasts add those chocolate or coffee flavors to stouts, usually without adding actual coffee or chocolate.

Hops are tiny vine buds that add bitterness to beer, while also acting as a preservative. (India Pale Ale got its name because the beer brewed in England had a lot of hops added so that it could make the voyage to India without going bad.) Hops also can add pine, citrus and/or floral flavors and scents to beer. Most brewers add hops twice during the brewing process—once early on to add a bitter bite to the flavor, and again just before wrapping up to add some citrus and/or pine scents to the finished brew.

Yeast is critical. Live yeast eats the sugars in beer during the fermentation process, releasing alcohol as a byproduct. No yeast, no alcohol. There are hundreds of different kinds of yeast commercially available, many of which add their own subtle flavors to beers. When you hear a beer snob talk about estery, bready or clove flavors in beer, they're likely talking about the flavors imparted by yeast.

Know Your Beer

Before you start making your own beer, it's good to know about different beer styles. You think SF/F subgenres are tough to keep track of? There are literally hundreds of beer styles; here's a quick rundown:

- **Pilsner:** Golden color, white head, highly carbonated, bitter. This is what Budweiser claims to be. Pilsner Urquell or Bitburger are far better choices.
- **Lager:** Amber color, white head, slightly less carbonated, a little sweeter. Think Samuel Adams or Brooklyn lager.
- **Ale:** A catch-all term for beers neither pilsner or lager, but for our purposes, an amber-to-red beer with a white or cream head, a bit more malty sweetness, and hops ranging from mild to biting. Varieties include amber ale (Fat Tire), pale ale (Sierra Nevada), or brown ale (Newcastle).
- **IPA:** Stands for *India Pale Ale*. A very hoppy, bitter beer, ranging in color from golden to amber. There are also double and triple IPAs. The latter varieties are very hoppy and definitely an acquired taste. Dogfish Head and Stone make wicked IPAs.
- **Stout:** Black in color, tan head. Very malty, with flavors varying from sweet to dry, often with coffee or chocolate flavors in the mix. Guinness is the standard bearer, but sit back with an imperial from Brooklyn Brewery or North Coast some time.
- **Belgian dubble/tripel/quadruple:** Belgian styles are known for their high alcohol content, along with a generally sweet taste, not a lot of hops. Ranging in color from dark burgundy to golden. Dubbels are strong, tripels are stronger, and quadruples should require you to surrender your car keys before the first sip. Belgian styles made by Trappist monks (Orval, Westmalle, Westvleteren to name a few) are outstanding, though many ambitious U.S. brewers successfully riff on the style.
- **Wheat/witbier/hefeweisen:** Beers made with wheat instead of/alongside barley. They tend to be milder and lighter, with less carbonation. Sometimes combined with fruit flavorings, such as apricot or raspberry, but good on their own. Hefeweisens are kind of a class to themselves, with more interesting flavors and a bit more carbonation.

There are tons more, and I'm not doing it justice here, but this should get you started. Craft beer is an inexpensive luxury, especially compared to high-priced wine. Before you brew, try a few different styles to see what you like. You can discover more about good beer on sites like *Beer Advocate* or *Rate Beer*, and you can see what your friends are drinking on the social media site *Untappd*.

Get Your Gear

Once you've decided that beer is good (duh) and you want to try brewing your own, you'll need some equipment. I recommend the beginner's brewing kits from either William's Brewing williamsbrewing.com) or Northern Brewer (northernbrewer.com). Both will run you about $100, give or take. They come with two large plastic buckets, tubing, a bottle-capper˙and caps. You'll need your own bottles; you can buy them on line, but the cheaper way is to save your empties. (If you're reading this, chances are you empty a few bottles from time to time.) You'll also need a big pot—there are big ones for sale on both sites, but I use a lobster pot I picked up at Target for $15.

The introductory packages also come with ingredients for your first batch of beer, and you can choose from many different types. My first was an IPA. You can go with everything from a typical American craft ale to an English or Belgian style.

These ingredient kits are pretty easy. They come with either malt syrup or powdered malt extracts, a few pouches of hops and a packet of yeast, along with instructions. If you can follow the recipe on the back of a cake mix, you can brew beer.

Generally speaking, you boil a big pot of water. Once roiling, add the malt extracts. A few minutes later, add your first round of hops. About 45-50 minutes later, add the second batch of hops. After an hour, take it off the heat and let it cool to room temperature. Transfer the unfermented beer (called *wort*) into your fermenter (i.e., the big plastic bucket). Add the yeast and seal it up. Wait two to four weeks for the yeast to do its work, then transfer the beer into bottles. Cap the bottles and wait two to four more weeks.

Then drink.

At most, you've spent two hours making the beer. It's the four-eight weeks of waiting that's a bummer, but it's totally worth it. Besides, you likely waited a lot longer to get your first fiction published.

Anyway, once you get through the first two cases (which I hope, for your health and wellbeing, takes more than a week), you can order another kit online, which typically cost around $35 to $45 each. Once you get practice with ingredient kits, you can look into creating your own recipes.

And your friends will find new reasons to invite you to parties.

AJVAR
K.V. Johansen

Two of my children's books have been translated into Macedonian, and I've had much wonderful food on my trips to the Republic of Macedonia; ajvar is one of the many dishes I encountered. It's found throughout the Balkans and all the lands once part of the Ottoman Empire. This is my very modified version of it, which doesn't involve stirring a simmering cauldron all day. And though the word ajvar looks rather like the name of Ahjvar, protagonist of The Leopard *and* The Lady, *the former is actually pronounced ay-var and the latter—ain't.*

Simplified Ajvar (Ajвар)
Pepper and Eggplant Spread (tasty . . . and full of vitamins!)

- 4 red, orange, or yellow bell peppers
- 1 large-ish eggplant (1 1/2 lb or so)
- 1/4 c olive oil
- 8 cloves garlic, unpeeled
- Parsley
- Cider vinegar or lemon juice
- Salt
- Pepper

Preheat the oven to 500°F. Cover a cookie sheet in aluminum foil (because the peppers will ooze and scorch and generally make a hideous mess of your cookie sheet otherwise).

Wash the peppers and eggplant. Cut the peppers in half and remove seeds; place on cookie sheet cut side down. Cut the eggplant in half and drizzle with a bit of extra oil, sprinkle with salt, and place on cookie sheet cut side up.

Put the garlic cloves, unpeeled, on the sheet as well. (This may even take two cookie sheets, depending on the size you have.)

Roast the vegetables in the oven for 20 to 25 minutes, until everything is soft. The peppers may scorch a little, but that's fine.

Quickly place the peppers in a bowl and cover, so that they will steam themselves a bit. (This helps to peel them afterwards.)

Scoop out the flesh of the eggplant. (Don't worry about removing the seeds.) Peel the roasted garlic. Once the peppers are cool enough to handle, get as much of the tough, membrane-like skin off them as possible.

In a food processor or blender, pulse the vegetable pulp, in batches if necessary, adding to each batch some of the oil and the liquid that collected in the bowl with the peppers. As each batch becomes fairly smooth, combine all in a large bowl, adding salt, pepper, a splash of cider vinegar or lemon juice, chopped parsley, Worcestershire sauce, and a dash of hot pepper sauce, to taste.

Serve with fresh bread or naan.

ANOUCHKA'S GRANDMOTHER'S SALMON PÂTÉ
Cat Sparks

Many years ago, at a friend's party, I encountered the tastiest dip in the universe. I hovered around the snack table shamelessly gobbling up crackerful after crackerful, ignoring the other guests and snacks—and even the fancy drinks tray! "Nice, isn't it?" said the woman standing next to me. Her name was Anouchka and it transpired that it was she who had provisioned the party with this delightful ambrosia—her grandmother's secret recipe which she was more than happy to share with the rest of the world. So here I am now passing it on to SFWA.

- 375g cream cheese
- 2 270g tins of red salmon, drained
- 2 T sour cream
- 1/2 c chopped spring onions
- Cayenne pepper to taste
- Salt and ground pepper to taste
- 1 c chopped pecan nuts (or walnuts)
- 1/2 c chopped chives

Mix cream cheese and sour cream with 2/3 of salmon in food processor, with salt and pepper and cayenne pepper.

Stir through spring onions and remaining salmon.

Mold into log shape on serving plate.

Cover with chives and pecans.

Easy peasy! Only tips are:
- It must be red salmon, not pink.
- Mix the nuts and chives up in a bowl before attempting to coat the log.
- Press the nut and chive mix on firmly with your hands, get it right into the mixture or it won't stick.
- You can make either one big roll or two smaller ones. It doesn't sound like it makes that much but something magic happens in the food processor and the mixture expands to mammoth proportions. Can be frozen.

BASTILLA
Erin M. Hartshorn

For party food, I find that almost anything becomes festive in a wrap. My favorite, albeit time-consuming, recipe is bastilla.

Bastilla (which is a transliteration, and may also be spelled b'stilla, Pastilla, Bsteeya, Bastilla, or Bstilla), *is a northern African dish that my husband and I first encountered in the Moroccan restaurant at Epcot Center. (We went to Disney World for our honeymoon.) We bought their cookbook as a starting point for Moroccan cuisine at home. Bastilla is often made in a large pie shape and served as a main course; I've adapted it to make finger food appetizers.*

Take a box of phyllo dough from the freezer and allow it to thaw while you prepare the filling.

- 3 1/2 chicken breasts (chickens have one breast; humans have two.)
- 2 c water
- 1/4 c butter (I suppose you could use olive oil for this.)
- 1 medium onion, chopped
- 1 t ground ginger
- 1 t ground cinnamon
- Pinch saffron
- 2-3 cinnamon sticks
- Salt and white pepper, to taste
- 6 whole eggs, well beaten
- 3/4 to 1 c chopped almonds
- 1/4 c granulated sugar
- Box of thawed phyllo dough
- Melted butter or butter-flavored cooking spray

Combine above ingredients and bring to boil; lower heat to simmer. Cook until chicken is tender. Remove chicken from liquid and set aside to cool.

Add eggs to reserved liquid; simmer over low heat ten-15 minutes, stirring occasionally. Strain, reserving liquid. Remove cinnamon sticks from eggs.

Shred chicken. Mix in cooked eggs. If mixture is dry, add some of the reserved liquid. Add almonds and granulated sugar

Okay, that's the easy part. Next is the time-consuming bit.

Preheat oven to 350°F (That's about 175°C, or what truly old-fashioned cookbooks refer to as "a moderate oven.")

Lay out a sheet of phyllo dough. Brush with melted butter or spray with butter-flavored cooking spray. (You'll go through a lot of cooking spray, but it's faster and easier.) Lay another sheet of phyllo on top and repeat the butter or spray. Keep the sheets you're not currently using covered—dried phyllo doesn't work. I cut the sheet in quarters, parallel to the short ends. (Given the size of the counter I use, I actually have three pairs of sheets laid out side-by-side and work on them all at once.)

Place a spoonful of filling toward the end of each quarter. Fold the end over to cover the filling. Then fold over a thin strip (no more than 1/4 inch) along each side to make sure the filling doesn't slip out. Roll the folded end over until there's no more dough left. Put the bastilla on a cookie sheet.

When the cookie sheet is full, stick it in the oven and bake until the bastilla are golden. Let cool. Remove bastilla to a serving platter and dust with powdered sugar and ground cinnamon. (Really—don't skip the powdered sugar. The combination of sweet and savory is perfect!)

This recipe makes a lot. Dozens and dozens of the size I've specified. If you take them to a party, make it clear that this is an appetizer, not a dessert. The cinnamon and powdered sugar tend to confuse people.

BIG BANG BRUSSELS SPROUTS
Sean Williams

The most maligned vegetable in the world is also one of the best for us, rich in (among other things) sulforaphane, a chemical that protects us from cancer, atherosclerosis, and UV radiation damage. The traditional way of cooking them, however—setting them to boil until all texture and color is eradicated—has led them to be widely reviled. Fortunately, a plethora of delicious alternatives exist. This party favorite in our home recently converted one of my closest friends, a sprout-hater of some forty years, into a staunch sproutophile.

Why "Big Bang"? Nothing to do with the flatulence some people suffer after eating this superb vegetable (no one's perfect, sulforaphane). Viewers of the TV show The Big Bang Theory *will know that scenes are separated by renderings of particles whizzing across the screen. Some of these particles are green. To me, they look like sprouts. That is all.*

- 4 c brussels sprouts, cut in half
- 2 T peanut oil (more if needed)
- 1 egg
- Lemon juice (about half a lemon's worth)
- 1 c extra light olive oil (not extra virgin)

- Salt
- 2 t spice mix (I use Keen's Curry Powder or The Mushroom Man's Eurasian spice mix, but they're not universally available so go with what you know)
- 1/8 t cayenne pepper (to taste)
- Handful coriander (cilantro), chopped

Brussels sprouts

Preheat your oven to 200°C (400°F).

Place the sprouts in a bowl with the peanut oil and toss until completely covered.

Transfer the sprouts to a non-stick baking tray, spread out evenly so they'll bake rather than steam.

Place in the oven and cook until crispy, around 20 to 25 minutes depending on the size of the sprout.

Dipping sauce

Crack the egg into a tall cup or container that's wide enough to accommodate the business end of a stick blender.

Add lemon juice and salt, then pour in the extra light olive oil and wait for the egg to settle.

Put your blender right down to the bottom of the container, so it's covering the egg, and only then switch it on.

Blend for about 20 seconds. (This is my favorite part—magic mayonnaise!)

Add spice mix, cayenne pepper and coriander, and mix well.

Present the warm and crispy brussels sprouts to your guests and watch them dip away. The leaves will have parted slightly, for maximal scooping efficiency. Delicious and efficient! Thank you, *Brassica oleracea*.

C3PO
Ef Deal

My husband and I don't just throw parties—we send those suckers hurtling through space. I've hosted 27-hour Christmas celebrations for over one hundred, and our backyard Summerfest is epic.

For me, preparing outrageously wonderful food is an exciting adventure. We've had a Victorian Christmas, a Mardi Gras Christmas, a Three-ring Circus, even a Santa Borg. So I've routinely roasted turkeys, prime ribs, whole pigs, and hams. Less routinely, I've made jambalaya, paella, and mountains of crawdads. One year I wrapped a canned ham in pastry and dyed it like an Easter egg, then surrounded it with little nests of homemade nutmeg pasta on which sat dinner-roll chicks.

I may have lost my ability to write, but my imagination is still being poured out—in my kitchen.

This recipe is great for dipping veggies in or spreading on crackers. Simple and delicious!

- 1 8-oz block of cream cheese
- 1 small can of crushed pineapple, drained
- 1 small green pepper, diced
- 1/2 c (or more, if you want) chopped pecans
- 1/2 onion, minced

Mix all ingredients together.

"CHILLY" SAUCE
Nancy Springer

I may be a fantasy writer, but I am not a fantastic cook. Most of the serious cooking around my place is done by my husband, Joel, who cheerfully produces such Pennsylvania Dutch delights as soft pretzels, boiled pot pie, and stuffed hog maw. (Hog maw is good. I was tempted to send the recipe, claiming it as my own, but it is impossible to pin down a true Pennsylvania Dutch cook as to measurements of ingredients. It all depends on the size of the pig's stomach, of course. And anyhow, where but in this area could one buy a pig's stomach in the supermarket?) Joel comes from a family of committed cooks, and I come from a family of microwavers.

However, I do have a few modest specialties of my own, picnic fare such as deviled eggs, "cannonball" hamburgers, and—the centerpiece of my cooking existence—Chilly Sauce.

Actually (thank goodness), Chilly Sauce gets cooked only once every two or three years, and enjoyed the rest of the time. It is a cold relish to be eaten on hot dogs and hamburgers, and it is heavenly. I got the recipe from my mother, who got it from one of her well-meaning friends, and as her cooking skills, like mine, consist nearly exclusively of things that can be thawed at the last minute, I was virtually raised on the stuff.

Chilly Sauce is traditionally cooked (amid grumbling) on the hottest day of August, because that's when the vegetable garden has provided the necessary superfluity of ingredients. They are:

- 25 tomatoes, peeled and quartered
- 10 large onions, peeled and quartered
- 6 sweet peppers, either red or green, cored and quartered

These veggies must be put through some sort of food mill or grinder on the coarse-chop setting. The resulting juicy slush should be placed in a huge cooking pot, along with:

- 2 heaping T salt
- 1 T cinnamon
- 1/4 t clove
- 1/4 t allspice
- 4 c (2 lbs) brown sugar

And (this is the grumbly part) the whole mix must be simmered on the stove for maybe four hours, maybe more, stirring occasionally, until it has cooked away to half its original volume and turned into a brown glop thick enough not to slide off a hot dog. Dole the glop into mismatched containers and freeze it to be thawed as needed for future use (if you're like me) or can it in sparkling glass bell jars and display it at the county fair (if you're like my mother-in-law).

My husband, who was raised on sour pickles and such, suggests cutting the amount of sugar in the recipe for a more adult taste. This notion is, of course, blasphemy.

"Chilly" Sauce looks awful but tastes sweet and cool and wonderful. Actually, the proper name is "Chile Sauce," but the sauce bears no resemblance to anything having to do with chili or Chile as I know them. From childhood on I have called the stuff "Chilly" Sauce. Perhaps contemplating this word play during hot dog meal after hot dog meal as a youngster started me on the way to being a writer.

CONFEDERATION SALMON MOUSSE
Mary Mason

This was created at the Atlanta WorldCon. I was throwing a party for Tor Books and had gone shopping for supplies at a local superstore. In the seafood section they had lox trimmings on sale for four dollars a pound. I asked the fishmonger if that was a mistake and he said, "No. In Atlanta they don't know from lox, much less lox trimmings." I bought five pounds, then tried to figure out what to do with it. I made this dish and served it. That night the head of catering was making trash runs on the party floors (they were running short of help) and came by the suite. He named it a salmon mousse and bought the recipe from me. Once I gave it to him, I offered to return the money since it was so simple. He said it was worth it to be reminded of the lesson that simple is sometimes best.

- 2 lb lox trimmings (Or lox, if you're rich enough.)
- 1 lb cream cheese
- 6 lemons
- 1 red onion, capers, 2 tomatoes, 4 dozen mini bagels or 2 dozen regular bagels split and cut in two pieces, 1 dozen green onion brooms or parsley, sliced green olives stuffed with pimento

Trim all skin, tendons, and dark parts off the salmon pieces. Mince, by hand—*do not use a processor*—the salmon into very fine but not totally uniform bits. Work the cream cheese with your hands until soft. Add the salmon and the juice of four of the lemons. Fold gently with your fingers until the salmon is evenly distributed throughout the cream cheese. Chill for at least an hour.

On a large platter shape the chilled mass into a fish shape. Serve with remaining ingredients.

MY GREAT-GRANDMOTHER'S CORN BREAD
Jaime Lee Moyer

A recipe my mother and grandmother made all my life, handed down from my great-grandmother.

- 1/3 c butter, softened
- 1/2 c sugar
- 1 egg
- 1 c yellow cornmeal
- 1 c flour
- 1 t salt
- 1 T baking powder
- 1 c milk

Preheat oven to 400°F. Cream together butter, sugar, and egg. Mix in dry ingredients and milk; mix until well blended. Batter will be thick, but shouldn't be lumpy.

If you have a 9-inch cast iron skillet, that is the perfect pan to use for baking this cornbread. You can also make muffins with this batter. Otherwise, use cooking spray to grease any 9-inch square or round baking pan.

Pour batter in the pan. Bake until the top begins to brown and a toothpick inserted in the middle comes out clean.

If you like your cornbread a little sweeter, you can increase the sugar to 3/4 cup.

CRACKER SNACKERS
Vylar Kaftan

- Some sort of medium-size cracker. Water crackers work great. You want them fairly thin and large-bite sized.
- Cheese (usually a good sharp cheddar)
- Sliced turkey (the good kind will make these better)
- Some sort of flavorful goop or relish. Olive tapenade works well. Red pepper spread is good (if you have a Trader Joe's nearby). Chutney could work. Anything like that.

Put the crackers on a platter. Make small bricks of cheese, a bit smaller than the crackers, maybe 1/2 inch thick. Crumple up some turkey and pile it on top. Add a dollop of goop. *Voila!*

You might want to make some without turkey for vegetarians, and some without cheese for the lactose-intolerant.

CREAMED SPINACH WITH JALAPEÑOS
Sharyn November

From *Home Cooking: A Writer in the Kitchen* by Laurie Colwin (Knopf, 1988)

I am someone who can happily eat the same thing night after night after night. (Often this is salad. Sometimes it is fruit and a bunch of candy.) One of my favorite recipes— for myself, and for company—is Laurie Colwin's Creamed Spinach with Jalapeños from her first cookbook, Home Cooking. It's easy, it's comfort food with a little bite, and you can eat it for days. At the height of my obsession with this dish, I made it every Sunday and as a side dish for every dinner party I gave. That is a lot of creamed spinach. (NOTE: you can substitute Pepper Jack for the cheese/jalapeño combo below. I also always put in more garlic and black pepper.)

Makes 8 servings (or 4, if you are me)
Preparation: 1 hour 10 minutes

- 2 10 oz packages whole-leaf frozen spinach (do not thaw)
- 4 T butter, plus additional for buttering pan
- 2 T all-purpose flour
- 2 T chopped onion
- 1 clove garlic, minced

- 1/2 c evaporated milk
- Black pepper
- 3/4 t celery salt
- 6 oz Monterey Jack cheese, cut into cubes
- 1 pickled or fresh jalapeño pepper, chopped, or more to taste
- 1/2 c soft buttered bread crumbs (see note)

Heat oven to 300°F. Meanwhile, cook spinach according to package directions. Drain, reserving 1 cup of liquid, and chop finely.

Butter a shallow 8-inch-square casserole dish or other shallow 4- to 6-cup baking dish. Melt remaining 4 tablespoons butter in a saucepan and add flour. Blend and cook 2 to 3 minutes. Do not brown. Add onion and garlic.

Add the spinach liquid slowly, then add evaporated milk, some black pepper, celery salt, and cheese. Mix well and add jalapeño and spinach. Cook until all is blended.

Turn into the casserole dish, top with buttered bread crumbs and bake until lightly browned, about 45 minutes.

NOTE: To make buttered bread crumbs, combine 1/2 cup fresh soft bread crumbs with 1 to 2 tablespoons melted butter and toss well.

DUKKAH
(A highly mutated interpretation of an Australian version of an Egyptian spice mix)
Liz Argall

Good with bread and olive oil, vegetables, adding as a crust to fish before cooking, sprinkling on chicken or on rice.

Ingredients for Christmas Dukkah
- Almonds (freshly toasted in the oven)
- Sesame Seeds (freshly toasted in the oven)
- Cumin Seeds (toasted in fry pan)
- Dried Parsley
- Dried Oregano
- Dried Thyme
- Salt (In this case Murray River Red Salt and a bit of Jamie Oliver seasoned salt mix that was a gift from my mother in law—adds a bit of ground bay leaf, thyme, lemon to the mix. Dukkah loves salt and I'll often add a bit of extra salt to the top of Dukkah dish when serving.)

- Cinnamon (freshly grated into the mixing bowl using a microplane)
- Nutmeg (freshly grated into the mixing bowl using a microplane)

Ingredients for Spicier Christmas Dukkah

Same as above, but add
- Extra Cumin
- Anardana powder (ground pomegranate seeds)
- Cayenne
- High quality, unsweetened cocoa powder (This pairs well with the cayenne and makes the spicier mixture look different to the plain version.)

Toast nuts and seeds in the oven. Don't try to toast them all together; they're all different sizes and you run the risk of burning. Toast almonds with just almonds, sesame seeds with just sesame seeds. After burning walnuts badly I now set a timer and check on the guys every few minutes. You can also toast things in a frying pan. And according to this tutorial—mybakingaddiction.com/how-to-toast-nuts-tutorial—you can also toast them in the microwave.

I always toast my cumin seeds in the frying pan as I always burn cumin if I try to do it in the oven.

Once the nuts or seeds are done I chuck them in a bowl and stir them around with a pinch of salt.

Put almonds in food processor and chop until they're fairly small pieces. Then add the other things, pulse the blender and taste. I taste regularly, adding one ingredient at a time and tweaking. To taste I'll get a rough feel by dropping a pinch into my mouth, but to fine tune I'll put some into a dish and then try with olive oil and bread. This is especially important when using dried ingredients that will come to life with the extra moisture.

(Instead of a food processor you can use a mortar and pestle to break down the big ingredients and then combine in a bowl instead.)

I've listed the ingredients I used on this occasion. I'm always changing it, depending on what I have in the cupboard and how I feel like experimenting. Once I have a base I sometimes decant my dukkah into different jars and then add extra spices to each jar. That way I can explore different variations and not wreck the whole thing.

If this big list of ingredients intimidates you, try mixing sesame seeds, cumin seeds, and salt together and just eating that. If you don't like cumin seeds, try coriander seeds or dried oregano as your base instead.

EMERGENCY SALSA, NEW MEXICO-STYLE
Sarah Goslee

I learned this recipe, such as it is, while I was living in southern New Mexico. It was a party staple, partly because it is so ridiculously simple, but also because it is far more delicious and addictive than the ingredients would suggest.

It's a perfect recipe for those times when you are so busy writing that you've utterly forgotten a social event, and tasty enough that it looks like you've made some effort even when you haven't. It scales easily for larger groups.

- 1 large jar of your favorite brand of salsa. (Regular salsa is tasty; hot fruit salsa is brilliant.)
- 1 package of cream cheese
- 1 bag of tortilla chips

Panic. Run to the store for ingredients. Only three things: you can be in and out in no time. You might want to double the amounts, because my experience suggests this will disappear quickly.

Put the cream cheese in your most attractive flat-bottomed sturdy serving bowl. This recipe works best if you have time to let the cream cheese come to room temperature so it's soft enough to cut easily with a tortilla chip, but if you had that much time you wouldn't need an emergency recipe. Add a serving knife to compensate.

Dump the jar of salsa on top.

Put the tortilla chips in your second-most attractive serving bowl.

Serve.

FORMER IN-LAW PARTY CRACKERS
Charlaine Harris

I got this recipe from a former sister-in-law, and I have no idea where she found it. (Or why she chose to part from my wonderful brother-in-law, for that matter. Though he's dating someone really nice now, and their daughter is grown and cool with it. If you want to know more about my former sister-in-law, catch me later.) This is one of those unhealthy recipes that I only make once a year, usually around the holidays. No, it doesn't make any difference which holiday. As you can see, this recipe dates from the time when Mini-Ritz crackers were easy to find. Now you have to make do with some off-brand. Any plain cracker will do; it's the size that really does matter. Of course, no one makes just one batch of these; it's easily doubled or tripled. People eat these by the large handful. They'd be perfect for con suites. I'm just saying.

- 1 10-oz package Oyster crackers
- 5 oz mini-butter crackers, like Ritz
- 5 oz Cheezits
- 1 c vegetable oil
- 1 t lemon pepper
- 1 t garlic salt
- 1 t dill weed
- 1 package ranch dressing (dry)

Spread crackers on a baking sheet. Bake at 300°F for 15 minutes, watching closely during the last five minutes.

While crackers are baking, mix all the other ingredients in a large mixing bowl. Add crackers to the mixture and toss well until all the crackers are well coated. Pour on paper towels to cool, and seal in an air-tight container when thoroughly cooled.

GOGI WANJA JEON
(Pan-fried Meat and Tofu Cakes)
Yoon Ha Lee

I actually didn't learn to cook until college (in the USA), so my first attempts were things like macaroni and cheese. Nevertheless, a few years back my mother sent me a bilingual (English/Korean) cookbook of recipes that don't take all day to make. (She also sent a cookbook from some foundation that tries to preserve traditional cooking. I can't even figure out what some of the ingredients would be called in English, if anything.) This is simple, tasty even if you can't make round shapes (that would be me), and reasonably fast.

I am not sure I ever mention food in writing (what, characters need to eat?), except in the Unsold Space Opera I have a space military running around serving gimchi *(described only as "cabbage pickles") because dammit, if people can have Western fruitcakes and steaks in their space operas, I get to have Korean food in my space opera.*

Meat/Tofu Mixture
- 1 lb ground beef or similar
- 1 package hard tofu, mashed into small pieces with a fork and water squashed out (Seriously, it's really helpful the more of the water you can get rid of.)
- 4 green onions, green parts only, chopped
- 1/3 carrot peeled and chopped (The original recipe calls for this; I omit it because I can't chop carrots without slicing my fingers off.)
- 1/2 onion, chopped

- 2 T flour
- 2 eggs, beaten with a pinch of salt
-

Marinating Sauce
- 1 t salt
- 1 t sugar
- 1 t ginger juice (Our local Korean supermarket sells pre-grated ginger in a jar, which is convenient for this, as I am too lazy to grate my own ginger and squeeze out the juice.)
- 1/4 t black pepper
- 1/2 T toasted sesame seeds
- 1/2 T sesame oil
- 1 T mirin

In a large bowl, combine ground beef, tofu, green onion, carrot, and onion with marinating sauce.

Mix well and shape mixture into a cylinder, wrap tightly, and freeze.

After about 1 hour (this might take longer), unwrap the cylinder and cut into 1/4 inch thick slices.

Put flour in a separate bowl and dredge each piece until all surfaces are lightly covered.

Heat a large frying pan over medium heat with 2-3 tablespoons of oil. Place each flour-covered slice into the beaten egg, then into the pan and cook until both sides are golden brown, about 1-2 minutes per side.

Place the cooked patties on a paper towel to drain. Add new oil as needed and repeat until all slices have been cooked.

MOMOS
Jay Lake

Momos, as modified by Jay Lake, from Jody Lake, from Fern Wofford, from traditional Tibetan cuisine. Makes about 24 momos, feeds 4-6.

Bread Dough
- 2 T (1 packet) yeast
- 3 T sesame oil
- 1 1/2 T sugar
- 1 1/2 t salt
- 3 to 5 c all-purpose flour

Place the yeast into 1/2 cup hot water. Place the oil, sugar, and salt into 1 1/2 cups hot water. Mix yeast, water, and flour to make a stiff dough. Turn out onto floured board and knead until very stiff. Set aside and let rise to double (about 1 hour).

Meat Filling
- 1 lb ground buffalo
- 1 T soy sauce
- 1/2 t salt
- Ground black pepper to taste
- 3 to 4 green onions, chopped small
- Small bunch cilantro, chopped fine

Mix meat ingredients together. If using ground beef, consider adding bouillon cube to simulate the richer taste of buffalo (or yak meat in the original). Also, consider substituting ground turkey or vegetarian ground beef substitute, with the addition of an egg in either case.

Divide risen dough into quarters. Continue to divide dough until each piece is about the size of a golf ball. (Use wax paper on a plate or tray to hold the balls.) Roll out dough balls into a rectangle.

Place approximately 1 to 2 teaspoons of meat filling onto each rectangle. Fold corners inward (like the back of an envelope) and roll flat so there is no open seam. (Don't worry if a little meat is exposed.)

Cooking Method One (Traditional Frying)

Heat thin coat of cooking oil with splash of sesame oil in frying pan. Insert momos in hot oil folded side down, fry until golden brown on bottom, then flip once to fry other side. Turn oven on "Warm"; stack cooked momos in layers on a baking sheet with paper towels under each layer to keep warm until serving. Do this even with the last batch—it helps drain the oil.

Cooking Method Two (Baked)

Egg Wash
- 1 large egg
- Splash milk
- Splash water
- Sesame seeds

Prepare an egg wash from above ingredients (except sesame seeds). Drop momos in boiling water, folded side down. Boil sixty to ninety seconds. They should float.

Transfer to cookie sheet covered with baking parchment. Brush or coat with egg wash. Liberally shake sesame seeds over egg wash coat.

Bake for 15-20 minutes at 400°F, until bottoms are brown. Move to broiler for 3-5 minutes, monitoring carefully, until tops are brown.

If needed, keep warm (or rewarm) per above directions.

Serving

Serve hot with a dipping sauce of equal proportions of soy sauce and vinegar. May be frozen and reheated later if you have leftovers; approximately 20 seconds on medium power in the microwave followed by toaster oven.

NUTS & BOLTS
James Sutter

Okay, so this is basically just my family's take on commercial Chex mix, but I always thought it was significantly more interesting than the stuff you can buy in the store. When I was a kid, you could sit me down in a chair with a coffee can full of this and a new science fiction novel, and I'd be set for set for the day. Christmas afternoons, summer vacation days, family boat trips—regardless of the occasion, "Nuts & Bolts" and a fresh book to curl up with was all I really wanted in the world. (Honestly, it still sounds pretty nice.) Of course, Nuts & Bolts also work great for parties, but if you find yourself slipping off with a handful to go read . . . well, you're just following tradition.

Melt 1/2 stick butter, and add:
- 1 t celery seed
- 1 t garlic powder
- 1/2 t onion powder
- 1/2 t cayenne
- 2 t Lawry's seasoned salt
- 1 t Worcestershire sauce

On two large cookie sheets, mix:
- 9 c Chex cereal (Usually 6 of wheat and 3 of corn, but rice is good too.)
- 1/2 bag of stick pretzels
- 1 c peanuts
- 1 c almonds

Drizzle the Chex with the sauce and bake for 45 minutes at 250°F, stirring every 15 minutes.

RICOTTA CHEESE
Mary Rosenblum

Ricotta is a quick, easy cheese that requires nothing other than milk, heat, and a pot. If you can get local milk from cows or goats out on grass pasture, this cheese is wonderful in the spring, when the pasture is full of tender young plants and the milk is full of aromatic compounds from those fresh young greens. In any case, you'll be amazed at the difference between store bought and fresh ricotta. And it takes no more than a half hour to make a batch. Easy!

1. Heat the milk on the stove to a temperature of at least 190°F. (Any temperature between 190°F and boiling is fine—to a simmer if you don't have a thermometer). Keep stirring over medium/medium-high heat so that it doesn't scorch.

2. Add enough vinegar, lemon juice, tartaric acid, or citric acid dissolved in water to cause white curds to form, leaving free yellowish liquid. You can find citric and sometimes tartaric acids in high end groceries, pharmacies, and beer/wine supply stores. Start with about a tablespoon of vinegar or lemon juice per quart of milk or 1/4 teaspoon citric acid or tartaric acid dissolved in water and add it little by little. If you don't get a solid, clear separation of curd and whey, add more. Stir very, very gently so you don't break up the forming curd.

3. Allow the curds and liquid to cool to a safe handling temperature. Okay, if you decided to do this at the last minute (the way I usually do) you can drain it right now, but don't complain to me if you splash scalding whey onto yourself! I always manage to. Dip off free whey, then pour the curds and whey left in the pot into a colander or strainer lined with wet muslin or even that crummy packaged "cheesecloth" from the local store. (It is fine to let the pot of curds and whey sit overnight to cool. Just cover it.)

4. If you used vinegar or lemon juice, rinse the curd thoroughly with cold water to remove any vinegar or lemon flavor, if desired. Usually you can skip this step with citric or tartaric acid. Taste the curd to see. If you like it, you're good!

That's it, you're done! If the milk is from grass-fed cows, it can be a delicate and lovely appetizer drizzled with a bit of basil-infused olive oil or any aromatic olive oil and served with crusty bread or crackers. Layer it between ripe halved strawberries or pit fat Bing cherries and stuff a bit of Ricotta inside. Use it in a wrap with baby lettuce, basil, and good prosciutto. On hot pasta with good olive oil and a crushed clove of garlic or two you have an instant Alfredo. Whipped with some fresh herbs it's a fabulous omelet filling, and low fat if you use low fat milk. Try it drizzled with good local honey on bread or crackers.

It's great stuff when it's fresh!

SEARED PEACHES WITH PROSCIUTTO AND BASIL
Rebecca Gomez Farrell

A coterie of writers hovered over the dining table, their senses dulled by an evening spent listening to their peers read from a podium. In their weakened states, the vibrant appetizer bundles arranged on a glass tray confounded the group. After striving in vain—it was always in vain—to retain their focus the last few hours as wizards had thrown flaming bolts that slew overgrown, omniscient Venus flytraps, these sunset-colored half-moons, wrapped in strips of seared meat and wilted basil and dotted with deep purple gems of vinegar, were too much to take in.

In their miasma, the scribes instead reached for the squares of pizza covered in geysers of grease that had spouted from cooling cheese. Familiar to them from when they emerged from dark caves of creation, eyes blinking and stomachs clenching, the pizza had always treated them well. It did not require further contemplation.

One daring soul, the sharp tug of hunger dispelling his haze faster than that of his compatriots, reached for the foreign items wedged between the multitudinous cardboard boxes. He sniffed, he sampled, he declared the mysterious savory treats delightful.

The ravenous hordes, bolstered by his bravery, dropped their limp slices and descended. In moments, only a Pollockian pattern of balsamic smears remained on the serving platter.

In other words, this recipe comes to you approved by the speculative fiction writers of North Carolina's Research Triangle Park.

(A variation on a *Food + Wine* recipe)

Makes 16 appetizers

- 8 slices prosciutto (about 3 ounces)
- 2 large, ripe peaches
- Salt and pepper
- 16 large basil leaves
- 1 T olive oil
- Aged balsamic vinegar, for drizzling

Carefully separate and cut the prosciutto slices in half. Lay them out on a work surface. Pit and cut the peaches into eight wedges each. Place one peach wedge at the end of each prosciutto slice. Season the peaches with salt and pepper. Place one basil leaf over each peach slice. Roll the peaches up in the prosciutto, making sure to enclose the fruit as well as you can.

Heat the olive oil in a sauté pan over moderate heat. Lay each bundle in the pan, seam-side down at first to seal the wrap. Turn the peaches to brown all sides, taking about five minutes in all. Transfer to a serving platter, drizzle with aged balsamic vinegar, and serve.

SALMON "PUFFS"
Julie Czerneda

My mom would bring these out, hot from the oven, the moment she felt someone at one of our frequent parties was steering conversation in a less than convivial direction. Too much politics (or not enough), too much sports (or too much of any one topic), or perhaps simply not paying attention to whatever the party was about. You know what I mean. I grew up calling these treats "salmon puffs," though we didn't have fancy pastry at hand so technically they're salmon-rolled-up-in-bread-things, and they're quick, tasty, and cheap to make. Oh, and they work. That mouth filled with one of these? A guarantee of the party getting back on track.

Later, as a writer who hosted a virtual party for 11 years at sff.net, it seemed natural to me to invoke "salmon puffs" to divert any thread of conversation that wasn't on topic or pleasant. No, I'd no idea about the use of the same hardy fish elsewhere by SFWA members. I just felt that my newsgroup was a gathering of friends on my online deck, to be fed appropriately.

Here you go. Since I cook by dumping stuff in, then eyeballing the result, I make no promises regarding the measurements. They'll be close.

Heat oven to 325°F if planning to bake immediately. (The daring can bake them on the BBQ.)

Filling
- Contents of a small tin of salmon, drained and squished into submission (Crab works too; I don't believe in tuna.)
- 1/4 c of something gooey to hold things together (I've used, depending on what's in my fridge that day, either: cream cheese, grated cheddar, softened butter, or mayonnaise)
- Seasonings (I've used, not all at once, cayenne pepper, horseradish, minced chives, ground black pepper, or powdered mustard. Suit yourself.)
-

To make filling: Dump into bowl, eyeball as you mix. It should be spreadable. I recommend nibbling to check the taste.

Scaffold (as I call it)
- White or brown squishable bread, crusts removed
- Butter or olive oil

To make scaffold: Flatten slices with a rolling pin or similar blunt instrument. (See? I said it was easy.) Butter both sides. (If you want. If that's too messy for you, just butter the side that's up.) Could use olive oil. This is what will brown and be extra yummy, so your call.

Assembling your salmon puffs: Spread filling on buttered, flattened slices, about as thickly as you'd spread jam. Leave room for sprawl along one edge (experimenting is also tasty). Firmly roll each slice towards that edge, like a jelly roll. (If you're a prep ahead person, like me, this is where you bust out the waxed paper and wrap the rolls for use later. When you whip them out the next day, you've gained the element of surprise.)

To bake: Cut into slices. If they try to fall apart on you, toothpicks work, but usually they'll stay together. Bake on a greased pan or parchment paper (or BBQ) until the bread just starts to toast and the filling bubbles a bit.

Smile and offer to the loudest talker in the room first!

SPINACH ARTICHOKE DIP
Mary Vigliante Szydlowski

Though this dip is really delicious when baked and browned in the oven, in a pinch you can do it all in the microwave with nobody the wiser. If you're a procrastinator, feel lazy, and don't want to exert yourself, can't figure out how to turn on the oven, or if your guests rudely arrive a half hour early and you're pressed for time, just forget the oven part entirely. Simply microwave the dip two or three minutes until the edges bubble, then serve it. Since it doesn't brown, it won't taste quite the same as the baked version, but it will still taste great and unless you've invited the Queen or the culinary police to your gathering, if you don't tell them who's to know!

- 12 oz cream cheese
- 14 oz can of marinated artichoke hearts, drained and chopped.
- 1 10 oz package of frozen chopped spinach
- 1 t lemon juice
- 1/4 t garlic powder
- 1/2 c grated Parmesan cheese
- 1 large bag of scoop-type tortilla chips

Preheat oven to 375°F. Cook spinach in microwave-safe container according to package directions. Drain using a fine mesh strainer, squeezing out as much liquid as possible.

Place cream cheese in covered casserole dish and microwave 1-2 minutes until soft.

Add spinach and artichokes to cream cheese. Stir mixture. Add lemon juice, garlic powder, and Parmesan cheese. Stir well.

Bake 20-25 minutes until dip bubbles and browns slightly at edges.

Serve with tortilla chips.

(IF YOU CAN SING "THAT'S A MORAY" YOU CAN) TUNA SALAD
Elizabeth Ann Scarborough
(The recipe comes from the author's mother.)

Tuna salad seems to be the redheaded stepchild on everyone's menu. It's never anyone's first choice. It's what you order at the deli when you don't know what else to have, when you're not in the mood for a Reuben sandwich or the blintzes with sour cream or the bagel and lox and cream cheese, or when you just want something light and quick. Too often, tuna salad is the, "Oh well . . . " pick.

This recipe is no different. It's quick and easy and light. There is nothing special about it. It's for people who are hungry and lazy—mostly single men who are watching their wallet and their waistlines. (Or writers who resent spending any time away from the keyboard.)

Tuna salad is never going to create orgasms of pleasure on your palate, but it will satisfy your hunger without guilt. If you're on a diet, it's healthy, filling, and painless— and if you're not on a diet, why are you eating tuna salad?

By the way, I find the analogy in the first sentence both puzzling and annoying. What's wrong with either redheads or stepchildren?

- 2 or 3 cans of dolphin-safe tuna (Figure out how much tuna salad you are going to eat. How many people are there in your household? How many will eat tuna salad the second day? Chunk white tuna in water is my usual choice, but this recipe will work with just about any canned tuna. Or salmon for that matter.)
- Shredded cabbage that they sell in packages for homemade cole slaw. (Or you can shred your own.)
- Green onions or chives
- Mayonnaise (The real stuff, please!)
- Yellow mustard

- Sweet pickle relish (The kind you put on hot dogs.)
- Anything else you want to add: celery, carrots, chopped olives, red or yellow bell peppers, cucumber, whatever. It's your tuna salad.

Get a big bowl and a big wooden spoon.

Now, it doesn't matter which order you put the ingredients into the bowl; I've tried it all different ways and I can't tell the difference, but if it makes you feel better, start with the tuna. Empty two cans (and the watery residue) into the bowl. Keep the third can handy in case you miscalculate on the ratio. (At the moment you run the can opener, you will gain an immediate audience of cats and/or dogs. This is your fan club. You do not owe them anything, no matter what they say.)

Now add the shredded cabbage.

Let me explain this. The local supermarket used to sell little tubs of "salad confetti." I never looked too closely, but there were little bits of shredded cabbage, broccoli, carrots, cauliflower, and I'm not sure what else. One tub of that and two cans of tuna was my basic recipe. But they stopped selling "salad confetti" because not enough people were buying it. So I had a choice—either lug out the Cuisinart and shred my own ingredients or take the path of least resistance and just grab a bag of shredded cabbage and carrots they now call "three-color cole slaw." (Just add dressing.)

If you're up for it, you can shred cabbage, broccoli, carrots, cauliflower, bell peppers, kale, green onions, cucumbers, and celery, and make your own salad confetti. The problem there is that you will likely end up with a lot more than you need for a bowl of tuna salad, and this is intended as a lazy man's recipe—quick and easy.

Dump the shredded cabbage onto the tuna and you're halfway finished. How much? It's your tuna salad, mix it to your taste. I usually go for equal amounts of tuna and cole-slaw mix.

Now chop up the green onions or chives. (I am told that green onions are not the same thing as chives, but I've never been able to tell the difference.) Chop as much as you want to add. Maybe a half cup. Add those to the mix.

If you're up to it, you can add chopped celery, but that crosses the line from "quick and easy" to "let's put on a show." And if you go beyond that, then it's a damn pageant. Forget it.

Now add equal amounts of mustard, relish, and mayo. Please use real mayonnaise, not that artificial processed crap. It *does* make a difference. Again, how much? Two or three big tablespoons of mayo, maybe the same amount or less of relish and mustard. You're the one who's going to eat it, adjust to taste. Too much relish makes it too sweet, too much mustard makes it too sharp, too much mayo makes it too sloppy, so start with small amounts and only add as you need.

Serving Suggestions

My preferred way of serving is to grab two pieces of rye bread and slather a thick layer of tuna salad into a sandwich. Rye bread tends to get hard quickly, even if you keep it in the fridge, so give it ten seconds in the microwave first to warm it up and freshen it.

If you don't want a sandwich, lay a few tomato slices onto a plate and pretend you're being fancy. If you really want to be fancy, hollow out half a tomato (or bell pepper) and call it "Tomato Surprise." (If you hollow out half a bell pepper, you can't call it "Tomato Surprise." You have to call it "Tuna Surprise" because a "Pepper Surprise" is usually administered by a hostile law enforcement officer.)

A piece of rye bread has about 75 calories. So, with two pieces of rye bread and a thick slather of "You Can Tuna Salad," you're looking at 300-400 calories. If you're serious about losing weight, make this tuna salad once or twice a week.

WHATURWANTIN'
Cie Adams

- 1 Egg
- 1 T of chili powder
- 2 lb 90% lean ground beef
- 1 15.5-oz jar medium salsa
- 8 oz Velveeta (cut into cubes)
- 1 c crushed corn chips

Preheat oven to 350°F. Mix egg, chili powder and meat together. Split meat in two parts. In a loaf pan, use the first part of the hamburger mix to put a layer of burger around the bottom and sides. Pour a layer (apx. 1/2 jar) of salsa over the meat, covering the bottom of the loaf pan. Put a layer of Velveeta cubes over the salsa. Put remaining meat over the top of the layers.

Pour corn chips over the top of the meat. Press lightly into the surface.
Bake for approximately 1 and 1/2 hours or until done.
Serve hot with the rest of the salsa on the side.

WIZARD'S PIGLETS IN BLANKETS
Rosemary Jones

Long before I went to cons or wrote fantasy, I attended Oogaboo parties. This Northwest branch of the International Wizard of Oz Club (ozclub.org) hosts regular potlucks where we still gather to talk about our book collections, the latest pop culture references to Dorothy and friends, and end the day in proper Ozian fashion with games and eating. This dish got its name from the Wizard's nine little piglets in *Dorothy and the Wizard in Oz*, the fourth book in the series. Those piglets were nearly eaten by Dorothy's kitten Eureka. These piglets never survive the party.

If you've never read the Oz books, or only seen the 1939 movie, L. Frank Baum's fantasy series began in 1900 with the publication of *The Wizard of Oz* and continued for forty-four "official" volumes written by Baum and his successors. Even before his death in 1919, his works inspired popular stage musical adaptations, silent movies, comic strips, toys, and more.

I received my first Oz book at the age of five. A personal library full of all of Baum's books and related early 20th century children's fantasy certainly led to writing a series of books about collecting children's books. While I try to stay away from overused Ozian tropes in my fantasy, the hardcore collector might spot the occasional tip of the cap to Mr. Baum in some of my stories.

Serves: A large group of Oogaboos or one hungry kitten.
Preparation: About 30 minutes to prep and 15 minutes cooking time.

Ingredients:
- 2 cans refrigerated crescent roll dough
- 2 packages of hot dogs

Equipment:
- Sharp knife
- Cookie sheet

Heat oven to 375°F. Unroll crescent roll dough. Wrap one hot dog in one crescent (triangle wedge of dough). Cut in the dough-wrapped dog into thirds.
Place on cookie sheet.
Repeat until all hot dogs and crescents are used.*
Place sheet in oven and bake for 12-15 minutes, or until dough is puffy and golden brown around each hot dog piece. Serve hot or cold. Mustard optional.

*The real magic in this is getting the number of hot dogs and crescents to come out even! You can vary these by using turkey dogs, veggie dogs, or, my personal favorite, Trader Joe's mini dogs.

• SWEET SNACKS & DESSERTS •

APPLE CRUMBLE
Chet Gottfried

Shortly after graduating college and living in my first apartment, I read that the odds of being successful in any of the arts are minimal; therefore, if you want to eat well, you learn how to cook. I've taken that advice to heart. A hot apple crumble straight from the oven with a scoop of vanilla ice cream along the side . . . now that's life. Cheers!

Topping
- 6 oz unbleached flour
- 3 oz butter
- 3 oz granulated sugar
- 1 t cinnamon

Filling

- 1 1/2 lb Granny Smith apples
- 4 oz dark brown sugar
- 1 t ginger
- 2 t lemon juice
- 4 T water

Preheat oven to 400°F. Sift the flour and cinnamon into a bowl. Rub or cut the room-temperature butter into the flour until the mixture resembles crumbs (or sand). (If you've never rubbed butter into flour, you're missing a treat, a massage that feels especially good after a hard day at the keyboard.)

Gently stir in the sugar, and then place the bowl aside.

Core, peel, and slice the apples and place into an 8x8x2-inch pan. (For 1 1/2 pounds, I buy three apples; I get around 20 or so slices from each apple. The pan is large enough to have three rows of slices.)

In another bowl, put the brown sugar; add the ginger, lemon juice, and water; and stir the mixture until everything is dissolved. Pour the mixture over the apples as evenly as you can.

Add the crumb mixture over the apple mixture. (Easiest method: Go for the center, and then level the "mountain" with the back of a wood spoon.)

Bake in center of oven for 30 minutes. Or 31 or 32 minutes, but I find 30 minutes works very well.

Six portions, unless you're greedy or hungry.

PUDDING COURSE: APPLE FRITTERS
Gail Carriger

COOK'S NOTES:

You want small dense sour cooking apples for this, the kind you might use for pie. Grannys are too wet. We used pippins. Only needed about 5 apples, billiard-ball sized, to make three fritters each plus extra for a party of 12.

There were no less than four different apple fritter recipes in my Victorian cookbook! This is a batter from one recipe combined with the apple preparation style from another.

We made the batter ahead of time and kept it in the fridge for several hours before using. Batter does not need salt if you use salted butter for frying. Even then I suggest 1 1/2 cubes of unsalted to 1/2 salted instead of 50:50.

The glass of brandy in the recipe probably implies half or three-fourths of a cup, not a whole cup. We ended up adding lots of flour to compensate, but it still worked out.

I would suggest a little more nutmeg and/or cinnamon for modern taste.

The fritters are beautiful but do take a while to make: took us three or four batches. We found the timing perfect if one cook makes fritters while other does custard.

This is British-style liquid custard. I used Bird's Custard powder with half whole milk, half cream, a half teaspoon less the recommended sugar, and a little lemon zest. But, of course, you could use homemade and do ahead of time with ease. Ice cream might also work for the American audience.

The original 1876 recipe, annotated, was as follows:

- Peel and core 1 dz small cooking apples but do not divide.
- Slice into (doughnut-like) 1/2 cm thick rounds.
- Pat apple rounds dry with napkin (Can just cut 2 hours ahead of time and leave out to dry, worked great).
- Beat well 3 eggs and 4 egg yolks with a small quantity of grated nutmeg, pinch of salt (see cook's note), some cornstarch, glass brandy.
- Add gradually sufficient flour to make thick batter (like pancakes).
- Get frying pan quite hot, melt 1/2 lb butter in it! (used 1/2 salted 1/2 sweet, see cook's note).
- Coat apple rounds in batter.
- Drop into pan; flip as needed until golden brown and crispy.
- Remove and place on paper napkin to absorb fat.
- Powder with sugar and serve with wedges of fresh lemon and dollop of custard with more custard in a gravy boat.

Serve hot with champagne or dessert wine or brandy.

APRICOT MASCARPONE POPPERS
Julie Jansen

I've been part of a writers' group for several years. We're six ladies with busy schedules and when we meet once a month, we talk about writing, books, and life in general. We critique our current projects, offer each other support and advice, and we eat! Our dinner meetings usually have a theme: Southern home cooking, Italian, Thai, Turkish, etc. They've led me down paths into other cultures and other worlds I might not otherwise have thought of and have inspired many ideas for writing and art.

As far as Apricot Mascarpone Poppers go, I don't think they really need to fit any particular theme, but I happened to first make them for a Mediterranean-themed dinner.

This dish is one of my favorite party hors d'oeuvre recipes. It uses few ingredients, is simple to make, and guests gobble it up. The poppers are somewhat sweet, somewhat healthy, gluten-free, and vegetarian.

- Sun-dried apricot halves
- Mascarpone cheese
- Salted shelled pistachios, crushed
- Toothpicks

The amount of apricot halves you use depends on the number of guests. When I prepare these for a party, I usually go with the Costco-sized bag of sun-dried apricot halves (usually the best deal) and buy two small 6 oz tubs of mascarpone cheese. This is plenty to make two large plates of poppers, and you'll have plenty of apricot halves (and some mascarpone too) left to snack on. I can't always find crushed pistachios, but do recommend buying the shelled variety. If you have to crush them yourself, place them in a freezer bag and pound on them with the flat side of a meat tenderizer, hammer, or hefty book.

Apricot Mascarpone Poppers can be made several hours before an event, but should be covered and refrigerated until ready to serve.

Instructions
Spread some mascarpone on dried apricot halves. Arrange the apricot halves on a serving plate. Sprinkle with crushed pistachios. Poke each apricot half with a toothpick so they're easy to grab off the plate. *Et voilà!*

AT THE FRUITCAKE OF MADNESS
Esther Friesner

First, chase all shoggoths out of the kitchen and invoke the Black Goat of the Woods with a Thousand Recipes as you preheat the red-litten fires of your oven to 325°F. Next, summon the following ingredients:

- 1 c brown sugar
- 1 c water
- 1 c golden raisins (though plain ol' mundane raisins are also okay). See to it that these have been first sunken (like the lost city of R'lyeh) in rum or brandy (like great Cthulhu) for at least a day before. Drain before using in this recipe. (*Remember, the Perpetrators of this cookbook are Not Responsible for the consequences if the shoggoths get into the jazzed-up raisins. Come to think of it, Not Responsible is pretty much the default setting for said cookbook Perps. But I digress.*)
- 1 c candied fruits
- 1/2 c butter or margarine
- 1/4 t salt
- 2 c flour
- 1 t baking soda
- 2 t baking powder
- 1 t cinnamon
- 1/4 t nutmeg
- 1/2 t ground cloves
- 1/4 t allspice

Boil the sugar, water, raisins, candied fruits, and butter or margarine for 3 minutes. Allow to cool and add the sifted dry ingredients.

Grease a loaf pan and line with parchment paper. It will make extraction so much easier!

Pour batter into prepared pan and bake for 45-60 minutes, or until done.

Test for doneness with a toothpick. When it comes out not dripping with eldritch goo, you're good to go.

Variations: You can get creative and add a tablespoon or two of cocoa to the dry ingredients. You can also add half a cup of chopped walnuts or pecans.

If you decorate the top of this cake with candied cherries and walnut or pecan halves it either comes out looking very pretty or they sink into the batter as in quicksand and are never heard from again. But they still taste good!

CARROT PIE THAT NISI INVENTED
Nisi Shawl

Pie Is the Best Food!

My former roommate and longtime friend Gaiya has a huge crush on carrots, so I created this recipe in her honor. I make carrot pies whenever she visits. One year, I offered the recipe and a singing performance as a Con-or-Bust auction item. I'm so happy that "Carrot Pie That Nisi Invented" is benefiting the SFF cause yet again by appearing in this collection.

Pies evoke in me such sensawunda: beneath their mysterious lattices or golden top crusts could lie almost anything. I once shared a Thanksgiving meal consisting entirely of pies with my Clarion West classmate Holly Wade Matter and her husband Brad Matter. I have enjoyed bean pies, peanut butter pies, grapefruit, parsnip—as a concept, pie is full of potential.

That said, there are some pies I loathe rather than love. Raisin pie is the most disgusting thing to come out of Canada ever. Ever. Mince pie, a close relative, is nearly as regrettable; I've never met a mince pie I liked.

Perhaps, also, some pies are better as theories than praxes. Walking with Eileen Gunn one morning, I listened in fascination as she described the filling of the traditional Cornish Stargazy Pie: pilchards with bobbed tails standing upright, staring heavenward. An arresting image, though not, I think, a guarantee of deliciousness.

But then, what is?

Ingredients:
- 4.25 c organic carrots cut in pretty small pieces
- Nice-looking carrot cross sections
- 2 c vanilla soymilk
- 1.375 c brown sugar
- 6 T canola oil
- 2 T molasses
- 1 t salt
- 1.5 t cinnamon
- 1 t nutmeg
- 0.25 t cloves
- 0.15 t cayenne pepper (or to taste)
- 0.5 c cornstarch
- 2 gluten-free vegan frozen pie shells (The ones from The Flying Apron in Seattle are great!)

Steam the 4.25 cups of carrots for about half an hour. While they are steaming, preheat the oven to 350°F, then stick the pie shells in to bake for maybe five minutes. When you take them out, pump up the oven temperature to 425°F.

Also use this interval in time to mix the salt, cornstarch, and spices together thoroughly in a small mixing bowl.

In a very large mixing bowl, stir the soymilk and brown sugar together. When the carrots are done steaming, plop them in that same bowl. Then put the pretty carrot cross sections on the stovetop to steam, adding more water if necessary. You're only going to let them go for about 20 minutes.

Meanwhile, mash up the 4.25 cups of carrots with the sugar and soymilk using a mashing thing, until all the pieces are small, like crumbs. Then add the oil, then the molasses. If you do the oil before the molasses using the same spoon, the molasses will slide right off the spoon most elegantly.

Once all that's mixed together, add the salt/spice/cornstarch stuff and mix everything up some more. Then pour that mixture into the pie shells. Decorate the tops with the steamed circular and rhomboidal carrot cross sections.

Bake the pies at 425°F for ten minutes. Lower the temperature to 350°F and bake them for another 40-50 minutes. You can check to see if their fillings are "set" in the middle by poking them with a wooden chopstick. If the holes you make disappear immediately, the answer is "no." Let the pies cool when they're through baking. Give them at least another thirty minutes before you eat them.

CADBURY EGG BROWNIE
Beth Cato

(Modified from *Love and Oil*)

Confession: I used to be a total Cadbury Egg junkie. As a kid, they were one of my very, very favorite seasonal candies—up there with Brach's Mellowcreme Pumpkins at Halloween.

When I delved into my Easter basket, these were what I wanted most of all. I always traded with my brother—Reese's Peanut Butter Eggs for Cadbury Eggs. I ate them in particular ways, too. The goal was to eat them without getting any of the egg ooze on my fingers. I'd try to eat the chocolate shell part way down and then suck out the center.

For a number of years, I would buy Cadbury Eggs at Easter and keep them in the fridge for months.

Then came adulthood and the awareness that this stuff wasn't so good for me. About ten years ago, I found that the eggs made my teeth hurt horribly. So I stopped eating them.

I came across this recipe last year, though, and knew I had to make them. The joy of baking this stuff is that I can have a tiny sample and then foist the rest on my husband to take to his work.

These really do taste like Cadbury Eggs, but better. Why? Because they have the sweetness of that gooey center but it's reduced greatly by the brownie layer. It balances more. Mind you, it's still not the slightest bit healthy, but it's more like getting slapped by the sugar rather than knocked upside the head with a two-by-four.

Brownies
- 2/3 c flour
- 2 T cocoa powder
- 1/2 t salt
- 6 oz milk chocolate, chopped
- 1/2 c (1 stick) unsalted butter, cut into cubes
- 1/4 c granulated sugar
- 1/2 c light brown sugar, packed
- 2 large eggs, at room temperature, lightly beaten
- 1 t vanilla extract

Cream Filling
- 1/4 c light corn syrup
- 2 T unsalted butter, room temperature
- 1/2 t vanilla extract
- 1/8 t salt
- 1 1/2 c powdered sugar, sifted

Glaze
- 4 oz milk chocolate, chopped
- 2 T unsalted butter, cut into cubes

Brownie Stage
Preheat oven to 350°F. Line the bottom and sides of a 8x8-inch pan with aluminum foil or parchment paper, making sure to overlap the sides to create handles. Cover with nonstick spray.

Sift together flour, cocoa, and salt in a small bowl and set aside.

Melt chocolate and butter together in a double boiler or in slow increments in microwave. Stir until smooth. Whisk in sugars and stir until dissolved and mixture has cooled slightly, then add eggs and vanilla extract until just combined.

Fold together the chocolate and flour mixes until just incorporated. Pour into prepared pan.

Bake for 25-30 minutes or until toothpick inserted into the middle comes out clean. Transfer pan to a wire rack and allow to cool completely.

Cream Filling Stage
Beat together corn syrup, butter, vanilla, and salt on medium-high speed until smooth. Add powdered sugar, a little bit at a time, mixing until creamy.

Dump three-fourths of the cream mixture on top of cooled brownies and spread into an even layer. Add a drop of yellow food coloring to remaining cream mixture and stir until evenly colored. Drop dollops of yellow cream on top of white layer, and then swirl gently with a spatula. Refrigerate for at least 2 hours or until set.

Glaze Stage
Slowly melt the chocolate and butter together in a double boiler or microwave bowl. Stir until smooth. Pour over cream filling, carefully spreading into a thin, even layer.

Let set in fridge about 15-20 minutes and then use the foil/paper to lift the entire block out of the pan. Using a large sharp knife, cut into 2-inch squares. Keep in sealed container in fridge; brownies will keep upward of a week.

OM NOM NOM.

CARDAMOM BREAD
David Brin

- 1 pkg dry yeast, dissolved in 1/4 cup lukewarm milk and 2 t flour, and left to sit for half a day
- 2 c milk
- 1 t salt
- 1/4 c shortening or butter
- 3/4 c sugar
- 1/2 t cardamom (preferably freshly ground)
- 2 eggs
- 6-7 c flour

Scald the milk; add sugar and shortening and salt. Cool to lukewarm; add cardamom, beaten eggs, and yeast. Add flour and knead, folding several times. Place dough in refrigerator and allow to rise slowly until it approximately doubles in size. Punch down the dough, divide into thirds. Roll each third into long strips. Braid the strips together. Set in a greased pan and give time to rise again.

Preheat oven to 350°F.

After dough has risen, bake to suit.

For an interesting effect, divide in thirds before adding flour. Make one or two of these segments out of a 50:50 mix of white and whole wheat flour. When finally braided together, the thirds combine with a multicolored, multi-textured effect.

CHEATING ON CROQUEMBOUCHE
Brenda W. Clough

A croquembouche is constructed out of a number of small cream puffs, stuck together into a Christmas-tree-like structure. It is the sort of thing that Martha Stewart makes, and if you want to do it her way, many recipes are available via Google. Do it her way, and dedicate a day to the project. However, I have invented a horrific cheat. This takes about half an hour but looks exactly the same, and tastes just fine. Make it the day you plan to serve it, because it does not keep at all. Because of the Christmas-tree pyramid shape, it makes a fine show at holiday parties, and everyone will believe you worked like a dog.

- 1 tub frozen mini cream puffs (I buy mine from Costco—there are 100-odd in each tub.)
- 2 c plain white sugar

Take the tub of frozen cream puffs out the night before and thaw them in the refrigerator.

Select a serving plate for this confection—about dinner-plate-sized is right. You will attach the croquembouche to it, so choose well. It should be reasonably heat-proof and heavy—not plastic, in other words.

Put the 2 cups of sugar into a heavy 2-quart saucepan and heat it on a medium flame. Add nothing and do not stir it. Keep an eye on it when it starts to caramelize. It'll turn brown and start to bubble at the edges. At this point, you can carefully shake it to encourage it all to melt down. It is ready when all the sugar is melted and the entire mass is dark brown. This will take at least 15 or 20 minutes. Handle the pan with oven mitts and be very, very careful not to splash the liquefied sugar—it can give you a nasty burn.

When it is ready, turn the flame down very low. Set your plate by the pan, and have the cream puff tub open and on hand.

One by one, take a cream puff and swipe its bottom through the hot caramel. Stick it onto the plate. You want to create a circle with about eight or nine puffs. The sugar will set as it touches the cool plate, and glue the puff tightly and instantly down. If you make a total error you will have to pry the puff off the plate with a metal fork. (All mistakes can be eaten.) Be very careful not to touch the liquid caramel with your bare fingers.

When you have a nice circle of puffs firmly affixed to the plate, it's time to go up! Glue a slightly smaller circle of puffs on top of the first one. Get enough caramel onto each puff so that it can stick to the one below, and also to the one beside it. If your bottom circle had nine puffs, the second could have eight. And then a third round of seven, and six, and so on up to the top! The very top puff will be a single one, sitting on top of perhaps three puffs in a triangle. This is fine. Keep the structure as symmetrical as you can, and use a lot of caramel so that it'll be reasonably sturdy.

If there is caramel left, pour it on top of the entire structure. If you are deft, you can use the fork to draw out strands of spun sugar to swirl around the pyramid, but you have to work quickly since the caramel tends to set up very fast. But drips and drabs of caramel are perfectly acceptable, and help structural integrity.

You will find that you do not use all of the puffs. Leftovers can be refrozen and eaten later. The recipe scales up to a degree—your pyramid can be shorter and wider, but there is a limit on how high you can go. It looks best if the base is not very wide and the tree is as tall as possible—I have gotten it about 20 inches high on a standard sized dinner plate. If you are making it much bigger, be sure and use more sugar. Plenty of caramel is necessary.

Further refinements could include chocolate sauce—squirt it extravagantly on top. If you want to add rum, I would use a turkey baster or even a hypodermic syringe (no needle) to inject a couple drops into the individual puffs. If you were properly generous with the caramel the structure will not pull apart for serving all that easily, but you will find that people do not complain if they are forced to eat two or three puffs.

Serves a large party, 12-30 people. Anything left over should be stored in the fridge. Leftovers vanish within a day.

DOOM COOKIES
Steven Saus

Let me spare you the forced jokes and stale humor about coffee, whether or not it has traveled through a vole's intestines. I will not make some dark reference to chocolate's past. I won't even attempt to lie to you about my love for cookies, though I might about cakes.

Instead, I will share with you this gift of a recipe. These Doom Cookies are easy to make, and will stimulate your gathering. Initial skepticism gives way to delight as the ingredients blend on the palate . . . and in the central nervous system.
Makes about 18 cookie bars.

- 2 c graham crackers crumbs (about 32 graham crackers)
- ·1 c (6 oz) semisweet chocolate chips

- 1 t baking powder
- Pinch of salt
- 1 can (14 oz) sweetened condensed milk
- 1/8 c fresh coffee grounds (may be adjusted upward to taste)

Combine all ingredients in a mixing bowl; stir to combine. Spread into a greased 8x8x2 inch square baking pan.

Bake at 350°F for 30-35 minutes, or until toothpick inserted near center comes out clean.

Cool cookie bars on wire rack.

FALLING CLOUD CAKE
Fran Wilde & Miriam Weinberg

(With the addition of espresso and Grand Marnier, this recipe has been altered to two different variations from an Alison Roman *Bon Appétit* recipe called "Fallen Chocolate Cake")

One of us (the editor) is a baker; the other (the writer) has rarely dared it (due to a preference for savory food, improvising in the kitchen, and a slight aversion to measuring). This recipe for Falling Cloud Cake is a perfect balance of light and dark, improvisation and structure, sweet and savory. Especially when you note that both the espresso and the Grand Marnier have a "to taste" option. ~ FW

Chocolate Cake
- 1/2 cup unsalted butter, cut into 1 inch pieces, plus more for pan
- 3/4 cup plus 2 T sugar, divided
- 10 oz semisweet chocolate, coarsely chopped
- 2 T vegetable oil
- 6 large eggs
- 2 T natural unsweetened cocoa powder
- 1 t vanilla extract
- 3/4 t kosher salt
- 1 t espresso, or to taste

Cloud Top
- 1 c chilled heavy cream
- 1/2 c mascarpone
- 1 T Grand Marnier, or to taste
- 3 T powdered sugar

Cake

Preheat oven to 350°. Butter 9-inch springform pan and dust with sugar, tapping out any excess.

Combine chocolate, oil, and a half cup butter in a large heatproof bowl. Set over a saucepan of simmering water and heat, stirring often, until melted. Remove bowl from saucepan.

Separate four eggs, placing whites and yolks in separate medium bowls. Add cocoa powder, vanilla, salt, 1/4 cup sugar, and remaining two eggs to bowl with yolks and whisk until mixture is smooth. Gradually whisk yolk mixture into chocolate mixture, blending well. Blend espresso into chocolate mixture.

Using an electric mixer on high speed, beat egg whites until frothy. With mixer running, gradually beat in 1/2 cup sugar; beat until firm peaks form.

Gently fold egg whites into chocolate mixture in two additions, folding just until incorporated between additions. Scrape batter into prepared pan; smooth top and sprinkle with remaining 2 tablespoons sugar.

Bake until top is puffed and starting to crack and cake is pulling away from edge of pan, 35-45 minutes. Transfer to a wire rack and let cake cool completely in pan. (Cake will collapse in the center and crack further as it cools.)

Topping

Using an electric mixer on medium-high speed, beat cream, mascarpone, Grand Marnier, and powdered sugar in a medium bowl until soft peaks form.

Remove sides of springform pan from cake. Mound whipped cream mixture in center of cake.

FRESH GINGER CAKE
Lee Hallison

Even more delicious the second day!

Preheat oven to 350°F. Line bottom of 9.5-inch springform pan with a circle of parchment paper.

Mix together:
- 1/2 c minced fresh ginger (Grated is fine too, but I can never get the whole root grated, so end up chopping fine instead.)
- 2/3 c mild molasses
- 1/3 c honey
- 1 c sugar
- 1 c oil

Stir in separate bowl (I use a whisk, gently, to combine ingredients and aerate flour):
- 2-1/2 c flour
- 1/2 t cinnamon
- 1/4 t ground cloves
- 1/4 t fresh ground black pepper (or more if you like a peppery cake)

Boil 1 cup water; add 2 teaspoons baking soda. Add to molasses ginger mix.

Combine wet and dry ingredients; mix well.

Add two eggs; mix well.

Pour into prepared pan and bake for one hour at 350°F, until top springs back or when toothpick comes out clean. It's perfect if it's moist on the bottom and sides but fully cooked through the middle. (Don't overcook!) Let cool 30 minutes, take out of pan and peel off parchment paper. Serve with lightly sweetened whipped cream.

GRANDMA'S CREAM CHEESE CRACKERS
Pat Cadigan

This is a piece of Genuine Depression Era cooking that has actually been in my family for about five generations. The cholesterol-conscious will shudder, and a steady diet of this stuff will probably give you a heart attack, but my grandmother found it was the best way to make a short supply of milk and eggs go around seven kids, a husband, and others who dropped in unexpectedly. If you have a kid at home who won't touch eggs or milk and you're worried about it, this is a great way to sneak it in. Kids think it's junk food and snarf it up. (Used as hors d'oeuvres at parties, they're the first to disappear—the crackers, I mean. Not the kids.)

Make a dipping batter of eggs and milk in a bowl: two to three tablespoons milk to one well-beaten egg, well-mixed.

Make "sandwiches" of soda crackers or saltines and cream cheese.

Dip sandwiches in milk and egg mixture and fry slowly in butter or margarine.

NOTE: the finished product will be kind of soft. May be stored in the fridge for several days, enjoyed cold or heated up.

GRANDMA'S MAGIC ALMOND COOKIES
Stina Leicht

When I was a kid, my grandfather worked for Chevrolet in St. Louis, and my family traveled from Texas to Missouri once or twice a year. Every holiday season we were there, Grandma Leicht would bake an entire vat* of holiday cookies—yes, even the iced ones—in spite of being surrounded by a raiding horde of about twenty grandkids, hovering close like agitated hummingbirds. We targeted the pre-baked cookies on the baking tray. We hit the mixing bowl before the dough landed on the cookie sheet. We even snatched up cookies before they were finished cooling. She never got angry. She would just smile, laugh, and continue baking. She'd take requests too. All without help. And she still managed to fill that plastic vat. I've never seen anyone else do it. I always assumed she had some sort of magical powers. It wasn't until recently—when my mother was going through her recipe files and came across Grandma's holiday cookie recipe—that I finally understood how Grandma did it. Turns out, she had a base cookie recipe she could pre-make in bulk and then change out the extra ingredients as needed. That is, my grandma had applied assembly-line tactics to cooking. I'm not going to give you that recipe now. Legally, I can't, but what I will give you is my own variant on that recipe—a variant my Grandma never made.

*Grandma had a Tupperware™ cake-keeper which she'd invert and use as a temporary cookie-keeper.

- 1 1/2 c butter
- 1/2 c almond butter
- 1 T salt
- 1 c brown sugar
- 2 t baking powder
- 1 egg
- 6 c all-purpose flour
- 1/4 c whole almonds

Preheat oven to 375°F. Mix butter and almond butter together in a large bowl with an electric mixer for about a minute. Then add salt, sugar, and baking powder. Lastly, add the egg and mix well. With that done, stir in as much flour as you can with the mixer—switch to a spoon when the dough is too dense for the mixer. Place in fridge to chill for a bit until the dough is easy to handle. Form into balls and flatten with a fork as you would peanut butter cookies. Center a whole (or half) almond on top. Bake for eight to twelve minutes until slightly brown. Should yield about four dozen cookies.

GRAVEYARD PUDDING
JG Flaherty

Graveyards are interesting places, at least to me. As a boy, I played in one with my friends. As an adult, I can appreciate them for being oases of serenity on a summer afternoon or solemn muses on a wind-swept gray winter morning. At night, they can force you to relive your childhood by delivering a chill up your spine when you dare walk through one. And, of course, what is Halloween without graveyards? With that in mind, every Halloween I serve my Graveyard Pudding as part of our dessert table.

Ingredients:
- Chocolate pudding mix (instant)
- Milk
- Oreo cookies
- Gummy worms

Additional Items:
- Plastic bugs or zombie toys or other tiny monster toys
- Cardboard
- Magic Marker

Directions:
Prepare enough instant chocolate pudding to fill your favorite cake or brownie pan about two inches deep. Let it set in the bowl, and then before pouring into the pan, crumble up half a package or so of the Oreos into crumbs and mix three-quarters of it with the pudding. Pour the pudding-cookie mix into the pan and then press several of the gummy worms under the surface. Put the pan into the fridge, covered, until just before the guests arrive.

Before the party, use the Magic Marker and cardboard to create tiny (2-inch tall) headstones with funny inscriptions.

An hour or so before putting it on the table, top it with the rest of the Oreo crumbs. Scatter the bugs and/or monster-related decorations on the top. Set the tombstones up. Place the dish in a prominent place on the table. Warn the kiddies not to eat the toys!

JOYCE'S PRALINES
Victoria McManus

I make pralines for my family in my home state of Louisiana every Christmas or New Year's, but I've also occasionally made them for writerly parties in my current home, Philadelphia. It's very important to pronounce the name correctly—they're prah-leens, not pray-leens. This recipe was perfected by my father's younger sister, Joyce.

- 1 c brown sugar
- 2 c white sugar

- 3 c pecans, halved
- 1 c evaporated milk
- 2 T butter
- 1 t vanilla
- Dash salt

In a saucepan, cook sugar and milk over medium heat, stirring occasionally, until it boils gently. Add pecans, lower heat, and stir gently until the mixture makes a soft ball in cool water (i.e., drip a bit into a cup of water, and if it sticks together, it's about right. The soft ball will deform into a lozenge-shape as it sinks). Remove from heat and stir in butter, vanilla, and salt, stirring until mixture thickens—you will feel the change. Drop quickly by spoonfuls onto greased cookie sheets or wax paper. Allow to harden.

—

LIME PIE
James D. MacDonald

A short story is like a pie because, first, you can do one relatively quickly. Second, everyone likes pie. Third, with both short stories and pie, you can use the finest ingredients in the world and still come up with an inedible mess. Fourth, if you come up with a mess, you have to get brand new ingredients and try again, using what you learned last time to make a better pie.

For example: if you make an apple pie, and things go badly, you cannot take those now-cooked apples and cook them again. They'll be soggy, limp, and burned around the edges. And the spices will be all wrong.

With some pies, like the lime pie (recipe below), you don't know if you've got a pie or a messy soup until you put it in front of your dining companions and cut it open. Same with a story. When your beta readers read your story, they will tell you whether the story works or not.

If a story doesn't work, you've got to start fresh.

[Excerpted from *Cooking the Books* (franwilde.wordpress.com/cooking-the-books)]

Pie Shell
- Whites of 3 large fresh eggs, at room temperature
- 1/4 t cream of tartar
- 1/8 t salt
- 3/4 c sugar

Heat oven to 300°F Lightly grease a 9-inch pie plate.

Beat egg whites in a medium bowl on medium speed until frothy.

Add cream of tartar and salt and beat on high speed until soft peaks form when beaters are lifted.

Beat in 1/4 cup of the sugar, 1 tablespoon at a time, until blended. With mixer on low speed, sprinkle on remaining sugar and beat until blended.

Spread meringue over bottom and sides of prepared dish.

Bake until lightly browned, about 45 minutes.

Cool in dish on wire rack.

Pie Filling
- 6 egg yolks, slightly beaten
- 1/3 c lime juice
- 2 1/2 T grated lime rind
- 1 c granulated sugar
- 1/4 t salt
- 2 T cold water
- 6 egg whites
- 1/8 t baking powder
- 1/4 c granulated sugar

Beat egg yolks until thick and lemon-colored.

Add lime juice, rind, sugar, and salt; beat mixture until thoroughly blended. Cook mixture in a double-boiler until very thick, stirring constantly.

Now add the cold water to the egg whites and beat until stiff but not dry.

Combine baking powder and remaining 1/4 cup sugar and add to beaten egg white mixture. Beat until stiff.

Fold hot lime mixture into half the egg white meringue; fill pre-baked pieshell. Cover with remaining meringue.

Sprinkle lightly with sugar and bake 15 minutes in a moderately slow oven (325°F) or until meringue is delicately brown. Chill and serve cold.

LOVE & ROMANPUNK MACARONS
Tansy Rayner Roberts

This recipe is not mine, but provided by a dear friend, Terri Sellen, on my behalf. Terri works for the Australian boutique publisher Twelfth Planet Press in publicity and marketing, and for the last few years has been providing Extreme Cake Support for TPP's book launches. For the Twelve Planets series of miniature short story collections by Australian women writers, she has designed a series of cupcakes, and more recently, macarons, to match the cover and theme of each book. My own contribution to this series, Love and Romanpunk, *is a book that takes extreme liberties with the history of the Julio-Claudian family in ancient Rome. (Honestly, that period of history makes so much more sense if you add werewolves.) The cover is purple, which is extremely relevant to the interests of these delicious macarons! The macarons are gluten- and dairy-free.*

Macarons
- 65 g almond meal
- 80 g icing sugar
- Purple food coloring—powdered or gel
- 50 g egg white
- 40 g caster sugar

Filling
- 3/4 c raw cashews
- 2 T olive oil
- 1 T honey
- 1/4 t fresh lemon juice
- 2 t fig paste
- 40 ml port wine

To Make Filling:
Soak cashews for two to three hours and then rinse thoroughly.

Combine all filling ingredients in a blender and blitz until smooth and creamy. Add water, or more wine, as necessary.

Chill in the fridge for at least an hour. The mixture will thicken as it chills.

When thoroughly chilled, spoon into a piping bag.

To Make Macarons:
Place almond meal and icing sugar in a blender or food processor. If you are using a powdered food colorant, add it to this mix. Blitz mixture until very fine. Put aside.

Pour egg whites into a clean mixing bowl and mix on a low speed for three minutes.

Turn mixer up to medium speed; pour in caster sugar. If you are using a gel food colorant, add it to this mix now. Mix for another three minutes.

Turn mixer to high and beat for a further three minutes. Mixture should be dry and very stiff.

Pour almond meal mixture into the bowl with egg whites.

Using your spatula, mix almond meal into egg whites. There is no need to be overly gentle, but be very careful not to over-mix. (This is the step that will most likely determine if your macarons will fail. There is a fine line between under-mixed and over-mixed. One will leave your macarons with nipples, the other will turn the mix into a pool of liquid that runs everywhere.)

When mixture is combined, drag your spatula through the center of the mix. It should slowly close and after about twenty seconds you shouldn't be able to see where your spatula went.

Fit a piping bag with a large round tip and spoon mixture into it. If you want to let your colors develop, place in the fridge for a few hours or even overnight (colors tend to lighten as the mixture cooks).

Pipe onto your macaron mat or prepared baking paper. (To prepare baking paper: Measure your baking tray and tear a length of baking paper three times as big. Fold it into thirds. Open the top leaf and, using a dark pencil, draw 1.5-inch diameter circles a minimum of one inch apart. When you are finished, fold leaf back again. You should be able to see the circles through the paper.) Don't over-fill the circles.

Slide the mat or paper onto a baking tray. Holding the tray firmly, bang it down on your bench top. This will pop any air bubbles that may expand and crack your shells. Let sit for at least 20 minutes. If it is particularly humid, you may need to leave them longer.

When the macarons are dry to a quick, gentle touch, you can place them in the oven.

Cook at 130°C for 15 minutes. (Know your oven. This is the other likely area that will make or break your macarons.)

To test if they're done, tap one of the macarons lightly—it should sound hollow. Or hold one of the corner macarons and gently try to peel the baking paper or mat off. If it comes away easily, it is done.

When done, remove from the oven and slide the mat or paper onto a cool surface.

Leave the macarons until completely cool before trying to remove them.

When completely cooled, lay out in pairs. Try to keep each pair even in size.

Pipe filling onto half the shells. Place the tops on each.

Now for the hardest step. Macarons may be eaten immediately, but are better if they're given around 24 hours to "ripen." Put in an airtight container and refrigerate.

NOTE: Macarons freeze beautifully. Make a batch, store them in an airtight container, and pop them in your freezer. Then pull out a couple just before you make a cup of tea. By the time the tea is ready, they should be ready to eat.

MARS COLONY CAKE
Or, How to Bake a Cake When You Don't Have Any Cows or Chickens Handy (i.e., butter, milk, or eggs)
Connie Willis

- 1 1/2 c flour
- 1 c sugar
- 3 T cocoa
- 1 t baking soda
- 1/2 t salt
- 5 T cooking oil
- 1 T vinegar
- 1 t vanilla
- 1 c cold water

I know, I know, but trust me. Just mix everything together and bake in a 9x9 inch pan that you've buttered first, and then, if you're feeling industrious, make some chocolate frosting (mix 1 tablespoon butter, 3 tablespoons cocoa, 1 teaspoon vanilla, a dollop of milk, and some powdered sugar in a pan over low heat). If not, put some canned frosting from the store on it. That's what the colonists at Bradbury Base would probably do. Either way, it's a great, dark, chewy cake.

Take it from an old punster; bash cake is good for what ails you—and your bash. It has the food of the gods—chocolate—and no butter. And best of all, you can make it (indeed you *should* make it) when you are angry.

EDITOR'S NOTE: *Jane Yolen agrees. Her account of the same cake contains the following:*

As SFWA president for two years, I had plenty of times to need to bake this cake. There was the John Shirley/Scott Card bash cake. There was the Blue Jay books bash cake. There was the Nebula controversies (redux) bash cake. There was the who-hung-up-on-me-this-time bash cake. If I had been Grievance Chair, I would probably have made even more bash cakes.

I got this recipe from a good friend of mine, a writer of little prominence and no ulcers. The following limerick goes with it.

> *There once was a writer of trash*
> *Whose insides were knots, kinks and mash.*
> *So I taught him to make*
> *A delectable cake*
> *Now instead of an ulcer—there's Bash!*

It's especially useful after a rejection letter (did you know Madeleine L'Engle had 29 rejections on *A Wrinkle in Time?*), bad reviews (Howard Pyle's first books were greeted coolly by critics), or poor sales.

MOONBUCKS
Toni Weisskopf

Makes 180 balls, give or take, and you will want to give; this is a ridiculous amount for one person. I used these at parties to promote DeepSouthCon 50, which had a lunar theme. These are a variation on regular chocolate buckeyes. It's a simple recipe but as with many simple recipes, technique and attention to detail make a difference. Note also this is anti-health food. Will counteract the benefits of many salads and tofu patties.

Insides
- 1 t vanilla
- 1 lb butter, softened
- 2 lb creamy peanut butter—use Skippy
- 3 lb powdered sugar

Mix above ingredients thoroughly, until mixture is uniform. You can use a heavy duty mixer, like a KitchenAid, but dough will be very stiff, so you probably will need to end with hands. If you do the whole thing with hands, you will feel like Rosie the Riveter. It will take a while. A long while. Roll into small balls, about cocktail meatball size, and place on wax or parchment paper over cookie sheets to await dipping. Too small won't work, too big won't work.

Dip
- A couple of packages of white chocolate bark (commonly found in the baking goods aisle). Best to buy three, just in case. You can always dip pretzels into it if there are leftovers.

Over a double boiler, melt chocolate. (My double boiler is a regular pot with a metal mixing bowl plopped over it.) Once water is boiling, lower heat so a gentle steam is maintained so chocolate stays melted while you are dipping.

Bring one cookie sheet's worth of innards to the stove at a time. Taking a wooden toothpick (plastic ones are okay, but the innards slip off more easily and you can lose them in the hot chocolate, which then makes the outsides lumpy, and you don't want that), inserted about a third to half of the way into the ball, dip into chocolate and swirl around, coating most of the ball, but leaving the top open. (Hence "buckeye": the chocolate ones look like chestnuts called "buckeyes." Ohio is the "Buckeye" State, by the way, which is why Ohio State's football team is nicknamed the "Buckeyes." So now you know.) Place back on waxed cookie sheet.

Let sit until chocolate is set. Store in a tightly covered container; if stacked, use wax paper between layers. They will last weeks. They can be frozen; will last until the heat death of the universe. Approximately 75 cals/moonbuck; no redeeming nutritional value to speak of.

MISS MURDER'S BLACK FOREST TRIFLE
Mercedes Yardley

There are few things more dark and delightful than the Black Forest. It's treacherous; rife with goblins and monsters, faeries and werewolves. The forest has teeth and claws, and yet in the midst of this danger are lovely things. Queens who choose to do good. Brave soldiers like Bearskin. Little girls who want nothing more than to bring Grannie a basket, even if it means braving the wolves. There's a sweet note that blends well with the horror of this magical forest.

I've learned to savor the darkness along with delight. This is an easy, rich trifle based on the sexy playfulness of the Black Forest. Chocolate, cherries, and whipped cream make this a beautiful and appetizing dessert. You can layer the ingredients into one large trifle dish, or into individual clear glasses for something that will give you a taste of the dark divine.

- 1 jar maraschino cherries
- 1/2 c sugar
- 2 c heavy cream
- 1 c powdered sugar
- 2 T vanilla extract
- 1 lb chocolate cake
- Chocolate shavings

Drain the cherries, reserving the liquid. Mix the liquid in a small sauce pan with half a cup of sugar. Simmer until the liquid becomes thick and reduces to about half. Don't reduce too much, or the liquid will harden later. Let it cool and then mix the cherries back in.

Whip the heavy cream, powdered sugar, and vanilla extract until it forms stiff peaks. The whipped cream will turn dark in color, but it's absolutely delicious and still looks beautiful.

Layer the trifle with the cake, cherries, and whipped cream, and then repeat, topping with the whipped cream. Grate chocolate shavings on the top, and top with a remaining cherry, if you'd like.

OATMEAL CAKE
Vylar Kaftan

This is a family recipe that's been served at all our birthday parties and math department potlucks. Instead of frosting, it has melted chocolate on top. Because why bother interrupting pure chocolate?

Cake
- 1 c oatmeal
- 8 T butter (one stick)
- 1 c sugar
- 1 c brown sugar
- 2 eggs
- 1 1/2 c flour
- 1/2 t salt
- 1 t baking soda
- 1 t cinnamon

Topping
- 6 T butter
- 2/3 c brown sugar
- 1/4 c evaporated milk
- 1 c shredded coconut
- 1 t vanilla
- 1 bag chocolate chips

Combine and let cool: one cup oatmeal with one and a half cups boiling water.

Cream a half cup butter, one cup sugar, and one cup brown sugar.

Add two eggs.

Sift in one and a half cups flour, a half teaspoon salt, and one teaspoon baking soda.

Bake at 350°F for 45 minutes. Let cool in pan.

For topping: melt six tablespoons butter, two-thirds cup brown sugar.

Add a quarter cup evaporated milk, one cup coconut, and one teaspoon vanilla. Spread on cooled cake.

Sprinkle cake with chocolate chips. Broil briefly (a few minutes) and watch the cake so you don't burn it. Very gently, spread out the melted chocolate just a bit (it is okay if it's lumpy).

PEANUT BUTTER BARS
Bonnie Jo Stufflebeam

This is my mother's recipe, a childhood favorite of mine. My mother, too, loved these as a child; she tells me that she and her sister, Linda, ate a similar peanut butter bar in elementary school. For years they tried to find the recipe. Finally, in her twenties, my mother found this recipe in a cookbook. Over the years, she modified it according to her memory of the peanut butter bars she and her sister loved, until it became her own. From her modifications I too made my own, and so the recipe, much like SFWA, has grown and changed over the years.

Bars
- 1/3 c shortening
- 1 c sugar
- 1/4 c brown sugar, firmly packed
- 1/2 c peanut butter (creamy or crunchy)
- 2 T applesauce
- 1 t vanilla
- 1 c flour
- 1 t baking powder
- 1/4 t salt
- 1/2 c quick oats
- 2 T water

Chocolate Frosting
- 1/4 c shortening
- 1/4 c margarine
- 1 1/4 c powdered sugar
- 3/4 t vanilla
- 1/2 c cocoa powder
- 1/8 c almond milk

Preheat oven to 350°F. Cream together shortening, sugars, and peanut butter until light and fluffy. Add applesauce and beat well. Add vanilla and blend.

Mix flour, baking powder, and salt. Add to creamed mixture. Mix. Stir in oats and water. Spread batter in greased 13x9x2-inch baking pan.

Bake 15-20 minutes. Let cool. Spread with frosting. (For frosting, combine all ingredients and cream until smooth .) Cut into bars. Makes two dozen.

PEANUT BUTTER DIP WITH APPLES
Rosemary Claire Smith

This recipe shows that sometimes the simplest food combinations can be among the best. It's quick and easy to make, and that means more time for writing!

Speaking of writing, when I'm getting to know my point-of-view characters, I need to determine a few of their food preferences and idiosyncrasies. What vicarious fun it's been to let my characters enjoy a dish that my own food allergies prevent me from eating. When it comes time to torment these characters, I have no problem with making them eat something they loathe, but I've never yet been able to force a single one of them to go hungry.

- 2/3 c smooth peanut butter
- 2/3 c honey
- 1/4 c lemon juice (fresh or bottled)
- 2 or 3 eating apples such as Granny Smiths, sliced, but not peeled

Make sure the honey is at room temperature. Beat together the peanut butter, honey, and lemon juice using an electric mixer at low speed. Transfer to a nice serving dish. Just before serving, place the dip on a round platter and surround with apple slices.

ALTERNATIVE: Use sliced bananas instead of apples.

TIP: Don't slice the apples too soon or they'll turn brown.

PRINCESS ALETHEA'S FAMOUS BAKLAVA
Alethea Kontis

My author bio boasts that I make "the best baklava you've ever tasted." For years in my family, my Aunt Theda (Theda C. Kontis, MD) was always known for making the best baklava in the world. My parents disagreed once, boasting that I could beat Theda hands down, even though I was only a teen. The resulting heated discussion led to The Great Kontis Baklava Bake-Off of 1989 . . . which I ultimately won.

It's not a particularly difficult dish to make, just incredibly time consuming, so I only ever trot it out for very special people or very special occasions. Without fail, every time I make this recipe, I receive a proposal of marriage. The irony is . . . baklava is really not my favorite Greek pastry. I prefer kourambiethes.

- 1-2 sticks melted butter
- 1 box phyllo sheets

Nut Mixture
- 1 bag (16 oz) walnuts, crushed
- 1/4 c sugar
- 2 t cinnamon

Syrup
- 1 c water
- 1 c sugar
- 1 T lemon juice
- 3/4 c honey

Prep time: A good long while. Have some good music and comfortable shoes.

Cook time: One hour, plus cooling time, plus time for the syrup to sink in.

Best when made the day before eating. Eat within seven days. (It won't last that long.)

Yield: about 48 small pieces

Quantities in this recipe vary, as do the methods of baklava assembly. The first time you make this, just assemble the baklava until you run out of something (phyllo or nuts) and then alter future ingredients to your taste (different nuts in the mixture, almond flavoring in the syrup, etc). If you run out of butter, however, just add more. Yiayia always said, the difference between a good cook and a great cook is half a pound of butter.

Brush butter into a 9x13-inch glass baking dish. Lay three to five sheets of phyllo at the bottom. (Trim to size. Phyllo should be kept beneath plastic wrap and/or a dish towel during assembly so it doesn't dry out.) Brush phyllo with butter. Then:

1. Sprinkle a thin layer of nut mixture onto buttered phyllo.
2. Add one sheet of phyllo.
3. Brush with butter.

Repeat steps 1-3 until either phyllo or nut mixture is gone. Top with three to five sheets of nice, unbroken phyllo, and butter the top.

Cut the baklava before you cook it. Using a very sharp knife, cut into small squares, then cut each square into triangles. pour any leftover butter onto baklava. Bake at 350°F for about an hour (until brown).

Syrup: Boil sugar and water until sugar is fully dissolved . . . plus two minutes. Take the saucepan off the burner, then stir in the lemon and honey.

Pour syrup over cooled baklava and let stand overnight. (Leave it on the counter, covered in plastic wrap.) For a party, serve individual triangles in foil muffin tins.

PUMPKIN CRANBERRY BREAD
Nancy Kress

I have always loved pumpkins. I love their look and smell, the way they epitomize autumn. Pumpkins are right out there: bright orange, unabashedly round, aggressively hard to carve into jack-o'-lanterns.

Pumpkins have attitude.

Not incidentally, they also taste good. When I was in Chengdu, China for the 2008 International Science Fiction Convention, I was delighted to discover that the daily breakfast buffet included squares of steamed pumpkin, which I gobbled every morning.

Unfortunately, I've never been able to duplicate them at home.

This pumpkin-cranberry bread, however, is just as good: moist, sweet, the perfect thing to accompany a Thanksgiving or Christmas dinner or to bring to a potluck anywhere between October and January. I also cut each slice in fourths and serve them as snacks at our annual Christmas party. Or you can bake them in small loaf pans (see recipe), tie a ribbon around the pan, and bring them to the hosts of other people's parties. Or you can just eat both loaves yourself with the doors locked and blinds drawn.

Nobody will ever know.

Makes 2 loaves

- 3 c flour
- 1 T + 2 t pumpkin pie spice
- 2 t baking soda
- 1 1/2 t salt
- 2 3/4 c granulated sugar
- 1 can (15 oz.) pumpkin puree (NOT pumpkin pie filling)
- 4 large eggs
- 1 c vegetable oil
- 1/2 c orange juice or water (orange juice is better)
- 1 1/2 c roughly chopped cranberries

Preheat oven to 350°F. Grease and flour two 9x5-inch loaf pans or six very small loaf pans.

Mix flour, pumpkin pie spice, baking soda, and salt in a large bowl. In a large mixer bowl, combine sugar, pumpkin, eggs, vegetable oil, and orange juice; beat until just blended. Add pumpkin mixture to the flour mixture and stir just until moistened. Fold in cranberries. Spoon batter into prepared pans.

Bake for 60-65 minutes for the 9x5-inch pans, until wooden toothpick inserted in center comes out clean.

For the six small pans, keep checking after 30 minutes until they're done. Do not over-bake. Cool in pans on wire racks for ten minutes, then remove from pans to cool completely on the racks.

RICOTTA PEARS AND APPLES
(AKA: A World Away from Fruit Salad)
Sarah Pinsker

I like to make things that are delicious but don't take much effort to prepare. If somebody asks me to make a dessert—particularly in the fall—this is the perfect thing. You can prep the first part, get in two good hours of writing, come back and do the last bit and done!

I know a lot of people who don't like fruit salad, but the crisp fruit and the tart apples seem to elevate this. The recipe serves about six.

- Six apples and pears (preferably Asian pears and Granny Smith or Pink Lady apples—something with crunch)
- 2 c ricotta
- 1/3 c honey
- 1 t vanilla
- 2 t lemon juice

Blend ricotta, honey, and vanilla in a food processor until it's smooth. Cover it and put it in the fridge for about two hours. Get some words in. Come back and cut up the fruit. I do cubes, but you could do slices if you preferred. Toss the fruit in lemon juice. Just before serving, toss the fruit and the ricotta mixture together.

ROASTED CHERRIES
Jaym Gates

Pit two cups of cherries; toss with one cup honey, a dash of red wine, two tablespoons ground vanilla or vanilla extract, a quarter teaspoon of salt, a few grinds of black pepper, and a quarter cup of balsamic vinegar.

Roast in the oven at 400°F for approximately 20 minutes, stirring frequently.

Use on top of cheesecake, ice cream, oatmeal, Black Forest Cake, or any other dessert. For the adventurous, top pork chops or a good, toasted bread with goat cheese and these cherries.

SALTY PIRATE BALLS
Jeanne Cavelos

Chocolate fosters creativity. This is one of the principles we discuss at the Odyssey Writing Workshop, a six-week program for writers of science fiction, fantasy, and horror held each summer in New Hampshire. You might think that at one of the premier workshops in the world for writers of the fantastic we have more important things to discuss than chocolate, but let's face it: few things in life—or writing—are more important than chocolate.

Chocolate stimulates the production of dopamine; dopamine helps the prefrontal cortex to focus. A focused prefrontal cortex allows writers to impose order on their ideas: to gain incremental insights, to focus on story elements, and to identify significant details. This Apollonian type of creativity is often most helpful in the revision stage and works in concert with Dionysian creativity, which is usually more helpful in the draft stage, allowing writers to discover associations between disparate elements and fostering breakthrough insights. Dionysian creativity reveals the big picture; Apollonian creativity reveals the details. Since Dionysian creativity arises from Alpha waves in the brain's right hemisphere, stimulated by relaxing activities like taking a walk or a warm shower, we haven't yet worked out a recipe for that.

But we spent Odyssey 2014 tirelessly searching for the best recipe to stimulate Apollonian creativity. Every Friday, at our class cookouts—occasions for bizarre discussions and crazy writing games—we held a contest to find the most delicious and creativity-inspiring treat. After much testing, the class chose this recipe by students Olivia Fowler and Cecilia Dockins as the winner.

- 1 box Betty Crocker Cookie Brownie Bars (any cake mix may be substituted)
- 1/2 package of bacon
- 2 bars semisweet baking chocolate (non dairy)
- 1 shot of espresso
- 1 cake ball pan
- 1 package lollipop sticks
- 1 or 2 blocks of craft Styrofoam or anything that will provide a stable base, such as upside-down paper cups with holes in the bottom

Precook bacon to crispy texture; drain or blot and set aside.

Mix the brownie batter as per packaging, and spoon into bottom of buttered cake ball pan. Attach top and bake for 17 minutes at 350°F. While these are baking, crumble/crush the cooked bacon.

Melt the baking chocolate with the shot of espresso.

When the balls come out, place on a wire rack to cool. When cool, dip the lollipop sticks in the chocolate, and stick the chocolate-coated tip into the ball and place in the freezer for ten minutes. When ten minutes has elapsed, dip the cooled balls in the melted chocolate, and roll in the bacon crumbles. Place the sticks with the decorated balls through the bottom of upturned cups or into a block of craft Styrofoam and place in the refrigerator to cool for ten minutes. Then serve.

SCHADENFREUDE PIE
John Scalzi

Let's face it, schadenfreude is a dark emotion. It deserves a dark pie. Here are your ingredients.

- 1 c dark brown sugar
- 1 c dark corn syrup
- 1/2 c molasses
- 1/2 c (1 stick) butter
- 1/2 c semi-sweet chocolate chips or chunks
- 3 large eggs (I used brown eggs in keeping with the spirit of things, but white eggs are fine.)
- 2 t cinnamon
- 1 splash Kahlua or other coffee liqueur
- 1 graham cracker pie crust (9 or 10 inches) (Choose regular or chocolate graham cracker crust according to taste.)

Preheat your oven to 375°F. Melt butter in large-ish mixing bowl; add in corn syrup, molasses, brown sugar, and cinnamon. Mix well. Melt chocolate; fold into existing mixture. Add eggs and Kahlua; mix vigorously until mix has an even consistency. Pour into pie crust (depending on size of crust you may have a little filling mix left over).

Shove into oven, center of middle rack, and bake for about 45 minutes. At 45 minutes, poke pie with butter knife. If butter knife comes out clean, your pie is done; otherwise give it about another five minutes.

Once you take the pie out of the oven, let it set at least 20 minutes before you dig in. It's really good when still warm, however.

Serving recommendations: small slices (this is an awesomely rich pie) and an ice cold glass of milk to go with it.

SOFT OATMEAL COOKIES
Jaime Lee Moyer

I can't remember a time when my mother didn't make these cookies. They are soft and almost cake like, and full of spices.

You can vary the recipe by using all brown sugar, doubling the spices, or adding raisins or chocolate chips.

- 1 1/2 c butter
- 1 c white sugar
- 1 c brown sugar
- 4 eggs
- 1/2 c milk
- 3 c flour
- 2 t baking soda
- 2 t salt
- 1 t allspice
- 1/2 t clove
- 1 t nutmeg
- 6 c rolled oats
- Optional: raisins or chocolate chips

Preheat oven to 375°F.

Cream butter, brown sugar, and white sugar together. Beat in eggs and milk. Blend in flour, spices, baking soda, salt, and oatmeal. Mix well. Dough will be sticky.

Cover cookie sheet with parchment paper or use cooking spray to keep cookies from sticking. Drop rounded teaspoons of dough about two inches apart. Cookies will both spread and rise during baking.

Bake for 10-12 minutes, until edges are golden brown and cookies begin to firm in the middle. Don't over-bake. This is one of those recipes where you learn when the cookies are done by trial and error.

SFWA DIY FORTUNE COOKIES
Scott Edelman

I first baked these more than 30 years ago, and what I enjoy about them is more than just that I end up with the freshest fortune cookies ever—it's that I get to adapt the fortunes to the audience that'll be cracking them open.

If you're going to bake them for a book club, you can write fortunes about book clubs in general or the book of the week in particular. If they're for a block party potluck, you can joke about all your neighbors. And if they're for a science fiction writers group, as my last batch was, you can joke about Hugos, Nebulas, Locus, agents, and more. Samples of my recent fortunes are below. But first—the cookies themselves!

Makes approximately 60 cookies

- 1 2/3 c white sugar
- 3/4 c unbeaten egg whites
- 1 c melted butter
- 1 c flour
- 1/2 t vanilla

Stir 1 2/3 cups white sugar into 3/4 cup unbeaten egg whites. Once the sugar has dissolved, beat in remaining ingredients in order until well-blended.

Drop by teaspoons, with sufficient space between, onto greased cookie sheets.

Bake in a 375°F oven until the edges begin to curl, which should be around five minutes.

Immediately lay your messages across the cookies.

Use a spatula to fold cookies in half once over the message, and then fold them over a wooden spoon handle.

Tip: If the cookies harden before you get a chance to fold them, return them briefly to the oven to soften.

Sample Fortunes

Here are ten fortunes I used for a batch I brought to my writers group. Feel free to use these, but remember to improvise, adapt, and be creative so that they fit your intended audience. That's what makes them so much fun!

Good news: Your writing will be chosen appear in a college textbook.
Bad news: It will illustrate what NOT to do.

Your favorite story that keeps getting rejected?
This is the year everything changes.

Your novel will win a Hugo Award. It will do so posthumously,
but hey, a win's a win!

Take heed—the person next to you will plagiarize that awesome idea
you were talking about.

Remember to back up your computer as soon as you get home. There's a hard
drive failure in your future.

Someday, you will appear on the cover of Locus.
You will be wearing a Hawaiian shirt.

You'll be nominated for a Nebula. The co-nominees that year will be
Connie Willis, Mike Resnick, and Neil Gaiman.

Finish the damn book.

You will win a Hugo Award. Bonus: It will be one of the year
the trophy is actually beautiful.

You next submission will be rejected. But the one after that . . . oh, boy!

TEATIME TASSIES
Mary Robinette Kowal

This was a standby of Grandma's that she made for, I think, every single gathering that our family attended or hosted. They are like miniature pecan pies and taste like childhood to me. I will go ahead and tell you, right now, to double the recipe, because they are just that good. So good. So very, very good.

- 1-3 oz cream cheese
- 1/2 c butter or margerine
- 1 c sifted flour
- 1 egg
- 3/4 c brown sugar
- 1 t vanilla
- 1 T butter
- Dash of salt
- 2/3 c broken pecans

Let cream cheese and butter soften to room temperature. Blend and stir in flour. Chill slightly until firm, about one hour. Shape into two dozen one-inch balls. Place in tiny, ungreased muffin cups. Press dough on bottom and sides of cups. Divide half the pecans among pastry lined cups.

Beat together remaining ingredients until smooth. Add to pastry cups and top with remaining pecans. Bake in slow oven (325°F) for 25 minutes or until filling is set.

TEDDY GRAHAM S'MORES
Mary E. Lowd

Whether you need to summon the magic of a campfire, ghost stories, and the deep dark woods, or are simply hosting a party for pixies, Teddy Graham S'mores are the perfect, tiny treat.

- Teddy Grahams
- Miniature marshmallows
- Chocolate chips
- Toothpicks
- Candle

Light your candle and skewer a mini-marshmallow on a toothpick. Roast the marshmallow over the candle's flame, turning to toast all sides. When the marshmallow is golden brown all the way around, squish it between two Teddy Grahams along with a chocolate chip.

NOTE: If you use a scented candle, make sure it has an appropriate scent as that will affect the flavor of your s'more. My favorites are hazelnut- and pine-scented candles.

TOASTED CAKE
Tina Connolly

Since starting the Toasted Cake flash fiction podcast, I get a fair number of questions about what is toasted cake and why should one toast cake and how do you fit a piece of frosted seven- layer cake into the little slots on your toaster and why is my toaster on fire?

Well. Let's first point out that the absolute best way to eat cake is, like all baked goods, warm from the oven. (Oh sure, it might be messy that way. So what.) Look, the cake comes out all warm and airy, and then you put your buttercream frosting on it and it melts a little, you know? And runs down the side of the cake and soaks into all the little cake pockets. Mmm. Cake pockets.

But you can only eat one piece of cake that way. (Okay, maybe two.) The point is, what do you do on day two? Well, here's the trick.

Step one: Make yourself a cake. Or cupcakes. (I like plain yellow cake. You can make a box cake if you want—I won't judge.)

Step two: Make frosting. (My favorite method is to whip one stick of butter with two cups powdered sugar and a teaspoon or two of milk.)

Step three: Only frost your piece. Sit down right now and eat it. Do not frost anybody else's cake. They can frost their own pieces. Keep the cake and the frosting separate.

Now, on day two, you don't have soggy stale cake with untoastable frosting. You can easily take a piece of cake (or cupcake, if that's what you made) and put it in your toaster oven. (Or under the broiler, if you don't have a toaster oven.) Now you have toasted cake, full of tasty, warm, sugary, crunchy bits on top, and now you take your bowl of frosting and smear it on and let it melt into your cake pockets and eat it all up.

Toasted Cake! It's not so much a recipe as a way of life.

VICTORIA SANDWICH CAKE
Rachael Acks

I needed something sweet and Victorian for a tea shop break in my novella The Ugly Tin Orrery, *and Victoria Sandwich Cake came up early on in a list of common desserts and sounded amazing. It involves fruit and jam and cream, all the sorts of things one of the characters, Mr. Simms, likes. (And I like them too!) Later, I couldn't help but wonder what it actually tasted like, and that led me to looking for the oldest recipe I could find—Mrs. Beeton's—and enlisting the help of my housemate Kathy, who is a fabulous cook. As I sat down to try my first slice (spoiler: anything involving this much butter is guaranteed to be sinfully delicious), I couldn't help but think about people 130 years ago taking in Mrs. Beeton's wisdom and sharing a similar, blissful experience with myself and the fictional Mr. Simms. It's a simple recipe, but perhaps that's why it hasn't had to change much in over a century; you don't need to mess with perfection.*

Four eggs, 200 grams* each of caster sugar, butter, and cake flour (preferred) or all-purpose flour, one teaspoon baking powder, a quarter teaspoon salt, plus any sort of fruit or jam you like plus freshly whipped cream for the filling. (*NOTE: Four large eggs will weigh about 200 grams total. For true accuracy in the recipe, weigh the eggs while still in the shell and then use equal weights of butter, sugar, and flour.)

Preheat oven to 350°F. Whisk eggs first. Cream the butter and sugar, then add the eggs, flour, baking powder, and salt. Split the resulting batter between two 8" cake pans. Bake for about 20 minutes. (Cakes will begin to pull away from the pan edges when they are done.)

After cooling completely, put jam, fruit, whipped cream, chocolate or Nutella, or some combination thereof which sounds pleasing to you, in between the layers. Dust the top with caster sugar or decorate with whipped cream if you're feeling fancy. Enjoy with tea or a glass of milk.

(This recipe is based closely on an 1874 recipe from Mrs. Beeton's *The Book of Household Management*. Mrs. Beeton's genius is available for all to peruse at any time for free thanks to Project Gutenberg: gutenberg.org/ebooks/10136.)

VEGAN STRAWBERRY CHEESECAKE
Cat Sparks

I'm not a vegan or even a vegetarian, but I like the inventiveness of vegan cuisine so occasionally dabble in it, especially as my partner Rob is dairy intolerant. This cashew nut cheesecake is astonishingly tasty. I'm a big fan of cheesecake in general and never thought I'd be happy with a substitute . . . until this cake came along. It's filling, but way less calorie-intense than regular cheesecake. Packed with protein, it pretty much counts as a meal in itself. The recipe I adapted it from called for multiple layers and twice as much filling—serious overkill, in my opinion!

Total time: 3 hours to soak cashews, 30 minutes preparation
(No dairy; no baking)
You will need a 9-12 inch springform pan.

Base Crust
- 3 1/2 c walnuts
- 12 soft seedless dates
- 1 T water
- 1/4 t salt

Strawberry Cashew Cheesecake Filling
- 1/4 c lemon juice (approx one large lemon)
- 3 c cashews, soaked in water for 3 hours
- 3/4 c maple syrup
- 3/4 c coconut oil, melted
- 1 T pure vanilla extract
- 1/8 t salt
- 2 c strawberries
- 2 T water
- Sliced strawberries to decorate.

To make the base, combine the crust ingredients in a blender or food processor. Mix to form a moist dough, use it to line the bottom of the springform pan, set aside.

To make the cheesecake filling, place the soaked cashews and other ingredients in a powerful blender, then blend until the filling is light and smooth. There should be no chunks at all. Pour the filling into the prepared crust.

Layer sliced strawberries over the top of the cheesecake. It's ready to eat, but if you prefer, put it in the fridge for a few hours to set firm, or freeze it for five hours for a result a bit like ice cream cake.

Tips:
- A powerful blender really helps, but if you only have a beat-up old one like mine, try blending the ingredients in small batches.
- You can use any nut for the base. Cashews work best for the cheesecake mixture but you could also try using almonds or macadamia nuts.
- To make a smaller cheesecake, halve the recipe.
- You can also make mini cheesecakes: just spoon a heaping of the mixture into mini cup cake holders.
- This cake will stay good in your freezer for three months.

"YOU CAN PRETEND THEY'RE HEALTHY" WHOLE WHEAT CHOCOLATE CHIP COOKIES
Kyle Aisteach

- 2 1/4 c whole wheat flour [CAVEAT: Choose carefully. The quality of the flour makes or breaks this recipe, and the leading brand (Gold Medal) for white flour makes a downright awful whole-wheat version. I'm particularly fond of the King Arthur brand, but I've had good luck with Arrowhead Mills and Stone-Buhr brands as well.)
- 1 t baking soda
- 1 t cinnamon
- 1/4 t sea salt
- 1 c (2 sticks) butter, softened
- 1 1/2 c packed brown sugar
- 2 large eggs
- 1 t vanilla extract
- 12 oz package dark chocolate chips (White chocolate chips give good results, too.)

Preheat oven to 375°F.

Combine baking soda, cinnamon, and salt, and then cream them into the butter.

Mix the brown sugar in with the creamed butter.

Beat together the eggs and vanilla, and then add to the mixture.

Add flour a little at a time, mixing thoroughly. Watch out for lumps.

Knead in the chocolate chips.

Roll into balls of the desired size (I prefer about 1 1/2-inch diameter) and place on ungreased cookie sheets.

Bake 10-12 minutes. (CAVEAT: If, like me, you're used to judging doneness by color, be careful! When whole wheat flour darkens noticeably, it's actually overdone. The color change when whole-wheat cookies bake is extremely subtle and hard to see. If you're not confident about your oven's temperature accuracy, I suggest testing five cookies, cooking them at 9, 10, 11, 12, and 13 minutes, and then seeing which doneness you prefer. With practice you'll be able to see the subtle color change, but initially you'll feel like you're undercooking the cookies. Take them out when they look like they've just begun to brown.)

Cool on a wire rack or on paper, not on the cookie sheet.

Store in the refrigerator. White flour was invented as a preservation technique, not to remove nutrients or to spike your insulin levels. Whole-wheat products must be kept at low temperature to preserve them.

Eat as you would any other cookie, with a trusted friend nearby to take them away from you when you've had too many.

• BEVERAGES: NON-ALCOHOLIC •

GINGER BEER (NON-ALCOHOLIC)
Nalo Hopkinson

This is emphatically not ginger ale. For one thing, it's not fizzy. It's sweet, but definitely not bland. It's a spicy beverage with a strong ginger bite that's traditionally served cold over ice in parts of the Caribbean. It can be served any time of year, but Christmas isn't Christmas without it.

- 1 lb fresh ginger root
- 12 c water
- 8 whole cloves
- 1/4 t ground allspice or pimiento
- 1 t vanilla
- 1/4 t nutmeg
- 1 fresh lime (use the peel and the juice)
- 1 1/2 c raw sugar (Demerara, turbinado or muscovado are best, but brown sugar will do)

You can leave the skin on the ginger. Wash, scrub and grate it.

In a large pot, bring water, cloves, allspice, nutmeg, and the lime peel to a boil. Turn off heat. Add the sugar and stir until dissolved. Adjust the sweetness to taste. Add ginger, vanilla, and lime juice.

Let the ginger beer cool to room temperature. Either leave it in the pot (covered), or pour it into a large, lidded jar. Refrigerate for one to three days. When ready to drink, strain through a fine strainer or cheesecloth, squeezing the solids to express as much of the liquid as you can. Discard the solids.

Serve cold, garnished with fresh mint or pineapple slices.

GINGER HORCHATA
Alaya Dawn Johnson

This is an agua de horchata that I made for the first time in Mazunte, Oaxaca with a crappy blender, and it tasted so good we drank it for breakfast, lunch, and dinner. For dessert, we added mezcal.

If you don't have a blender, you'll need a mortar and pestle, but be prepared for a workout!

- 1 c rice
- 6 c water (or more, according to taste)
- 1/2 c sugar
- 1 t vanilla extract
- 1 c whole milk
- 2 inches fresh ginger
- 2/3 stick cinnamon

Rinse the rice once, not too thoroughly. The starch that coats the rice makes the drink. Put the rice in the blender with the water. Blend until the rice has a sandy consistency (this may take a while with less powerful blenders). Pour the entire mix into a pitcher, cover and leave out for at least three hours. Six is ideal. After the soak, the rice water should look white.

In the meantime, prepare the ginger. Try to get ginger that's young and not fibrous. Cut off a good chunk (depends on how much you like ginger), peel the skin and crush the rest in a garlic press. If you don't have a garlic press, mash it under your knife.

Now, pour the water/rice mixture back in the blender. Add the milk, the sugar, the vanilla extract, and the ginger. Blend until the sugar is dissolved. Strain the mixture of most (but not all!) of the rice. Add the cinnamon, blend again. The cinnamon won't turn into powder, but it should be in pretty small bits. If you want powder, I suggest breaking out the mortar and pestle. (Yes, you could use powdered cinnamon, but it won't taste very good. Honestly.)

This goes back in the pitcher, the pitcher goes in the fridge for another hour or two, until everything has chilled and it tastes seriously good. And if you're feeling adventurous, or it's just that time of evening, try adding a splash of good Mexican mezcal.

Buen provecho!

HOT BUTTERED RUM FANTASY
Aly Parsons

On cold nights, I wander out to the kitchen after midnight to make a hot drink to bring back and sip while writing. I came up with this as an alternative to my usual decaf coffee and teas. It's also great as a holiday drink.

For my writing, the spices encourage creative moods. Cinnamon rouses memories back to early childhood. Cardamom evokes the exotic. Cloves bring remembrance of both stress while in dental chairs and relaxation when sipping mulled cider. Stirring up such memories aids in reaching the mindset of characters experiencing similar emotional states.

As a teen, while cooking a scrambled egg, I decided to add a touch of nutmeg. One shake of the jar sent its perforated lid flying, dumping the spice. Though I scraped off what I could, nutmeg saturated the egg. After wavering over consuming my hot meal or slipping it into the trash, I ate it.

Decades later, at one of Maria V. Snyder's poison-tasting workshops, when other participants identifications of ingredients in a chocolate bar petered out, I added, "Nutmeg." My nutmeg binge had sensitized me to detect it in minute quantities. To conjure the roller-coaster emotions of the adventurer taking a risk with uncertain consequences, I include nutmeg in my hot beverage.

- 8 oz soy milk (or milk)
- 1 t butter (or your favorite butter substitute)
- 1 t imitation/artificial rum flavoring
- About 1/8 t cinnamon

Optional additions:
- Cardamom, cloves, and/or nutmeg
- Diet sweetener, Splenda brown sugar, brown sugar, granulated sugar, raw sugar, or honey

Heat, but do not boil. Makes one serving. This recipe accommodates many restricted diets including lactose-intolerant and diabetic.

MORNING BEVERAGE
Talia Gryphon

- 1 c French roast coffee
- 1/4-1/2 c half-and-half
- 2 t Torani hazelnut syrup
- 1 package Truvia sweetener, if needed

Put half-and-half and Torani syrup in cup; fill with freshly-brewed coffee. Add Truvia sweetener if needed. Enjoy!

SCURVY CURE
Teresa Nielsen Hayden

I customarily make Scurvy Cure at the annual Viable Paradise writing workshop on Martha's Vineyard, since scurvy is a notorious danger of ocean voyages, and you can't get to Martha's Vineyard without crossing salt water.

Equipment
- Microplane grater/zester. In theory you could use an old-fashioned conventional grater or zester, but a Microplane grater is much better, and you want one anyway.
- Juicer. You want one with real squeezing power. Failing that, you need strong hands and wrists.
- Strainer. Must be made of non-reactive materials. Don't use muslin.

Ingredients
- At least a dozen citrus fruits, though 2-4 dozen are better. Of each dozen, six to eight should be oranges, one may be but doesn't have to be a grapefruit, and the rest should be lemons and limes in approximately equal quantities. Blood oranges, tangerines, and sour ornamental oranges are excellent additions. Clementines are better eaten out of hand. Do not use sweet limes.
- Granulated white sugar, one or two pounds
- 1 large can of frozen citrus concentrate. Cascadian Farm frozen lemon juice concentrate is best, but frozen limeade concentrate will do.
- Seltzer
- (Optionally, vodka or tequila or Everclear. Scurvy Cure doesn't have to be an alcoholic beverage, though it does make a good one.)

Procedure
Wash the fruit and remove any labels. Don't dry them off—the residual dampness is helpful.

Remove all the zest from all the fruit, tapping it off onto a plate or shallow bowl as you work. This will take a while. Stop at intervals to generously sprinkle sugar on the growing heap of zest. When you're done, sprinkle sugar onto both sides of the zester, then scrape it off onto the zest.

Refrigerate the denuded fruit, or run it through the juicer and refrigerate the juice.

Stir up the zest and sugar, then start working additional sugar into it. (How much? Until it be enough.) Ideally, the liquid given up by the zest should be enough to moisten and slightly liquefy the amount of sugar you use. If your bits of zest turn translucent and are starting to swim in a thick syrupy citrus concentrate, you're golden. If your zest isn't giving up any liquid, add a bit of juice or water to make it sticky enough to get the process going.

Science: The concentrated sugar pops the cells in the zest and sucks out their liquids.

Onward.

Pack the zest and sugar mixture into a non-reactive container, cover, and refrigerate for 2-24 hours. Juice the fruit if you haven't done that already.

Defrost the frozen juice concentrate. Add it to the zest and sugar mixture, stirring well. Mix this with the juice, stir very well, and let the whole thing sit for an hour, then run it through a strainer. Save the zest and freeze it in a tightly lidded container (see below).

What comes out of the strainer should be Scurvy Cure. Store in a lidded non-reactive container. Dilute before serving. One part Scurvy Cure to 3-5 parts seltzer is good. If you like, you can substitute distilled spirits for some of the seltzer.

Makes enough to protect an entire writing workshop from the dreadful perils of scurvy.

FURTHER NOTES: Why you save and freeze the used zest: there's generally some citrusy goodness left in it that you can extract by soaking it in more citrus juice and/or frozen juice concentrate. It'll yield a much smaller batch, but it's a freebie, and good to have around when your morale runs low.

Scurvy Cure mixes very well with elderflower syrups or liqueurs.

Half a cup or more of undiluted Scurvy Cure, mixed with powdered sugar until it reaches the right consistency, is great for icing or glazing dark gingerbread.

If you let your Scurvy Cure sit and it throws off a layer of citrus oil, you win. Whisk it back in and proceed as directed. If it throws off a layer of opaque pale yellow sediment that floats on top, you have two options. One is to stir or whisk it back in and proceed as usual. The other is to first spoon out a dab of it onto your toothbrush, then whisk in the rest. Brushing your teeth with that dab of sediment will remove plaque. I'm not kidding. It's like edible Citrusol.

If you freeze or semi-freeze Scurvy Cure, stir it well before using it. If you've added alcohol to it, I don't guarantee that it will freeze at all. If alcohol-enhanced Scurvy Cure partially freezes and you pour the liquid off the frozen portions, you are jacking it, and I refuse to be responsible for whatever follows.

———

STRAWBERRY SMOOTHIE
Chuck Wendig

During fresh strawberry season, this is an easy way to shove fruit into your mouthhole with great delight.

Put a pint of washed strawberries in a blender with:
- 2 c milk,
- 2 T honey,
- 2 T malted milk powder
- A small palmful of ice cubes.

Blend. Adjust sweetness to taste. Drink. Or, rather, guzzle greedily before your toddler can take it from your hands. Or, my toddler, at least.

———

WHOLESOME FRUIT-VEGGIE SMOOTHIE
Jennifer Stevenson

My husband gave me a blender for my birthday. I know, right? All those jokes about guys who give their wives vacuum cleaners for Christmas. But this blender is a Vitamix, the Cadillac of blenders with a ridiculous number of horses under the hood. My husband calls it The Woodchipper.

- 1 two-ounce bunch cilantro, cut in half and rinsed
- Equal amount flat parsley, ditto
- 2 inches whole ginger root, washed and diced
- 6 baby carrots
- 1/2 c fennel root, rinsed and chopped
- 1/2 c frozen pineapple
- 1 ripe pear, rinsed, de-stemmed, seeded, and cut in half
- 1 whole avocado, peeled, pitted, cut in half

Blend until smooth. This is green and healthy-looking but sweet!

• BEVERAGES: WITH A KICK •

THE ALGONQUIN COCKTAIL
Gregory Frost

The cocktail has been making a comeback the past few years. This is interesting, in that, as one friend pointed out, most of them were created during a time period where you couldn't get your hands on much that wasn't formulated in a bathtub, and so various exotic and imported liqueurs were thrown in to mask that bastard bathtub provenance. I figure if you're going to drink a cocktail, you probably want to feel a little bit special while you're at it. The Algonquin seems to me the perfect cocktail for burgeoning wits who know better than to cross Alexander Woollcott without an alpenstock. Remember also, the toast is "Dorothy Parker!" as you raise your glasses.

- 1 oz rye
- 1/2 oz vermouth
- 1/2 oz pineapple juice

Pour the ingredients over ice in a cocktail shaker, shake, and strain into a chilled cocktail glass. Imbibe.

DANDELION WINE
Natalie Luhrs

This is a family recipe for Dandelion Wine—no idea if it makes anything drinkable, but it seems like a SFWA Cookbook needs to have a recipe for it nonetheless! I'm also attaching a photo of the recipe in all its misspelled ungrammatical glory. Enjoy! Or not, as the case may be. Source: Mildred Luhrs (my great-grandmother).

- 1 qt blossoms, packed
- 1 gal water

Boil 1 hour, then add two lemons, then boil ten minutes longer, then drain and add 2 1/2 lb sugar. When lukewarm, add one packet Fleischman's yeast. Let stand one week and then bottle.

DARK AND STORMY
John P. Murphy

- 2 oz ginger syrup (below)
- 1 1/2 oz gold or dark rum
- Half a fresh lime

- Ice
- Soda water

Juice the lime and pour in the glass. (If you like, toss the lime peel in the bottom of the glass and muddle.) Add ginger syrup, rum, and ice. Fill with soda water to taste and stir.

OR... use vodka instead, for a Moscow Mule.

OR... skip the booze, use a little more syrup, and you'll have a darn fine ginger beer.

Ginger Syrup
- 1 lb ginger, scrubbed clean
- 1-2 c sugar
- Salt
- Allspice berries, cinnamon stick, peppercorns, whole cloves, orange peel, and/or cardamom pods

Chop ginger and add, with four cups of water, to a pot with a good lid. Add a pinch of salt and any whole spices (just a little bit for some background flavor), and bring to a simmer. Put the lid on and let it simmer for an hour or so.

Strain out the solids and bring the water to a very low boil. Boil it down to one to two cups of liquid. The more you boil it down, the stronger it'll be, but the less you'll have.

Measure the remaining liquid, and measure out the same volume of sugar. You can use turbinado or other raw/unrefined sugars, but those can add grassy flavors in large volumes like these. Dissolve the sugar in the hot ginger liquid to make a syrup, then cool and store in a tightly capped bottle in the fridge.

DRAGON'S BREATH
David Glen Larson

It's embarrassing to admit, but throughout much of my childhood I didn't read. Not because I didn't want to, but because I couldn't.

In elementary school I lagged behind many of my classmates, especially when it came to reading. So much so that when it was time to read aloud in class, I was often ushered into a special room that was only slightly larger than the janitor's closet. There, along with two or three other remedial outcasts, one of whom still couldn't tie his shoes, I would attempt to sound out a supposedly simple passage while an eager student teacher smiled encouragement. It was torture. And frankly, I was unmotivated to improve. After all, I had television, and my own considerable imagination. Besides, who the hell cared what those freaks Dick and Jane were up to, and who dresses like that anyway? Then I discovered fire-breathing dragons.

While rummaging through my older brother's belongings—as little brothers do—I came across Anne McCaffrey's Dragonriders of Pern. *The ferocious beast on the cover was all the encouragement I needed.*

Stumbling and faltering over words and concepts I had never before encountered, I made it safely through only to find that it wasn't the end of a journey, but the beginning. Now, when I ride from Rama to Mars, Dune to Middle Earth, back to a time that never was or a future that must never be, I do so on the back of dragons.

- 2 oz Vodka
- 1/2 lemon (cut into wedges)
- 1 oz Ginger Hibiscus Grenadine (see recipe below)
- 1 whole Thai chili pepper

In a shaker, add lemon wedges and chili pepper. Muddle thoroughly. Add ice, ginger hibiscus grenadine, and vodka. Shake well and pour into a chilled cocktail glass through a fine mesh strainer. Garnish with whole Thai chili. Makes 1 serving.

Ginger Hibiscus Grenadine
2 c 100% pure pomegranate juice (no sugar added)
2 c granulated white sugar
1 oz dried hibiscus flowers (available at many health food stores or online)
8 oz ginger (peeled and sliced thin)
1/2 lemon

Combine pomegranate juice, sugar, ginger, and dried hibiscus flowers in a medium non-reactive saucepan. Bring mixture to a boil and reduce heat. Continue to simmer for 20 minutes. Remove from heat and allow the mixture to steep and cool for 30 minutes. Add lemon juice before straining and bottling. Keep refrigerated. (Add soda water and a squeeze of lemon to a small amount of ginger hibiscus grenadine for a refreshing non-alcoholic beverage).

FEUERZANGENBOWLE
Larry Constantine

Back in the 1960s, when I was studying management at MIT's Sloan School, a German friend had a reputation for the best parties. Gerhardt believed that the secret of celebratory success was high density. An early quant wonk, he said that it was not the number of people at a party but the number of people per square meter that guaranteed good times. I don't remember the magic threshold number, but his parties were always wall-to-wall people, noisy, and great fun. They often climaxed with rounds of German drinking songs fueled by feuerzangenbowle, or "fire tong punch," a flaming German concoction that is a spectacle in itself.

Here is my adaptation. You will need a large glass (not plastic) punch bowl and the "tongs," an open frame filled with sugar cubes to span the top of the bowl. Holes in the bottom of the tongs allow flaming rum and melting sugar to flow into the punch. Makeshift but serviceable tongs can be fashioned by folding multiple layers of heavy aluminum foil and cutting the holes with kitchen shears.

Makes about ten servings (multiply accordingly for high-density parties)

- 1 1/2 liter red wine (nothing fancy)
- 1 orange, sliced thinly
- 1 T whole cloves
- 1 T whole coriander seeds
- 4 sticks cinnamon (approx. 3" long)
- 1/4 c honey
- 1/4 c rum

Mull above ingredients together, covered, over low heat for 45-60 minutes. Pre-warm the punchbowl to prevent thermal shock, then strain the punch into it. Arrange about 50 sugar cubes in the "tongs" suspended across the top of the punchbowl.

Gently warm three-quarters cup brandy, rum, or a mixture in a small, long-handled saucepan. Gather everyone around the bowl—but not too close—then turn out the lights and ignite the spirits in the saucepan. Very slowly pour the burning liquid over the sugar cubes, allowing molten sugar and spirits to drip in cascades of flame down into the bowl where the flames will skate and dance and slowly fade. Serve in mugs or heatproof glasses. *Prosit!*

H. BEAM PIPER'S KATINKA
John F. Carr

In the Afterward to The Early Letters *(the collected correspondence between H. Beam Piper and Ferd Coleman), Don Coleman shared his memories of H. Beam Piper, shortly after Piper moved to Williamsport in 1957:*

"So, as party times arose—regardless of those included in the gala—Beam was invited automatically . . . He truly loved these parties, and prepared and drank his Piper-made Katinkas at the den bar. Although wearing a fixed face and attitude of supposedly complete apathy, he was on top of the entire curriculum.

"Actually, when it came down to the subject of booze, Beam was a real judge of the stuff . . . In the 1950s, Piper could be considered a connoisseur; he would orate on the origin of, as well as savor, any type or classification of whiskey known to man . . . black rum continued to be his working-at-the-desk favorite. He also improved a concoction that proved to be a standout with the imbibing bunch . . . He called it the 'Katinka.'

"When I asked for the ingredients, Beam pulled out his multi-colored ink pen and a small scratch pad from his inside coat pocket . . . In giving me the recipe, he printed four lines of instructions, each with a different color . . . black, blue, red and green:

- 3 parts Vodka
- 2 parts Apricot Brandy
- 1 part Grenadine
- STIR over ice . . . DO NOT SHAKE!

"This conglomeration would then be strained into a brandy snifter. On one occasion, I dropped into the City Hotel lounge with Beam in downtown Williamsport, and upon becoming comfortable at the recently renovated bar—with the fork of his cane hanging over his forearm—he asked for a 'Katinka.'

"I remember turning to him dubiously and remarking, 'This guy wouldn't know a 'Katinka' any more than he'd know what he had for supper last Tuesday!'

" 'Oh HELL!' Beam burst. 'Tommy's been mixin' 'em for some time now.'

"The year was 1957 and Beam would properly appraise the going rate of his creation 'in the vicinity of seventy-five cents.' "

At SF cons Piper's signature drink was Jim Beam, but at home his favorite sipping drink was Myers's Rum.

HONEY BADGER
Andrew Penn Romine

Making the syrup with fresh ginger instead of using store-bought will help.
I've lowballed the lemon juice. You may be able to use as much as a quarter of an ounce to taste.

It's very reminiscent of a bourbon/whiskey sour!

- 1 1/2 oz bourbon
- 1/2 oz honey liqueur
- 3 dashes angostura bitters
- 1/4 oz ginger syrup (Commercial or handmade is better because easier to make it stronger.)
- 1/4 t lemon juice

Add ingredients to cocktail shaker with ice. Shake and strain into rocks glass, garnish with lemon twist, or better, a small slice of fresh ginger.

HOT TODDY CLASSIC
Eric J. Guignard

- 2 oz rum, brandy, bourbon, Irish whiskey, or scotch (I prefer rum.)
- 5 oz boiling water
- 1 T honey (or 1 t sugar)
- 1 lemon slice (or 1/2 t lemon juice)
- Cinnamon to taste

Bring water to boil. Add all other ingredients. Inhale before imbibing.

MAURICE'S VODKA SPECIAL
Maurice Broaddus

Now that you've had a meal with friends, you should relax with a drink. I have no idea what to call this drink, but one weekend me, Kyle Johnson, and Doug Warrick conducted a series of experiments involving vodka-related drinks. This is the recipe (from what we've been able to piece together from our collectively cobbled-together memory) of our main drink.

In a tall glass add:

- 1 oz vodka, either Whipped Cream or Cake
- 1 oz sweet 'n' sour mix
- Fill the rest of the glass with ginger ale

Stir and enjoy!

MINT JULEP
Stephanie Osborn

I learned this recipe from a delightful old Black bartender in Mobile, who was tending bar in the gala tent for a U.S. Polo Association tournament. It is excellent for imbibing while watching the Kentucky Derby, or reading the latest science fiction novel.

Serves quite a few.

Ingredients
- 1 qt water (filtered or distilled is best)
- 1 large bunch fresh mint or half a dozen mint teabags
- Sugar
- Ice
- Jack Daniels
- Small bunch fresh mint for garnish

Tools
- Saucepan
- Heat-resistant, cold-resistant pitcher
- Long spoon
- Tall glasses (about 12 oz) for drinks

Begin preparations the day before the drinks are needed.

Bring water to a rolling boil in a saucepan. While waiting for water to boil, place mint into a very clean, heat-resistant pitcher. When water is boiling, remove from heat and carefully pour over mint in pitcher. Allow to steep for 30 minutes. (Tea should be a dark olive green.) Remove mint (strain if necessary). Begin adding sugar, a quarter cup at a time, stirring between each addition until sugar is dissolved. Continue adding sugar and stirring until there is a slight residue of sugar at the bottom of the pitcher which will not dissolve. (The solution is now a super-saturated syrup.) Cover tightly with a lid or plastic wrap and refrigerate overnight.

Just before the drinks are served, set up enough tall glasses to serve all guests. Fill to brim with ice cubes. Place one shot Jack Daniels in the bottom of each glass. (You can use two shots, but be it on your own head.) Top glass with the mint syrup. Add a swizzle stick (you can use one of the rock candy sticks if you like), garnish with mint sprig, and serve.

(WARNING: Because of the high sugar content, this is a much stronger drink than it appears to be. Most people can only handle one full-sized glass, and may be tipsy after this. Two juleps made following this recipe have been known to put grown men under the table.)

THE MIRIAM NEGRONI
Chuck Wendig

- 1 oz dark rum
- 1 oz Campari
- 1 oz sweet vermouth
- The juice of a blood orange

You could go old school and just use gin. While rum fits the part of the book where Miriam descends to Florida, the book also is set around Christmastime and one cannot deny that gin sometimes tastes like liquefied Christmas tree.

To be really authentic you should probably also lacquer the edges with cremated human remains or cigarette ash.

Or just drink the whole thing through a human skull.

—

MUDDLE IN THE MIDDLE MOJITO
Kay Kenyon

This concoction may not solve that dreadful sag in the middle of your novel. But after a couple of these, you won't care.

Serves 6 (or 2, if novelists)

- 3 c fresh mint leaves
- 9 T sugar
- 1 1/2 c light rum
- 1/2 c fresh lime juice
- 6 c crushed ice
- 6 lime wedges
- 3-4 c club soda (taste at the 3-cup mark before adding more)

Reserve six mint leaves for garnish. Place remaining mint leaves in a glass bowl. Add sugar. Muddle with wooden spoon (that is, mash) until mint is fragrant.

Add rum and lime juice and stir until sugar dissolves. Strain mixture into pitcher. (You can prepare a couple hours ahead, but refrigerate.)

Add club soda to pitcher; stir. Fill each of six tall glasses with one cup crushed ice. Pour Muddle in the Middle Mojito over and throw in a mint leaf and a lime wedge.

—

OUZO: THE INDIGENOUS GREEK LIQUOR
John Walters

Having lived in Greece for over fifteen years, it was inevitable that I would get accustomed to the ubiquitous Greek drink ouzo. I consumed it in moderation—once a week or so on Sunday evenings—but I got so that I very much looked forward to my weekly dose of this aromatic but powerful liquor.

Traditionally, ouzo is not a liquor used in mixed drinks. Greeks drink it either straight in shots or half-and-half with water and ice. When you mix it with water, or when the ice begins to melt if you are having it on the rocks, it turns from clear to cloudy. Personally I don't like to dilute it with water; I prefer it on the rocks. I think the taste is too sublime to temper. It is flavored with anise and tastes a bit like licorice. Beware, though; it packs a hell of a punch.

My first experience with ouzo was in the mid 1970s when I was staying in a youth hostel in Athens preparing to hitchhike and hop local transportation farther east to India. I went out with a group of young travelers from a multitude of nationalities who were heading for all points of the globe. We sat for hours and drank glass after glass. Experienced ouzo drinkers told me it was strong and to beware of over-imbibing, but I didn't understand what all the fuss was about—until, that is, I tried to stand up. The moment I got to my feet I felt as if someone had hit me over the head with a sledge hammer, or a Mac truck had just struck me head on. I still don't remember how I got back to the hostel.

When Greeks go out to drink ouzo, they sit for hours in special restaurants that serve food that goes especially well with the drink. You see Greeks sitting at outdoor tables at these *ouzeries*, as they are called, with their glasses of milky beverage and the table heaped with dishes of octopus, squid, mussels, sardines, French fries, fried zucchini, feta cheese, tomato and cucumber salad, and tzatziki, a type of garlic-flavored yogurt. Ouzo brings out their personalities, so to speak, and as they remain there for hour after hour they get louder and louder, but all in the spirit of congenial camaraderie. Greeks are known for their loudness anyway under normal circumstances, but you can count on the ouzo to crank up the volume even more. At the same time, ouzeries often play traditional bouzouki music while the drinking is going on, further adding to the raucous confusion. If there's one thing that Greeks know how to do well, it's cut loose and relax, and that time-honored pastime is often accompanied by ouzo.

There are various types of ouzo on the market in Greece, and some famous brands are extremely pricey. On my English teacher's budget, I had to go for the moderate to low-priced brands, but even these are quite acceptable. For a time my preferred brand was Ouzo 12, which is in the medium price range, but once when I was particularly poor I tried the Alpha Vita, or AB supermarket chain brand, and I found I liked it even better. Who would have known?

Though I have kept my eyes open, I haven't yet found ouzo on liquor-shopping forays in the States. I'm sure it must be somewhere about; though I've been out of the country for thirty-five years and only recently returned, I have realized that you can find just about anything here in the States if you look hard enough. I'm living in a small town right now, but once I move to a bigger city I will launch a thorough search. It's my favorite hard liquor, and I would love to resume my

Sunday evening habit. My alternative plan is to have relatives bring a few bottles the next time someone visits from Greece.

In closing, let me re-emphasize that if you are new to ouzo, take it easy. Sip it and don't gulp it, and after you have had several, hold onto something and get up slowly.

A PERFECT GIN AND TONIC
Laura Anne Gilman

Writers write a lot about meals and great big feasts, especially in epic fantasy. But when you look at our society, when people gather outside of those feasts, we meet over coffee or we have drinks. It's a very social thing. We eat, and we drink water, in order to keep our bodies going, but we also drink in order to sort of smooth the passage of conversation.

If you want to schmooze someone, to get information, you buy them a drink. If you want to get someone drunk so they'll do something stupid for political reasons, this also requires libations. You don't do it over a hamburger. It's always struck me as an aspect of storytelling that tends to get overlooked. Everyone deals with the traditional food aspects of storytelling, but look at how many scenes take place in bars, coffeehouses, taverns, and tea houses.

It's a trope that is useful as opposed to just being fun. Really, if you think about it, you will be hard pressed to find a book that doesn't have drinks.

The Perfect Gin and Tonic starts with the most important ingredient. No, it's not the gin. It's the tonic water. Too many people use the cheapest tonic water they can find. That's always a mistake. You want to find a really good quality tonic that tastes good on its own.

Then find a good gin, one you like—preferably not flavored, keep it clean and simple, but if you like flavored gins, go for it. The percentage of gin to tonic for each drink depends on how much you plan to drink.

Never fill the glass all the way. Room to breathe, like with wine, and if you knock the glass over it doesn't spill as much.

Then, don't put lemon in it. Use lime. Lemon is too sharp. Lime has a more rounded taste to it; brings up the flavor of the gin.

We've test-driven this because it gets really hot in NYC in July and August. Gin and tonics are medicinal in hot climates. The tonic water keeps you from getting malaria. And the lime keeps you from getting scurvy.

(Excerpted from *Cooking the Books*.)

PERSEPHONE TAKES THE A TRAIN
Elizabeth Bear

I would like to introduce you to a delicious cocktail—a Manhattan variant that started as a riff on Peché Austin's Manhattanhenge cocktail. I call this, "Persephone Takes the A Train."

- 2 parts bourbon (decent bourbon, please)
- 1 part Amaro (a bitter herbal Italian liqueur)
- 1 part grenadine (Make and use real grenadine, which is just pomegranate juice cooked with an equal weight of sugar to make a syrup. If you use that corn syrup and red dye #5 crap, Persephone is going to look you in the eye and go right back to her mama.)
- 2 dashes orange bitters (Bitter Truth makes a lovely orange cardamom one that works well.)
- Half a clementine or mandarin orange
- Ice

Put the bourbon, Amaro, grenadine, and bitters in a lowball glass. Swirl to mix. Squeeze half a clementine into the glass and then drop the crushed fruit in so the peel oils infuse the drink.

Add a little ice, preferably in the form of a single giant ice cube.

Enjoy in a leisurely fashion while reading Langston Hughes and listening to Ella Fitzgerald.

SISTER MINT, SISTER DARK
(Created in Honor of Jane Yolen)
Andrew Penn Romine

- 1 1/2 oz chocolate liqueur
- 1 oz whipping cream
- 1/2 oz cognac
- 1/4 oz white creme de menthe
- 3 dashes Aztec chocolate (AKA mole) bitters
- About 5 of your favorite chocolate mint sandwich cookies

In a food processor, finely grind the cookies (scrape out the icing first). Pour crumbs into a shallow bowl and rim a chilled cocktail glass. (Five cookies will make enough crumbs for a lot of cocktails.)

Combine all liquid ingredients in a cocktail shaker with plenty of ice. Shake fifteen seconds or until well chilled, and strain into a cocktail glass. Garnish with a mint leaf or two.

VAMPIRE SUNRISE COCKTAIL
Carole Nelson Douglas

"Umm, subtle yet spicy . . . or modern women like us."
—Psychic psychologist Helena Troy Burnside in *Vampire Sunrise*

- 6 ice cubes
- 1 1/2 oz pepper vodka
- 1/2 oz DeKuyper "Hot Damn!" Cinnamon Schnapps
- 4-5 oz orange juice, well shaken
- 1 oz Alizé Gold Passion orange cognac
- 1/2 -1 oz grenadine
-

Put ice cubes in 12-ounce highball glass. Pour in pepper vodka and cinnamon schnapps; add orange juice to fill to desired level. Add two ounces of orange cognac. Last, pour in grenadine, which will settle to the bottom. Add ice to drink as it melts, creating a longer and more sensual experience. This drink is no hit-and-run vampire bite.

WHIMSY DIVISION COCKTAILS
Scott Lynch, Steven Brust, & Jennifer Melchert

(These two beverages were designed for an April 1 *Cooking the Books* post.)

The Fat Fantasy Series

- 1 part vodka
- 1 part rum
- 1 dash pomegranate liqueur
- 1 part fresh pineapple juice
- 1 part cranberry juice

Garnish with two cherries and an orange slice. *Must be on a little plastic sword.*

Mix all ingredients except pineapple juice. Serve.

Inform customer that the pineapple juice doesn't actually show up until the second drink.

Take order for second drink. Mix, then strain into equal portions in two glasses.

Serve first half of second drink. Inform customer the second drink has been split up, and the next half will be available in twenty minutes.

Serve second half of second drink. Take order for third drink.

To third drink, add Tabasco sauce, celery stalk, milk, and one part Coca-Cola. Serve.

Commiserate with customer. Agree wholeheartedly that third drink is a low point in the sequence and something of a failed experiment.

Take order for fourth drink. Agree wholeheartedly with customer that they don't have a problem and can quit whenever they like.

The Fate of Beloved Characters

- 1 highball glass
- 1 bottle of bitters

Pour all the bitters into the glass. Serve. Customer will garnish drink with own tears to taste.

—

WOODCHOPPER DRINKS
Jennifer Stevenson

Dark Berry Daquiri

- 3/4 c frozen mixed berries (blackberries, blueberries, raspberries; your choice)
- 1-2 c rum or vodka, depending how thick you like it
- 1/2 c dark brown sugar
- 1/2 c plain, full-fat Greek yogurt, sour cream, or coconut milk

Blend on 3/4-speed. Push whole berries down with food pusher to make sure it mixes. Turn it up to high speed at the end. When the Vitamix starts whirring helplessly, you're done. Random fruit chunks are a feature, not a bug. Serve with spoons, because it's too stiff to sip.

Piña Colada

- 2 c frozen pineapple
- 1 c coconut milk or cream
- 1/2 c brown sugar
- 1 1/2 c rum

Blend until sugar is dissolved. Serve immediately.

—

ZOMBIE BRAIN
JG Flaherty

What is a gathering of writers without a few cocktails beforehand (and during, and after)? This is a sweet after-dinner drink or conversation-sparking party shot for the adults. But beware, because too many will cause you to feel like a zombie in the morning! I first came across these at a bar in the 1990s, well before the current zombie craze had taken over the world. The best part is watching people cringe as they bring the glass to their lips!

- Peach schnapps
- Baileys Irish cream
- Grenadine syrup

Pour 2-3 ounces of peach schnapps into a large shot glass or apéritif glass. Very gently, pour about two teaspoons of Baileys into the schnapps. It should form a round, brain-shaped glob at the top. Drip 2-3 drops of grenadine onto the Baileys.

NOTE: to change things up, you can add a couple of drops of Blue Curaçao or Green Curaçao to the schnapps before the Baileys, and create an Alien Brain. Or add Yellow Curaçao and make it a brain in formaldehyde.

• BRUNCH DISHES •

ALIEN SCONES
Elaine Isaak

When my mother put together a cookbook for family members with recipes we enjoyed, she wanted to include a version of the scones. She listed them as "Elaine's Scones," and it didn't occur to her that perhaps spellcheck did not have her best interests at heart when she simply accepted all of its suggestions. As a speculative fiction writer, I'm fine with the fact that my name autocorrected to Alien—I've always claimed to have arrived here by flying saucer! Just didn't realize the saucer came with a teacup...

As E.C. Ambrose, I'm currently writing a series of historical novels set in Medieval England, necessitating lots of business trips (of course) and lots of tasty eating. I've been working on my recipe for scones since my first trip to England when I was about ten years old. Most American scones are just not very satisfying. With this version, I think I've finally got it! Of course, you can add crystallized ginger or blueberries or whatever you think is needed—mostly I just slather them with clotted cream.

Makes twelve

- 3 c flour
- 6 T salted butter, cut in small pieces
- 1 T baking powder
- 2/3 c superfine sugar
- Pinch of salt
- 2/3 c buttermilk (or whey from cheese-making)
- 2 extra-large eggs

Preheat oven to 400°F. Lightly spray cooking sheet or use parchment.

Use your largest bowl for the flour. Run your hands through it to aerate. Cut in the butter to fine crumbs.

Add baking powder, sugar, and salt. Mix well using a large spoon. Form a well in the center and set aside.

Whisk together the buttermilk and eggs. Pour into the well in the flour. Using a very large spoon and as few strokes as possible, mix the dough until just combined. It will be moist and sticky.

With lightly floured hands, transfer the dough to a floured work surface. Knead gently, then form a thick rectangle. Roll to about one inch. Use biscuit cutter or slice into wedges. Transfer to baking sheet. Bake 15-18 minutes.

ALMOND-OAT MUFFINS
Kathy Tyers
(Gluten-free, Lactose-free, FODMAP-friendly)

NOTE: This recipe was developed at a high altitude (about 4500 feet). Please take that into account when baking at your own altitude.

I could almost live on these. The inspiration was a Specific Carbohydrate Diet recipe in Elaine Gottschall's groundbreaking book, Breaking the Vicious Cycle—*but this version is modified with low-FODMAP ingredients. I generally bake a double batch, since these freeze so well. These are my lembas for traveling (fellow Tolkien fans will understand). I generally pack two for each day I'll be gone, and then I know I won't starve even if the only restaurant food I can find is a plain chicken breast. Or . . . an almond-oat muffin and a cup of tea can tide me over until I find other safe food.*

Yield: 12-18 muffins

Flours Mixture
- 2 c almond flour: blanched or unblanched, in any ratio you like
- 3/4 c gluten-free oat flour
- 1/2 t (scant) xanthan gum
- 1/2 t baking soda
- 1/2 t salt
- 2 t cinnamon
- 1/2 t (scant) ground cloves

Batter Ingredients
- 4 eggs
- 1/2 c sugar (I like to use about half dextrose when I bake, since dextrose is reported to help digest fructose.)
- 1/2 c cooked, cooled gluten-free oatmeal
- 3 T melted, cooled butter
- 1/4 c plain, unsweetened almond milk
- 3/4 t vanilla

Preheat oven to 375°F. Prepare muffin tins with 12-18 paper muffin cups, depending how large you like your muffins.

Combine flours mixture in a medium bowl, stirring well. Keep all liquids away from xanthan gum until it's well blended with other flours.

Beat batter ingredients with an upright mixer in a large bowl until smooth and fluffy. Gradually add the flours mixture. The batter should be thick, but if it's extremely stiff, add one to three tablespoons cool water.

Spoon into paper muffin cups. Bake about 25 minutes, until nicely browned. Cool completely on wire rack. These muffins tend to stick to the paper until fully cooled.

Gingerbread Variation
(Delicious!)

Flours Mixture

For the oat flour, you may substitute equal parts oat, sorghum, and sticky rice flour. Add 1 T ground ginger.

Batter Mixture

- Increase total sugar to 2/3 cup.
- Add another 1/4 t vanilla (total 1 t).
- Add 1/2 c chopped nuts.
- (Optional) Add 1/2 t Kitchen Bouquet or FODMAP-safe bottled browning sauce to the batter ingredients. KB contains a trace of onion. If you're excruciatingly onion-sensitive, don't risk it—but it helps the muffins look like gingerbread, and eye appeal is important.
- (Optional) Add 1-2 t grated fresh ginger.

Tips:

- These muffins freeze beautifully. Thaw in refrigerator for best results, or microwave one muffin about 15 seconds. Microwaving does toughen them slightly, but if I eat them warm, I don't notice.
- Here's a satisfying, FODMAP-friendly traveler's breakfast: One or two Almond-Oat Muffins, an ounce or two of meat, and a small bowl of berries or a quarter of an orange.

BUTTER ROLLS BREAKFAST
Eric J. Guignard

I was born with a genuine sugar tooth, and I think it must be in the genes, because my parents, brother, and children have it too. My wife, who is of the so-called "health-conscious" persuasion, doesn't understand that this is akin to pedigree breeding; it takes generations to build up a tolerance and appreciation for certain foods that'll rot your ivories just as soon as treat you to a glimpse of saccharine paradise. I mean, I take care of myself, eat my whole grains, veggies, and such, but occasionally, on dreary, lazy Sunday mornings, nothing goes better to loll about in stuffed armchairs than a pairing of Butter Rolls and Hot Toddies. I don't know the history of butter rolls, but my mother made them, and I suspect my grandmother passed the recipe on to her. They're a sticky, sweet mess and easy to make. They're soaked in milk and, of course, being a growing boy at the breakfast table, were served to me alongside a tall glass of milk to drink. My father's family is from Switzerland, so I can't fault this predilection for dairy. However, as an adult, it's a bit too much lactose, even for me. I prefer a hot, light liquid to wash down the patisserie and have found nothing better than a simmering rum toddy. If you're not familiar with the toddy, imagine a cup of tea, but instead of tea, it's alcohol. Toddies are relaxing, renowned for curative effects, and just plain indulgent. After a few butter rolls and a couple hot toddies, you'll be ready to watch Casablanca *or take a nap. You'll find my toddy recipe on page 114.)*

- Store-bought biscuit dough (or make your own)
- Butter (a stick or so)
- 1 qt milk (or just enough to cover rolls in pan)
- 1 c sugar
- 1 t vanilla extract
- Cinnamon to taste
- Nutmeg to taste

Roll dough thin in 3-inch deep (or greater) greased pan and cut to rectangular strips.

Spread butter over surface.

Sprinkle sugar liberally along with a hint of cinnamon and nutmeg.

Roll up each strip of dough.

In a saucepan, mix milk, sugar, and vanilla, and gently warm it. Pour the warm milk over dough rolls.

Bake until lightly browned; about thirty minutes at 400°F.

CRÈME BRÛLÉE FRENCH TOAST
Patrice Sarath

This is a no-fail brunch potluck recipe. Remember to start it the night before because it needs to soak overnight. I've made it with various different liqueurs, including Kahlua, for a richer taste. Based on a Food Network recipe and various similar recipes.

- 1/2 c unsalted butter
- 1 c packed brown sugar
- 2 T corn syrup
- 1 8- to 9-inch round loaf Challah bread
- 5 large eggs
- 1 1/2 c half and half
- 1 t vanilla

- 1 t Grand Marnier or other liqueur, such as Kahlua
- 1/4 t salt

In a small heavy saucepan, melt butter with brown sugar and corn syrup over moderate heat, stirring, until smooth and pour into a 13x9x2-inch baking dish. Cut six one-inch thick slices from center portion of bread, reserving ends for another use, and trim crusts. Arrange bread slices in one layer in baking dish, squeezing them slightly to fit. In a bowl whisk together eggs, half and half, vanilla, Grand Marnier, and salt until combined well and pour evenly over bread. Chill bread mixture, covered, at least eight hours and up to one day.

Preheat oven to 350°F and bring bread mixture to room temperature. Bake, uncovered, in middle of oven until puffed and edges are pale golden, 35-40 minutes.

Unlike revenge, this is a dish best served warm.

MIGAS
William Gibson

"She crushed dry tortilla chips into a black pan, over sizzling butter, and poured the eggs on top."—*Count Zero*

I first encountered this primordial Tex-Mex soulfood dish in an Austin restaurant near Bruce and Nancy Sterling's place; it subsequently became a family staple, and even made it into my second novel. Texturally, the nearest equivalent would be the matzoh scrambled eggs served in kosher dairy restaurants, but the salsa definitely vibes it up into a different category of breakfast eating. A friend of mine remembers it fondly from his prison stay in San Miguel Allende. Preparing it always reminds me of that great scene in Peckinpah's The Getaway, *when Steve McQueen, fresh from a successful jailbreak, cooks breakfast for his girlfriend.*

- 6 eggs
- 1 T butter
- 5 T salsa
- 1 1/2 c dry tortilla chips, lightly crushed

Avoid snackbag chips with additives, particularly the horrible flavored varieties; you want plain chips, reasonably fresh; the very best are the dark brown ones made with "blue" corn. Either make your own salsa or buy it by the jar; hotter is better, because the eggs and chips tend to cancel the pepper.

First, crush the chips. This is easy if they're still in the bag; just give it a squeeze or two. You don't want crumbs; you want smaller chips.

Break the eggs into a bowl and stir.

Heat the butter in a large skillet, as for scrambled eggs. Add the chips. Stir. Add the eggs. Stir. Add the salsa. Stir. The salsa slows the cooking process somewhat, so continue to stir. The chips should be thoroughly coated in the mixture. It's done when the watery bits are gone, but not too dry.

It may look disgusting, but try it. Serve immediately with a dollop of salsa on top. Fancier restaurant versions add diced bell peppers, peas, etc.

REBEL FIRE OMELETTE, OR
LOVE THE TASTE OF NAPALM IN THE MORNING
Spider Robinson

I had always rather assumed that an "omelette" was a small omel, and whenever it occurred to me to wonder exactly what an omel was, I simply applied Moebius logic and concluded that it must be an enormous omelette. A person eating an enormous omelette might easily make a sound spellable as "omel!"—which in itself could have spurred the creation of a small version for social dining.

But in settling the all-important question of how to spell "omelette," the first step in writing this recipe, I discovered that I have been mistaken all these years. In point of fact, according to The American Heritage Dictionary, *"omelette" comes "from Old French* amelette, *'thin plate,' alteration of* alumette, *variant of* alumelle, *from* lemelle, *from Latin* lamella, *'thin metal plate,' diminutive of* lamina, *'plate' or 'layer.' "*

Which is silly, since an omelette looks nothing like a thin plate. It looks like a fat plate, a plate which has swallowed a mouse, and only half a plate at that. (Okay, it's frequently eaten off of a thin plate—but so is everything.)

As near as I can figure, the name is an example of prescience. Somehow, the Romans knew that one day science would produce a lightweight frying pan laminated with a thin layer of Teflon (or equivalent), on which glorious day the omelette would finally come into its own, accessible at last even to the average klutz.

What they probably could not have suspected, in their wildest dreams (and the Romans had some pips), was the final stage in the apotheosis of the omelette. How could they, for whom pepper was an exotic spice, ever have foreseen the coming of Rebel Fire. . . ?

If you already know how to cook an omelette (or think you do), you need only read the next section of this recipe, concerning—

The Miracle Additive

There are as many omelettes as there are omelette makers—ludicrous understatement!

Every omelette is different, unique as a fingerprint or a lay. The reason omelette-making is an art rather than a science is that nothing about it is replicable. The maximum number of possible omelettes is greater than the maximum number of possible chemical compounds—since the periodic table provides a smaller menu than the average pantry. That is why, over the years, I have seldom attempted to repeat an omelette. So many possible combinations, so little time!

But recently I stumbled across a variant which reliably triggers *kenshō* (Zen: sudden enlightenment), and now I repeat it often. Each time I eat it, my hat size goes up an eighth or so, my vision sharpens, my IQ rises five or ten points, my complexion improves, my singing range gains two notes on either end, I feel a boundless sense of kinship to and compassion for all that lives, and my beard thickens. All because of a single miracle additive . . .

I found it by serendipity. I was wandering through the Mexican Food section of my local supermarket, searching without much hope for a hot chili sauce that would actually be hot enough to suit me. It had always been my custom to buy the hottest sauce the store could provide—and then take it home and put some spices into the sucker. (I am the kind of sap who walks into Mexican—or Thai, or Vietnamese, or Szechuan—restaurants and says, "Astonish me!" I like food that commands attention.) Suddenly my eye was caught by a new brand. *Rebel Fire*, the proud name read. Four different Rebel Fire sauces, numbered, in 250 ml (8.45 fl oz) jars. Rebel Fire #1 claimed to be a Mild Chili Sauce; I ignored it. Rebel Fire #2 looked better: Hot Chili Sauce. I began to reach for it, but my hand veered to the right of its own accord and selected a jar of Rebel Fire #3. In contrast to all the red sauces, this one was an intriguingly villainous mustard-yellow color, and was labeled, "Jamaican-Style Pepper Sauce."

I checked the label. The ingredients looked quite promising: vinegar, fresh onions, mango, Scotch bonnet peppers, cucumber, fresh garlic, yellow mustard seed, coriander seed, cumin seed, ascorbic acid, turmeric, bay leaf, fenugreek, cardamom seed, Spanish paprika, black pepper, cloves, and cinnamon. A description was provided which also sounded attractive: "Jamaican-Style Pepper Sauce is sweet with mango and hot with Scotch Bonnet chilies from the West Indies." But then, right beneath this precis, I saw the legend that made the sale.

It is to be found on every jar of Rebel Fire Sauce, this proud credo: "At Rebel Fire, our respect for peppers borders on worship."

I felt at once a sense of recognition and kinship. "These," I thought, "are my kind of people."

Nor was I disappointed. When I got home with Rebel Fires #2 and #3, I found each to be that rare and wondrous thing: a sauce that is not only hot enough to make you wonder what all the delay in fusion research could possibly be about, but profoundly and subtly delicious as well. Have you ever had food so good you not only wanted to meet the chef, but wanted to invite him out for a drink and get to know him, learn what he thought about life? That good. Someday, if God is kind, I will meet the wizard who developed Rebel Fire's recipes, and he or she and I will be old friends when we meet.

The same praise is due Rebel Fire #4, Hot Jalapeño Sauce. I cannot testify directly as to #1, which I have not yet tried, but I would be astonished if it were not terrific. Even on an off day, the artist who created Jamaican-Style Pepper Sauce simply could not have produced mediocrity.

Rebel Fire Foods Inc. is at 247 Roxton Road, Toronto, Ontario M6G 3R1. If you can persuade your local supermarket to order their sauces, and get your friends to try them, you will have helped to make the world a better, brighter place. I have no financial interest in the company and have never communicated with any of its representatives; my praise is sincere and heartfelt.

The Omelette Itself

Now we deal with what a programmer would call the "shell," the basic omelette itself. This requires two other kinds of shell: eggshells, obviously, and the above-mentioned lightweight Teflon-coated shell in which to cook the contents of the eggshells. The importance of this tool to omelette-making cannot be overstated; the thing is simply a breakthrough, like the zipper or the integrated circuit. It is possible to cook an omelette in a cast iron fry pan; it is not fun. Two aspects of the modern Teflon-shell fry pan make it an absolutely ideal tool for omelettes: its low coefficient of friction under rigorous conditions (stuff don't stick to it) and its gently sloping shape. Equally useful, by the way, is one of those new highly flexible plastic spatulas.

The size of the pan should vary with the size of the omelette. I find that a standard 10-inch diameter pan is just right for a 3-egg omelette (the smallest you should attempt) and a 12-incher will do fine for a 5- to 6-egg job. A small omelette in an overlarge pan will be paperthin and tear too easily; a large omelette in a too small pan will be a lumpy monstrosity shot through with horrid nodes of undercooked egg, than which few things are more disgusting.

Okay. You have already prepared and set aside whatever ingredients you prefer to fill your creation with—the ideal assortment I recommend below, or whatever crackbrained collage of groceries you prefer. Diced eggplant, shaved fish, minced broccoli, whatever.

Now: break your eggs into a bowl. Add a tablespoon or two of your favorite thinning-liquid (I use 18% cream, myself, but then I am 6'1" and weigh 125 pounds. Water is fine, or leftover gravy from last night's chicken, or whatever.) Whip everything into homogeneity with a fork. (Other schools of thought lean toward an electric mixer or blender, which produce a sort of foamy omelette similar in texture to the Styrofoam containers they serve Big Macs in, but even if I liked foamed eggs, I am not competent to operate electrical machinery before I have had coffee.) If you wish to add spices—salt, pepper, garlic salt, chili powder, etc.—the Constitution gives you that right.

Next: put the frying pan on the stove at fairly high temperature. I have an electric stove, and set the dial halfway between medium and high.

Next: spread a mess of butter around the pan. Yes, I know: with the Teflon frying pan you're not supposed to need any lubricant. What do you want, first thing in the morning—an ironclad warranty claim, or breakfast? Besides, the omelette will taste better. (And remember, I'm 6'1" and 125 pounds . . .) Be sure and get the sloping sides of the pan wet and slippery.

Now you must time things carefully. The egg-and-liquid mix should be introduced to the pan about five seconds before the melted butter begins to turn brown. (Rather like Dr. Asimov's famous thiotimoline reaction.) If you miss the tick and the butter starts to brown, rinse out the pan—with hot water—and begin again, paying closer attention this time.

Add the egg mix. If the temperature is high enough, it will sputter and fuss as it hits the pan. (If not, rinse and repeat as above.)

At once reduce heat to medium or a hair lower.

Within seconds you have a bottom layer of firmish egg, with a pool of uncooked egg swimming on top. You now work your way around the perimeter of the pan, sliding your flexible plastic spatula under the firm cooked egg, lifting the edge slightly, allowing the uncooked egg to run underneath, then move the spatula 45° counterclockwise and do it again—and again. If you can't get the edge to lift, that's okay: just scrooch it towards the center of the pan; again, runny egg will fill in the space. The faster you go, the more tender your omelette will be. (Perhaps this is where the name came from: you're building "layers" of cooked egg.)

When you have made one complete circuit, reduce the heat again, to halfway between medium and low. Keep scooping up edges and letting egg run underneath (or scrooching them toward the center and letting egg fill in behind), until there isn't enough runny stuff left to flow, even when you tilt the pan in the direction of the lifted edge. There will still be a few little bits of runny stuff on top, but don't worry about them; they'll be taken care of.

At once reduce the heat to low.

Now bisect the omelette in your mind, and spread your filling ingredients evenly across one half—but don't dawdle to get the artistic effect perfect. You've just got time for the Final Subtle Touch—sprinkling a teaspoon or so of water across the filling, so it can turn into steam and cook those last remaining runny bits—and then it's time to Fold The Omelette. Run your spatula under the half of the omelette that does not have ingredients on it, to make sure it isn't sticking anywhere. Then place the near edge of the spatula against the imaginary line down the middle, and fold the flap over in a quick decisive motion.

Without stopping to congratulate yourself, cover the pan tightly and go pour the coffee which has been dripping while all this was going on. By the time you have put away the cream and sugar, it's time to remove the cover and slide the omelette onto a thin plate.

But pause to pour a tall glass of your favorite fruit juice, and grab a couple of towels. You'll need them if you're using Rebel Fire in your filling . . .

Spider's Favorite Omelette

The Shell:
- 3 eggs
- 2 T 18% cream

The Filling:
- 2-4 slices Black Forest Ham, chopped or shredded fine
- 1/2 avocado, diced small
- One whack of Monterey Jack cheese, diced into half-inch cubes (The cheese should equal the half avocado in bulk.)
- 2 t Rebel Fire #3, Jamaican-Style Pepper Sauce (I recommend smearing it on the diced cheese and then stirring, to get it evenly distributed through the omelette.)

The Tools:
- 1 fry pan, 10 inches in diameter, with snug-fitting cover
- 1 flexible plastic spatula

PORTUGUESE SWEET BREAD
Steven H Silver

I first came across this bread at a coffee shop I used to frequent when I was in college. In those days of a teenager's metabolism, I would, on occasion, just buy a loaf and have it for a meal. It is great with preserves. More recently, I've been using it to make pizza crust, which is great, but makes for a very rich pizza.

- 3/4 c milk
- 2 eggs
- 1 1/2 T butter
- 2 1/2 c flour
- 1/4 c sugar
- 3/4 t salt
- 1 1/2 t yeast

Mix milk, 1 egg, and butter together. Add flour, sugar, salt, and yeast and knead. Allow to rise for 1 hour. Beat down, knead, and allow to rise for another hour. Beat down and shape into loaf. Brush the top of the loaf with a beaten egg and score the top three or four times. Allow to rise for at least half an hour. Bake at 350°F for 40 minutes.

• POTLUCK DISHES •

AFRICAN CHICKEN PEANUT STEW
Lawrence M. Schoen

In the winter of 2011, I hosted a small weekend workshop in my home. I'd like to think that people came for the insightful critique and warm camaraderie of fellow authors, but the real draw was that my ex-chef wife, Valerie, planned round-the-clock gourmet meals. We had everything from simple nibblies like grilled Halloumi cheese sprinkled with red hot peppers, breakfasts of savory Italian-style, caramelized onion, black bread pudding, and dinners of Feijoada (Brazilian black bean stew), to desserts like vanilla bean soufflé with crème anglaise sauce and cranberry-pecan duff. It's a wonder we managed to get any workshopping done at all.

But the best dish by far was the African chicken peanut stew. I recommend it for any and all SFWA functions. Here's the recipe:

Serves 6-8
Prep time: 20 minutes, Cook time: 1 hour, 55 minutes

- 3 lb chicken thighs, skinless, chopped into thumb-sized pieces
- 3 T vegetable oil
- 1 large onion, yellow or white, sliced
- 1 3-inch piece of ginger, peeled and minced
- 6-8 garlic cloves, roughly chopped
- 3 lb sweet potatoes, peeled and cut into chunks
- 1 15-oz can crushed tomatoes
- 1 qt chicken stock
- 1 c peanut butter, smooth or chunky, your choice
- 1 c roasted peanuts
- 1 T ground coriander
- 1 t cayenne, or to taste
- Salt and black pepper
- 1/4 to 1/2 c chopped cilantro

Begin by heating the oil in a large soup pot. Use a medium-high heat. Next, salt the chicken pieces thoroughly. Pat them dry, and then brown them in the oil. (NOTE: You're going to want to do this in batches so as not to crowd the pot. As the pieces brown, set them aside.)

Next, put the sliced onions in the oil. Sauté them for 3-4 minutes. Stir them frequently and scrape off any browned bits from the pot as you go. When the onions are done, add both the ginger and garlic, then continue to sauté for another one to two minutes. Now it's time to add the sweet potatoes. Stir until everything is combined well.

At this point, add in everything else except the black pepper and cilantro: the chicken, chicken broth, crushed tomatoes, peanut butter, peanuts, coriander, and cayenne. Stir, and stir, and when you think you're done, stir it some more. Keep at it until everything is well combined.

Bring the result to a simmer and taste; add salt as needed. Next, cover the pot and adjust the heat to simmer gently for 90 minutes (but check on it in an hour), or until the sweet potatoes have vanished, transforming into what appears to be a cream sauce!

Finally, tweak to taste with additional salt and cayenne. Now add the black pepper. Stir in the cilantro. The stew is ready to serve, either alone or over steamed rice.

ALTERNATIVE DAIRY MANICOTTI
Catherine Lundoff

After suffering from migraines for many years, I was diagnosed with a dairy allergy. This was about fifteen years ago, back before there were a lot of good substitutes for foods made with cow's milk. Soy cheese tasted like rubber to me and I disliked the aftertaste of most of the other alternatives. Goat and sheep's cheeses were both harder to find locally and harder on the wallet, so I started experimenting with alternatives. This recipe emerged as the result of a lot of trial and error experimentation with other lactose-free options. It's quite forgiving so you can also try other kinds of cheeses and cheese substitutes and still get something tasty out of it.

I'm originally from Brooklyn, NY, and while I'm not of Italian descent, I do enjoy good Italian food. I was pretty depressed at the idea of giving up all that yummy manicotti, lasagna, and stuffed shells, so I was pretty eager to find an alternative way to make food I liked. This one has become one of my favorites, and it has fed numerous fen and SF/F writers over the years.

- 12 manicotti shells (1 package)
- 2 pt jars or 1 qt of spaghetti sauce
- 1/2 t garlic salt or powder
- 1 t oregano
- 1/4 lb goat's milk mozzarella
- 2 lb ricotta without cow's milk

To make the ricotta, mix the following together in a large mixing bowl: a standard package of soft tofu, an equivalent size of goat or sheep's milk feta cheese, two eggs to serve as a binder and one to two teaspoons dried basil to taste. Stir until the mixture is thick enough to use as shell stuffing.

Boil water and a tablespoon of olive oil in a six quart pot and gradually add the first six shells. Cook per the package directions, generally about three to four minutes. You want them to be soft enough to work with but not so soft that they fall apart. I generally test by stabbing them with a fork: round holes from the tines are good, tearing is bad. When the shells are done cooking, drain the first six and put in the next six. Repeat the process for the remaining six shells.

Heat the sauce and add the oregano and garlic powder to it. When hot, place half the sauce in a baking pan. Wait until the shells are cool enough to handle or spray lightly with cold water. Then fill the shells with the cheese mixture and place them in the pan. Cover them with the remaining sauce and any remaining cheese mixture. Bake in the oven for 25 minutes at 400°F or until done. Serve with garlic bread and salad.

ASHBLESS PASTA SALAD
Tim Powers

I think it was in September of '86 that Jim Blaylock and I hitchhiked over to William Ashbless's Long Beach apartment to collect some money he owed us and get Blaylock's car back. Ashbless didn't have time to discuss these things, because he was expecting guests—Augustus Silver, William Hastings, and some transient called Cyclops, as I recall—but he did let us watch him cook, as he drank up the gin I had bought for my father; and by asking questions of the increasingly drunken poet I was able to get this recipe from him. He claims he got it from Percy Shelley's cook in Pisa in 1821, but I suppose that's a lie.

- 2 c semolina flour
- 2 eggs
- 2 bell peppers, with the seeds and all white membranes removed, cut into chunks
- 4 fat cloves of garlic, in all, peeled
- 3 steaks (New York, Spencer, Filet Mignon, or something comparable)
- 1 16 oz bottle of a good Italian salad dressing (he used Bernstein's Restaurant Italian Dressing)
- 3 or 4 T extra-virgin olive oil
- 6 green onions, finely sliced, including a couple of inches of the green sections
- A fist-sized chunk of blue cheese, crumbled
- 1 4 oz jar of marinated mushrooms, finely sliced

Mince two of the garlic cloves into the Italian dressing and then marinate the steaks overnight in it; the next afternoon, cook the steaks over very hot coals for four minutes, turning once and basting frequently with the marinade (Ashbless claims that a bunch of fresh thyme or rosemary makes a great basting brush, and that you can tear it up and throw it onto the coals just before the steaks are done, to bathe them in the resulting smoke). Cut the steaks into "cigarette-butt-size pieces", eliminating all fat, and wrap them in some clingy plastic wrap and refrigerate them.

Next day make the pasta: start by throwing the bell-pepper pieces and the other two garlic cloves into a blender or food-processor and rendering them into an only-slightly-textured paste.

Then dust a cutting-board with ordinary flour and dump the two cups of semolina flour onto it and make a baseball-size well in the middle of the pile, so that the semolina flour forms a ring. Break the eggs into the well, cover them with the garlic-and-bell-pepper-paste, and beat them with a fork, gradually knocking in sections of the flour wall, until you have a gluey, crumbly pile. Put the fork aside and begin kneading the mess with your hands. There will be unincorporated pieces of dough and stray drifts of flour—shove them all together and keep pushing the pile in on itself, and pretty soon—give it ten minutes—you'll have something like a green ball of putty.

Scrape the cutting-board clean and dust it again with ordinary flour.

Tear off a quarter of the dough-ball and wrap the rest in plastic. Roll the torn-off piece out flat, either with a pasta-machine or a rolling-pin, until it's about a sixteenth of an inch thick (roughly the width of five or six sheets of typing paper). If you've got a pasta machine, cut the sheet into fettuccini; if you don't, roll the sheet up into a cylinder and cut it into quarter-inch sections and then unroll the sections.

Tear off the other three quarters of the dough ball, one at a time, and do the same with them.

Set four quarts of lightly-salted water on high heat; when it's at a rolling boil, dump the pasta into it. The pasta will probably be done within seconds of when the water returns to a boil, so keep fishing pieces out and testing them for chewiness.

When the pasta's done, drain it in a colander, run cold water over it and shake all the water out of it; then pour the olive oil over it and toss it thoroughly with your hands. Put it into the bowl you want to serve it in, and add the onions, the mushrooms, the blue cheese, the steak pieces and the Parmesan cheese. ("A tablespoon or two of good balsamic vinegar wouldn't hurt, either," Ashbless told me. He apparently didn't have any that day.)

Toss it again, and serve at once. It serves, I gathered, four.

BEA'S SOMETIMES VEGAN BLACK BEAN CHILI
Maria Lima

In Texas, chili means meat and a lot of it. But if you're in the mood for something less primal, take a shot at this easy, savory black bean chili recipe . . . oh yeah, you can totally add meat.

Makes 8 hearty servings (AKA, this is a real meal).

Equipment
- Heavy-bottomed sauté pan
- 4-6-qt slow cooker

Ingredients
- Generous splash of olive oil (Use the good stuff!)
- 2 fist-sized onions (red or white), chopped
- 1 t dried oregano
- 1/2 t unsweetened cocoa powder
- 1 t cumin
- 1/4 t cinnamon
- Sprinkling of dried pepper flakes, to taste
- 1 med-large jalapeño, minced whole (Or, increase pepper flakes instead of jalapeño.)
- Cayenne to taste (Or, use smoked paprika for an extra nice flavor.)
- 1 large sweet pepper, chopped (red, yellow, orange)
- 4 large garlic cloves, pressed
- 2 cans black beans, undrained
- 1 28-oz can diced tomatoes with juice
- 1 28-oz can crushed tomatoes
- 1 c fresh or frozen corn kernels
- 1/2 c chopped fresh cilantro
- 1/4 c fresh lime juice
- Salt to taste

Heat oil in heavy-bottomed sauté pan over medium heat.

Add chopped onion. Sauté and stir until onion is translucent and has begun to caramelize.

Add herbs and spices; stir. This will release the aromatics.

Turn heat way down and stir until onion is completely caramelized and soft. Make sure you don't burn it!

Add jalapeño and red pepper; sauté until tender.

Stir in garlic and sauté for 30 seconds, just until it's a bit heated up.

Take everything off the heat.

In your slow cooker, dump the two cans of black beans, diced tomatoes, and crushed tomatoes.

Add the mixture from the sauté pan.

Stir everything well.

Set slow cooker to lowest heat and cook for eight hours.

At the very end of the cooking time (about 7.5 hours in or so, this doesn't have to be exact), stir in the corn kernels, cilantro, lime juice, and salt and let it finish cooking.

Toppings (Optional)
You can serve the chili using any of the below toppings . . . or not.
- Grated sharp cheddar
- Sour cream or greek yogurt
- Chopped avocado
- Sliced scallions
- Chopped cashews

If you want more protein (add these before you cook!)
Add one cup of textured vegetable protein plus one cup of veggie broth or water.
> or

Cube up some extra-firm tofu and add it.
> or

Brown some ground beef and add to spice mixture before adding to the slow cooker

Leftovers
This keeps very well in refrigerator or frozen. Serve leftover chili over rice or crumbled cornbread.

BLACK BEAN SALAD
Anna D. Allen

A-maize-ing grace! When I was two, my mother and I lived with my grandparents in what was then a very rural Alabama while my father was in Vietnam. My grandfather grew several acres of corn—sweet corn for the family and horse's corn for the livestock. For an entire year, I refused to eat anything but sweet corn (and Stouffer's spinach soufflé—but that's another story). My mother was just happy I would eat something.

Plus the corn was free. This childhood predilection ended up in my short story, "Lake People." Food always shows up in my stories, but this was more personal than usual.

Today, other than popcorn (with butter and Mexican-style hot sauce), polenta (deconstructed cornbread), and all the wonderful things made from masa harina, I don't eat much corn—mainly because the stuff found in grocery stores has been bred for shipping and is just horse's corn. The exception is salads like this one.

This is a wonderful side for a traditional cookout. It's also great when you have a mixture of vegetarians, meat-eaters, diabetics, and heart patients. It's shockingly healthy and vegan, too, but it's still oh-my-God good!

- 2 cans black beans, drained and rinsed
- 1-2 t adobo sauce from a can of chipotle chilies, or to taste (see note below)
- 2 c corn, cooked and cooled (I use frozen and just heat it up in the microwave and then rinse in cold water.)
- 1 bell pepper, diced (I recommend orange or red, but green works fine.)
- 1 red onion, diced
- Cilantro, chopped (The more the merrier, but at least a quarter cup.)
- 2 tomatoes, diced (I like Roma tomatoes and add more.)
- Salt to taste (At least a half teaspoon but probably more.)

Dressing
- 1 large clove garlic, finely minced
- 1 t ground cumin
- 1 t ground coriander
- Juice of 1 lime
- 2 T extra-virgin olive oil

Make the dressing by whisking all the dressing ingredients together. You can also add the salt to the dressing. Set aside.

Toss together the black beans and adobo/chipotle sauce (I recommend starting with just a teaspoon). Add the rest of the ingredients. Toss together. Add the dressing. Toss together. Taste for seasoning. If it's not really good, you haven't added enough salt. Might also need a touch more adobo/chipotle sauce.

NOTE: Originally, I just used the adobo sauce from a can of San Marcos chipotle peppers in adobo sauce. Now, I puree the entire contents of the can and then use a teaspoon or two of that (freezing the rest) as needed in my cooking. As the important flavor in this salad is that smoky chipotle, you can use any chipotle-based hot sauce to taste, but start with a small amount and work from there.

BOOZY BEEF
Joe & Gay Haldeman

Ready in: 30-60 minutes
Serves 10

- 3 lb filet mignon or filet of beef, cut in cubes
- 5 T butter
- 2 1/2 T olive oil
- 1/2 lb mushrooms, sliced
- 3 3/4 T shallots or green onions, minced
- 2 1/2 medium onions, to taste (optional), sliced
- 5 T flour
- 1 c bourbon
- 2 cans beef broth
- 2 t salt
- 1 t garlic powder
- 1/2 t freshly ground pepper
- 2 c sour cream

Sprinkle the steak cubes with salt and then dust with flour. In a large skillet, quickly brown them on all sides in the olive oil and butter. Remove the steak from the pan. Add the onion slices and mushrooms to the pan drippings. Sauté for a few minutes, until the onion is tender. Sprinkle with one tablespoon flour. Put the steak back into the pan with the onion and mushrooms. Add the beef broth and bourbon.

Cook over low heat for about 30 minutes, covered. Adjust seasoning to taste, adding salt and pepper as needed. Stir in the sour cream the last few minutes, right before you serve. Serve over cooked noodles.

CALDO DE POLLO
David Lee Summers

Caldo de pollo is one of those traditional meals that's so rustic and simple it rarely makes it onto the menu of Mexican restaurants. I first discovered it when my friend, singer/ songwriter Mónica Gómez, brought it to a party in Las Cruces, New Mexico. I've been a fan of this chicken stew ever since. It really is a great party food in that the portions are easily adjustable and you can do a lot of the time-consuming work well ahead of time. This would work well for an autumn or winter gathering when the weather turns chill. Use it for a smaller gathering where it's the star of the show or take it to a potluck where people will dole out smaller portions. Feel free to try different vegetables. Many cooks add corn, and some like to keep it on the cob. Other families add green beans. I like this dish so much, I recently featured it in a scene of my western steampunk novel Lightning Wolves when an unexpected guest pays a visit to the Morales family and they need something to feed everyone.

Makes approximately six 8-ounce servings.

- 1 T canola oil
- 1 onion, chopped fine
- 4 chicken leg quarters
- 48 oz chicken stock
- 1 c whole grain brown rice
- 4 cloves garlic, chopped
- 2 T New Mexico or Anaheim green chile, roasted and chopped
- 2 c water
- 1 c baby carrots
- 2 stalks celery, cut about an inch long
- 2 large potatoes
- 1/4 c cilantro
- 1/2 c salsa (Pick the flavor you like; I like a smoky, chipotle salsa.)
- 1 t garlic powder

Heat oil in four quart pot. Sauté onions until clear to lightly browned. Cut chicken quarters in half and add to the pot. Add chicken stock, rice, garlic, and green chile. Bring to a boil, then simmer until chicken is tender—about an hour. Allow to cool. The dish may be prepared to this point and refrigerated overnight. Remove chicken from pot. Discard skin and bones. Shred meat and set aside. Skim fat from broth. Add two cups water, carrots, celery, potatoes, cilantro, salsa, and garlic powder to the stock. Bring to a boil, then cook over medium heat until vegetables are tender. Add water as needed to keep it brothy. Add the shredded chicken back to the pot and heat through.

CHAMPAGNE CHICKEN
Vonda N. McIntyre

- 1 chicken, cut up
- 1/2 c lemon juice
- 1 c champagne

- 4 garlic cloves, chopped
- 1/2 t rosemary

Using a glass (not metal) dish, marinate chicken in lemon juice, champagne, garlic, and rosemary.

Bake covered at 350°F, until the chicken is tender. If the marinade doesn't completely immerse the chicken and you don't want to use up the rest of the champagne, add some chicken broth. (Otherwise it will be tough.)

Serve over rice or kasha.

The lemon juice is a good stand-in for salt if you happen to be cooking low sodium meals. If you refrigerate it overnight, you can skim off the fat before serving it reheated. (It reheats excellently.) You can also use broth instead of champagne. But it's a lot better with champagne.

CHICKEN CURRY
Ann Leckie

My recipe is one I got from my mom. She got it, I'm told, from The White House Chef Cookbook *by Rene Verdon. Or, more accurately, I think, from an excerpt from that cookbook that was published in a magazine around the time it came out. I can't find the photocopy of the original page that she gave me when I asked for the recipe, but this is how I make it, anyway. The recipe calls it "Chicken Madras" but we always just called it "Chicken Curry."*

- 1 whole chicken, cut up (Or the equivalent in pieces, if you just want/have thighs or whatever. Bone-in gives the best flavor, but you can even make this with pieces of already cooked, diced leftover chicken).
- 1/4 c flour and 1 T curry powder (For dredging the chicken, if you're using raw pieces.)
- 1 medium onion, chopped
- 3-4 apples, peeled and diced
- 1 can chicken broth (or around two cups of stock)
- 1/2 t of salt (or to taste)
- 1 T curry powder
- 2 T flour
- Oil (Though I'm fairly sure the original recipe called for butter.)

Trim the chicken if needed. Mix the first bit of flour and curry powder (and some salt if you want) and dredge the chicken.

Heat some oil in a large skillet (preferably one that has a lid) and brown the chicken on both sides. Remove from the pan and set aside. (You can actually skip this step and go straight to sautéing the onions and apples, but it's yummier if you brown it first).

Put the chopped onion and apple in the still-hot skillet and sauté it until the onion is, you know, done—translucent and soft.

Add the one tablespoon curry powder and stir around and let that cook a bit. Then add the two tablespoons flour and half teaspoon salt and stir that around and cook it a bit. (I sometimes add a nice dollop of ginger garlic paste here, but it's not in the original recipe and my mother knew nothing of the existence of ginger garlic paste).

Add the chicken broth/stock, and stir while it comes to a boil and thickens. Put the chicken pieces back in the skillet—be sure to get the sauce all over the parts that stick up—put the lid on, and simmer it until the chicken is done.

While the chicken is simmering, you're going to make some rice, and chop up a few hard boiled eggs, and put some raisins in a cup and pour boiling water over them and let them sit and puff up some. The rice and sauce is extra delicious with some egg and raisin sprinkled on it.

You might need to adjust the flour and/or curry powder if it's too hot/not hot enough the first time you make it, or if it's thicker/thinner than you'd like. I like the sauce fairly thin, and only a small tickle of heat, myself. I always get "mild" curry powder, or when I'm feeling extravagant, I get Penzey's Maharajah Curry Powder.

As I said above, this tastes its absolute best if you use chicken with bones in it, but it will work with basically any kind of chicken you've got on hand, including leftovers. Don't feel like peeling apples? You can leave them out, though it's not quite as yummy. It's really versatile—once you know the basic technique, you can essentially throw in anything you like. Throw in peas or carrots or whatever veggie seems good to you. Make it simpler or more complicated—stripped down to its simplest components (meat, curry powder, stock, flour to thicken, rice) it can make a pretty quick, good-tasting supper with very little effort. It's a definite fave of mine, and has been since I was a kid.

CHICKEN MOLE POBLANO
Greg and Astrid Bear

The Lost Secret of Martha Lake
by Greg Bear

Every year, in July, my wife and I hold a party to celebrate the Clarion West writers workshop—a six-week affair that allows beginning writers (or writers who want more familiarity with science fiction or fantasy) to spend days under the tutelage of six professionals in those fields. The workshop has been remarkably successful over the years—and a great deal of fun.

The party is held at our lakefront house, and Astrid usually serves a mouth-watering chicken mole to accompany the many salads and desserts brought in by guests.

One of my favorite incidents occurred over twenty years ago. A young writer had joined me at the end of the dock to dabble our feet over the water and talk theory. After a few minutes, she asked, "What's the real secret to writing and getting published?"

"Well," I began. "To tell the truth, it's . . . "

At that point, the four-year-old blond daughter of some dear friends pushed herself between us and said, "I know the Lithuanian word for tree!"

Obviously this was a coded message from the secret muses.

The young writer never did learn the secret, which has been kept safe ever since.

Serves the multitudes; leftover sauce freezes well.

- 8 roast chickens (I buy them at Costco.)
- 8 packages flour tortillas
- 1 recipe mole sauce

Mole Sauce
- 4 c chicken broth
- 1 c blanched almonds
- 2 T crushed, dried hot chilis
- 1/2 c sesame seeds
- 1 1/2 t ground cinnamon
- 1/4 t ground cloves
- 1/2 t each: ground coriander seed, ground cumin, anise seeds
- 1 lb fresh tomatoes, cores removed, or 1 14-oz can chopped tomatoes, with juice
- 1 c raisins
- 4 small, fresh hot chilis
- 1 large onion, chopped
- 1 T sugar
- 1/2 t freshly-ground black pepper
- 2-4 squares unsweetened chocolate

In a food processor, puree two cups broth, almonds, dried chilis, sesame seeds, cinnamon, cloves, coriander seed, cumin, and anise seeds. Pour into heavy, large saucepan.

Puree tomatoes, raisins, fresh chilis, onion, sugar, and pepper, and add to mixture in saucepan. Add remaining broth and two squares of chocolate, and bring mixture to a simmer, stirring occasionally. Taste and add salt as needed. After the chocolate has melted, taste to see if it needs more chocolate—I usually go with the full four squares as I like the deep note that it brings to the flavor. Simmer, stirring now and then, for about 30 minutes. Set aside until ready to serve.

Strip the meat from the chicken and tear into generous shreds, arranging artfully on two large rimmed baking sheets. If you need to keep things warm for a while until you are ready to serve, pour the juices over the meat, loosely cover with foil, and keep in 200°F oven.

Wrap the contents of one package of tortillas at a time in a clean dishcloth, and put in microwave for one or two minutes to warm tortillas.

Arrange the serving dishes so that guests place a warm tortilla on their plate, take a portion of chicken, then drizzle the mole sauce over it generously. Roll it up and eat, and come back for more!

―――

CHICKPEAS WITH BASIL, TOMATOES, PARMESAN & GARLIC
Fraser Sherman

This recipe is based on one from Readers' Digest's Live Longer Cookbook. *It's a good, quick potluck recipe for when you don't have time to cook anything elaborate—and much as I enjoy cooking something fancy, that's often a good thing. All the ingredients keep so I buy them whenever we're out of town and make it fast when we get home. It's also very flexible: I've upped the garlic from the original recipe and my wife LeAnn invariably adds extra Parmesan. When she grows basil and tomatoes, I use fresh ingredients. For a large pot, I just double the amounts shown here.*

- 6 cloves garlic
- 1 T olive oil
- 1 15 oz can tomatoes
- 2 15 oz cans chickpeas
- 1 T basil
- 1/2 c Parmesan cheese
- 1T lemon juice

Sauté the garlic in the olive oil until lightly browned. Add in the tomatoes, basil and chickpeas and stir over medium heat for about seven minutes. Add in Parmesan and lemon and stir until the cheese melts. Serves four.

―――

CHILI CON CARNAGE
Charles Sheffield

"Oh East is East, and West is West, and never the twain shall meet . . ." I don't think Rudyard Kipling had cooking in mind when he wrote "The Ballad of East and West," but his comment certainly applies to the world of spicy food. The East (Asian) palate is trained on curry powder. The Western world looks to chili peppers, cayenne, and Tabasco to add interest to bland ingredients.

I love very hot food (one of my favorite SFWA breakfasts was served in Anaheim in 1984: hot chili, moonshine, and generic beer.) A few years ago I set out to explore the union of East and West, and this is my favorite result to date.

- 2 large onions (strong, not Bermuda)
- 2 cans red kidney beans, including the liquid
- 1 clove garlic, finely chopped
- 2 lb ground beef (regular, not extra-lean)
- 2 c dry rice
- 1 t salt
- 4 T curry powder
- 4 T hot chili powder
- Tabasco sauce

Chop the onions into pieces no bigger than the nail on your index finger; set to one side.

Cook the ground beef in a skillet until lightly browned, stirring so that there are no large pieces.

While the beef is being browned, drop the rice into boiling (unsalted) water, cook until al dente, and strain.

Place the beef in a large (three quart) container over a simmering heat. Add the onions and garlic and stir. After five minutes, add the rice, and five minutes later the beans.

Add one teaspoon of salt.

Add the curry powder and chili powder.

Cook, stirring occasionally, for at least an hour, preferably two hours or more. Taste after one hour, and add Tabasco sauce to suit own preferences. (To be sure you do not burn it, you might want to use a double boiler.)

Serve in bowls with Ritz crackers or chapattis.

These amounts will feed eight, or a greedy six.

Have iced water ready. My own preference as accompaniment to this dish is very dilute Pernod and spring water (one ounce of Pernod, twenty ounces of water).

CHOW FUN NOODLES
Wesley Chu

I *would love to take credit for this recipe but this was contributed by my sister-in-law, Chef Beverly Kim of* Top Chef Texas (Season 9) *and owner of Parachute restaurant in Chicago.*

Serves 1-2 people

- 3 cloves garlic, finely chopped
- 1/4 c small-diced onion
- 1 1/2 t sweet soy sauce
- 1 1/2 T oyster sauce
- 1 full egg, mixed briefly
- 1 1/2 oz Shaoxing rice wine
- Dash salt and sugar
- 1/8 t white pepper
- 1/4 c seeded, diced tomatoes, or halved grape tomatoes
- Handful of sliced shitake mushrooms, or mushroom mix
- Handful bok choy or Chinese broccoli, sliced on the bias
- 4 oz phat rice noodles, briefly separated, flash fried
- Juice of 1/4-1/2 lime
- Sliced scallions, cilantro, crispy garlic, truffle oil

(NOTE: If adding chicken, cook chicken first.)
(*Crispy garlic*: Mince garlic evenly, and fry in sufficient medium oil until golden. Spread out on paper towels. Sprinkle a touch of powdered sugar on top to help separate and curb bitterness.)

Get wok hot. Add about 1 1/2 ounce oil. Add the egg, and it will puff. Quickly add mushrooms and greens, and sauté, and garlic and stir fry for minute.

Add Shaoxing rice wine (you should hear a hiss), then add the noodles (and chicken, if desired), the tomatoes, the soy sauce mixture, and seasoning.

With spatulas, push everything around briskly and rhythmically, until the noodles soak up all the sauce and are uniformly brown.

Finish with lime juice.

Top with fresh scallions, cilantro, crispy garlic, and truffle oil.

COUNTRY PUMPKIN CHICKEN CHOWDER
David D. Levine & Kate Yule

Serves 4; 274 calories per serving and only 23% from fat (if you use white meat)
From: *Oregonian FoodDay*, 1/97.

- 1 T vegetable oil
- 8 oz boneless, skinless chicken, cut into bite-size pieces (We used 2-3 frozen thighs.)
- 1 c chopped onion
- 1 c chopped red bell pepper
- 1 clove garlic, minced
- 2 cans chicken broth (3.5 cups)
- 1 lb canned pumpkin (1.75 cups)
- 1/2 c frozen corn
- 1/4 c long-grain white rice
- 1/2 t dried basil
- 1/4 t salt
- 1/8 t pepper

Heat oil in large, heavy saucepan over medium heat. Add chicken, onion, bell pepper, and garlic; sauté until chicken is no longer pink.

Stir in broth, pumpkin, corn, rice, basil, salt, and pepper. Bring to a boil; cover. Reduce heat and simmer for 20 minutes, stirring occasionally, until rice is tender. Serve warm.

CREAM CHEESE TOMATO STUFFED CHICKEN BREASTS
Russell Davis

NOTE: Using boneless chicken breasts will reduce cooking time. This recipe may be prepared using bone-in, skin-on chicken breasts (less expensive), by simply skipping the butterflying step and placing the cheese mixture beneath the skin.

Serves 4

- 4 boneless skinless chicken breasts, trimmed of any excess fat
- 16 oz (2 packages) plain cream cheese, softened
- 2-3 ripe roma tomatoes
- 1 fresh lemon
- Kosher salt

- Fresh-cracked mixed pepper
- 1 t each: fresh, chopped basil, thyme, and parsley

Mix the herbs into the softened cream cheese, then roll into a log, wrapping in waxed paper. Place the herbed cream cheese in the freezer until stiff enough to slice (about 1 hour). Preheat oven to 375°F. When cheese is ready, butterfly the chicken breasts. Slice the cheese in quarter-inch thick slices, and place on one side of each breast until covered (typically two to three rounds). Fold the chicken back together and secure with two plain, wooden toothpicks. Place breasts on a small roasting rack inside a lined baking dish. Brush lightly with olive oil; salt and pepper to taste. (Note: you should be able to SEE the salt and pepper.) Slice the lemon and place a lemon twist on top of each breast. Place in oven for approximately 20-25 minutes, until juices are clear or a meat thermometer registers 165-170°F. (For bone-in chicken breasts, the cooking time will be longer.) Place on a platter and serve with simple sauce (below).

Simple Sauce
1 stick salted butter
2 shallots (medium to large), diced
1 T garlic, minced
1/4 c sour cream
1 c white cooking wine
2 T sherry or Frangelico
Kosher salt
Fresh-cracked mixed pepper

Preheat a small sauté pan and melt two to three tablespoons of butter. Add the shallots and garlic, cooking until soft and beginning to brown. Add the cooking wine and the drippings from the chicken (above). Stir almost continuously. Add sour cream, continuing to stir until all ingredients are mixed. Top with the sherry or Frangelico, turn off the heat, and continue to stir. Pour on top of the chicken.

CROCKPOT 15 BEAN SOUP
Larry Dixon & Mercedes Lackey

This is one of Larry's favorites, and it is stupidly easy to make.

- 1 bag of 15 Bean Soup Beans (You can find them in the dried peas and beans section.)
- 1 ham bone and all the liquid from cooking the ham (plus any ham trimmings you want to add)
- Minced garlic and/or onion to taste (Like a lot, put in a lot. Don't like it, eliminate it.)

Soak the beans overnight, or for at least 8 hours. Rinse twice and drain.

Put the ham bone, trimmings, and all the liquid in the bottom of a crockpot.

Add the onion and garlic (if any).

Add the beans. Add water until the beans are covered. Cook on low for at least eight hours. Can be left to cook for as long as twelve.

Because you are using the liquid from the ham, which contains plenty of seasoning, you will not need to salt or season the beans.

CROCKPOT RED BEANS & RICE
Nicole J. LeBoeuf

This dish became a wash-day tradition in old New Orleans because it requires little supervision on the stove. Move it to the crockpot, and "little" becomes "none." Go away to your day job, lose yourself in your work in progress—the beans won't care. (Unless you short the water, that is, in which case I hope you like them scorched.)

The best red beans and rice of my childhood came from the kitchen of Metairie Park Country Day, my school from kindergarten through graduation. The consistency was perfect: creamy and smooth. I've spent years trying to recreate it and I think I may have succeeded.

Country Day also instilled strange condiment habits with this dish, at least for some of us. On a single plate, food gets a little mixed, fueling that classic childhood game of "What's too gross to eat?" I have a deep and abiding nostalgia for thousand island dressing and croutons on my beans. It's surprisingly tasty.

When I prepare this for a potluck, I do it up vegan. When I'm spoiling myself, I don't consider it done until shredded chunks of ham are falling off the bone.

Feeds 8-12 party-goers in a night, or one busy writer at home over the course of two weeks.

Put in crockpot:
- 2 c dark red kidney beans
- 6 c water
- 2 bay leaves
- couple sprigs of fresh thyme
- About 1 T instant espresso
- About 1 T Cajun Land crab boil seasoning (if unavailable, substitute other brand, or mix to taste some combination of cayenne, salt, black pepper, white pepper, paprika, garlic powder, onion powder)
- A few shakes hot sauce (I prefer Crystal.)

Going vegan? Add:
- About 1 t apple cider vinegar
- Small drizzle of cooking oil (e.g., canola)
- Enough vegetarian broth base to mix with 6 cups water according to package instructions (e.g. 2 T "Better Than Bouillon" paste).

Meat eater? Add:
- A ham hock or shank
- A few links andouille sausage

Cook on high until the beans are almost as tender as you want them and the broth is getting creamy; about four to six hours, but may vary. If this is your first time preparing it, check on it every hour or so to get an idea of how your beans are behaving and whether you need to add water. Don't worry about "overcooking." Overcooking is not an issue.

You might at this stage use a potato masher or the back of a spoon to mash some of the beans against the pot.

Now chop up and add your fresh veg:
- 1 large onion
- 2 to 3 celery ribs
- 1 green or purple bell pepper (though I usually don't)
- 2 to 3 green onions/scallions (or more)
- 3 garlic cloves (or more)
- Large handful of chopped fresh parsley

Keep cooking until veggies are pretty much indistinguishable in the broth. Beans and broth should be very creamy. Serve over a sweet long-grain rice, like jasmine or basmati. Offer guests several bottles of hot sauce and either a shaker of apple cider vinegar or a bowl of diced dill pickles, or both. Thousand island dressing and croutons is encouraged, at least once.

CUCUMBERS WITH CINNAMON
Barbara Hambly

Persian cucumbers—peel and cut up. I cut into quarter-inch slices, but the shape doesn't matter.

Spray with olive oil. Sprinkle with salt, sugar (a lot or a little, depending on the flavor you want. I go with about a half teaspoon salt, one teaspoon sugar), pepper if you like it (I don't).

Dump in three tablespoons seasoned rice vinegar (this is on five or six Persian cukes in a big bowl). Sprinkle—lightly or heavily—with cinnamon.* I use a lot of cinnamon, so I have no notion how much normal people would regard as normal.

This usually makes a couple of meals for me.

NOTE: Recipe testers suggest 1/4 tsp cinnamon or more to taste.

―

GA XAO DAM GUNG SA:
CHICKEN WITH LEMONGRASS & MACERATED GINGER
Aliette de Bodard

A wonderful mix, tart and spicy and redolent with the smell of lemongrass (recipe from Bach Ngo's *Classic Cuisine of Vietnam*).

Prep time: 20 mins
Cook time: 30 mins
Total time: 50 mins
Serves: 4

- 300 g chicken
- 1 stalk lemongrass
- 2 T fish sauce
- 2 T ginger, pounded with mortar and pestle
- 2 T rice vinegar
- 6 T water
- 1 t cornstarch
- 1/2 t sugar
- 3 cloves garlic
- 1 large onion
- Sprinkling of black pepper

Mix the ginger and the vinegar. Set aside.

Prepare the lemongrass stalk: discard any dried outer leaves, discard the upper two-thirds of the stalk, and slice the remainder paper-thin. Slice the chicken into bite-sized pieces. Put the chicken in a bowl along with one tablespoon of the fish sauce and sprinkle black pepper. Add the lemongrass. Mix, and set aside.

Mix the cornstarch, sugar, water, and remaining fish sauce, and set aside.

Chop the garlic, and slice the onion into wedges.

In a large-bottom casserole dish on medium fire, put in oil, and fry the garlic for about 30 seconds, until fragrant. Add the onion, and cook until soft. Add the chicken, and fry for five minutes, stirring constantly. Cover, and cook for an additional five minutes. Then stir in the ginger/vinegar mixture and the cornstarch/fish sauce/sugar one. Mix well. Cover again, and cook for five minutes. Then uncover, set heat until the sauce boils, and finish off by congealing the sauce (basically, make the cornstarch boil and thicken).

Serve with rice.

NOTE: The lemongrass stalk can be replaced with 1 tablespoon dried lemongrass, but it will need to be soaked in warm water for two hours and chopped very fine.

GAZPACHO TWO WAYS
Walter Jon Willliams

I. Red Gazpacho

Serves 4-6

- 4 or 5 large ripe tomatoes, peeled, seeded, and chopped
- 1 serrano pepper, minced
- 5 cloves garlic, minced
- 2 lemon cucumbers, peeled, seeded, and diced
- 1 red bell pepper, seeded and diced
- 1 red onion, peeled and thinly sliced
- 1 ripe but slightly firm avocado, peeled and diced
- 4 c light beef stock or chicken stock
- 2 T fresh lemon juice
- 2 T medium-acid red wine vinegar
- 2 T chopped fresh basil
- 2 T chopped fresh Italian parsley
- 4 T chopped fresh cilantro
- Kosher salt and black pepper in a mill
- 1/2 c best-quality extra-virgin olive oil

Combine all of the vegetables in a large bowl. Add the stock, lemon juice and vinegar and stir very briefly. Stir in the fresh herbs and season with salt and pepper to taste. Chill the soup for at least one hour before serving. Remove from the refrigerator, stir, let rest for 15 minutes and then pour the olive oil over the soup and serve.

II. Golden Gazpacho
Serves 4-6

Certain varieties of golden tomatoes have a rich, velvety texture; this soup highlights
that luscious quality.

- 4 or 5 ripe golden or orange tomatoes
- 3 c homemade chicken stock
- 1 small red onion, minced
- 2 t finely minced garlic
- Juice of 1 lime
- Kosher salt and black pepper in a mill
- 1 ripe avocado, peeled and sliced
- 4 T best-quality extra-virgin olive oil
- 2 T fresh minced chives

Peel the tomatoes and gently remove their seeds. Chop the tomato flesh very finely
or pass it through a food mill (do not puree in a blender or processor) and place it
in a large bowl. Stir in the stock, onion, garlic, and lime juice. Taste the soup and
season with salt and pepper. Fold in the avocado and chill the soup for at least one
hour. Remove the soup from the refrigerator, ladle into soup bowls, and top each
serving with a generous tablespoon of olive oil and a sprinkling of chives.

[Recipes by Michele Anna Jordan, author of the *Good Cook's Book of Tomatoes*.
All Rights Reserved. Reprinted with permission.]

GLUTEN-FREE CORN BREAD, TURKEY DRESSING, & GRAVY
Jerry Pournelle

*I write this for people of varied experience. We find that many gluten-free households
tend to give up on cooking, while others have great experience at it. And many are just
discovering that cooking gluten-free is a very different and baffling experience. For a
long time our family had strong long-standing holiday traditions centered on the meals,
particularly the dressing and gravy; then we had to go gluten-free, and it took a while
to adjust to that. This recipe solved one of the gluten-free problems of this household.*

*Note that gluten sensitivities vary, but it is safest to assume that even minuscule
traces of gluten will be more than enough to trigger an undesirable digestive event.*

*The key ingredient in these recipes is the flour. We have been fortunate in finding
a very satisfactory gluten-free flour: Bob's Red Mill GF Bread Mix. I have only seen it*

for sale in Whole Foods stores in Los Angeles, but it has been available there for many years, and many gluten-free cooks are aware of it; if you don't know of it and you are trying to do gluten-free cooking, it is very much worth your while finding it.

Bob's Red Mill GF Flour contains a very large number of ingredients, including corn starches. The result is that it has a taste much like that of a good wheat flour, and most breads hold together better than other GF flours we have tried, but it has some properties different from ordinary flour. In particular, it tends to thicken more when cooked with liquids. It works as a good general purpose flour for breads and cookies, and also browns for roux to make gravy, but it takes less GF flour to make a gravy than gravy with white flour requires.

Corn Bread

We use Albers Yellow Corn Meal (Harina de Maiz Amarillo), although doubtless other corn meals will work. Albers is definitely gluten-free. This recipe is derived from the recipe on the Albers box, altered for use with Bob's Red Mill GF Flour.

Preheat oven to 400°F.

- 1 c Albers Yellow Corn Meal
- 1 c Bob's Red Mill GF Flour
- 1/4 c sugar (Most recipes call for 1/4 cup sugar. We use considerably less. Some use none.)
- 1 to 3 T baking powder (Standard recipe is 1, but GF flour doesn't rise well. I use 3.)
- 1 t salt (Or less, as you please.)
- 1 c milk (See notes.)
- A bit more than 1/3 c vegetable oil
- 2 or 3 large eggs

NOTE: More egg makes a richer bread. Normal recipes want one egg. Two is enough, but three makes a better bread for eating. GF flour thickens more than wheat flour. More liquid may be needed, but if you use three eggs it isn't likely.

Put the milk and eggs, salt, and sugar in a medium bowl or the egg beater bowl. Pour the vegetable oil into the pan or pans you will bake it in, swish it around, then drain into the mixing bowl. Beat it pretty good. Put the baking powder in, stir, then add flour. Standard practice seems to be to pour liquid into some other bowl, put the flour and corn meal in the mixing bowl, and add the liquid to the dry flour. I just put flour and corn meal into the eggbeater bowl with the liquids and run the mixing machine on slow until it's all thoroughly mixed. If you beat the heck out if it, you'll use up the goodies in the baking powder, so don't be too vigorous about it. When you're done, the mixture should be a thick liquid that levels itself. If it doesn't level when standing, add (by spoonfuls) a bit of milk or even water to thin it just enough so that it pours. GF flour tends to make things thicker.

Pour it into baking pans. One 8-inch pan should do it for one recipe, but this does tend to make a bit more than you expected. Fill the pan no more than three-quarters full, as it's going to rise. Bake for 20-30 minutes; 25 is usually about right. You want it brown on top and done in the middle. Standard advice is to poke a wooden toothpick into the middle of the loaf and see if it comes out clean. Just be sure it doesn't burn.

Let cool a bit and you can have a slice.

NOTE: You can double or treble or quadruple this. It's not likely any will go to waste in a gluten-free household. If you add a bit more sugar and Red Mill flour, and a bit less corn meal, it makes a good cake. Up to half a cup more corn meal makes a "cornier" corn bread. Basic or altered recipe can be poured into muffin pans. Muffins take less time to bake so watch them after fifteen minutes.

NOTE ON SEASONING: We add a small amount—less than one teaspoon—of blackstrap molasses. It's very easy to get too much, so be careful or don't try it at all.

If this is intended to be stuffing for a chicken or turkey, you can stir half a cup of corn meal and suitable spices into the batter before baking. Obviously this will depend on what spices you like. We tend to use the Romany formula: parsley, sage, rosemary, and thyme, plus a bit of savory. The spice marketed as "poultry peasoning" works well. In California, sage and rosemary grow in yards as well as up on the hills, and we prefer that. We have not found spicing corn muffins to be a worthwhile activity.

Gluten-Free Cornbread Stuffing

Make sufficient corn bread a couple of days before you will use it. Make some to eat as bread, too.

The best dressing requires a pressure cooker. Get some chicken thighs, or half a chicken, or a whole chicken, depending on how much of this you're going to need. Too little doesn't ruin things, and too much can be a lot more than you think. Put the chicken, bones and all, into the pressure cooker. Add some chopped celery, onion, garlic, parsley, sage, rosemary, and thyme. Don't overdo it. Put in a cup of water. If your pressure cooker leaks, it will need more, but you're not making soup.

No more than a teaspoon of salt. The afternoon of the day before you cook the turkey, put all that stuff into the pressure cooker and cook under the highest pressure your cooker will work at for at least an hour. I generally let it go two hours, and sometimes three. The goal here is to really and thoroughly cook everything, including the bones. When it's done the bones must be edible without splintering.

Let it cool before opening it. That retains more of the flavor. If you're in a hurry the steam will make your kitchen smell pretty good. Open the pressure cooker and start taking out all the bones you can find. Put them in a bowl. Your dog, or the neighbor's dog, will love them, and if you've cooked them as long as I recommend they are perfectly safe. For that matter you can eat them yourself, and some people put backbone segments into the dressing. They have a nut-like consistency and flavor.

The night before you are going to cook the turkey, get a large pot, put a little butter in the bottom, and put it on the stove. Don't turn on the burner until you have something to put in there.

- Pressure-cooked chicken or much chicken broth
- 1 yellow onion
- 1 red onion
- 1-3 cloves fresh garlic
- 1 full stalk of celery
- 2 apples
- pecans
- 1 c chestnuts, peeled, and roasted or boiled
- Gluten-free corn bread
- Poultry seasoning
- Parsley, sage, rosemary, and thyme (Note that this is a real love potion.)
- Savory
- A bit of mace, but be careful.
- Same advice for allspice: use some but be careful.

Clean off your work surface. Make sure there's no trace of raw poultry left on your cutting board. The pressure cooking will have autoclaved the chicken, and your turkey ought to be well out of sight at this point. We'll be dealing with warm chicken (as the pressure cooker contents cool down) and we don't want anything from raw chicken getting into it while the dressing is waiting around to be stuffed into the turkey.

Start chopping. I begin with the onions, and when they're in there I get the burner going while I start in chopping celery. This whole mess needs to be reduced to small pieces that blend together. Most of the celery and onion and garlic ought to be in thinner slices than you think, but some thicker celery adds variety. Apples and pecans can be in larger chunks. As you chop, throw stuff into the pot and mix. When there are some vegetables in there, chop up the corn bread into small cubes and throw some in. Add chestnuts (good luck on peeling them, although we have found peeled whole chestnuts in Asian stores and at Whole Foods sometimes), chopped into quarters or so.

161

Now start adding the contents of the pressure cooker. I stir with a big spatula, sometimes using it to chop larger bits into smaller. You can start tasting now and making any corrections you think are needed. When you get it all mixed up, you may have a problem finding a place in the refrigerator for it, so be careful it doesn't get into contact with the turkey until everything is ready for the oven.

We stuff the front and back of the turkey with this, then put the rest into a casserole or baking pan. The neck of the turkey can be put on top of a casserole of dressing. The neck will be thrown away, but it will add some good turkey juices as it cooks. Cover the pans. If they don't have covers, use foil. Dressing in pans cooks faster than turkey. When you baste the turkey, put some of the basting onto the dressing in pans; watch to see it's not getting too brown at the edges. If it is, take it out, and put it back into the oven a half hour or so before the turkey is done. Or put it in a warming oven if you have one.

Gluten-Free Gravy

(This stuff keeps about as long as the turkey. It will also recover from freezing.)

- Butter
- Bob's Red Mill GF Bread Flour
- Turkey juice from your baked turkey
- Possibly salt, pepper, spices as you like; taste the gravy first.

Put a healthy amount of butter into a good frying pan. How much depends on how much gravy you want, and that depends on how much turkey juice you will have. You want to make enough for one good meal and perhaps one leftovers meal, but not more. Good gravy doesn't keep all that long.

When the butter is melted, start adding Bob's Red Mill GF Bread Flour, about a tablespoon at a time. Keep adding it until you have a liquid that's thick and is beginning to brown. Stir like crazy with a spatula; it will stick to the frying pan and burn if you aren't careful. Don't let it get so thick that you can't stir it. If it gets too thick, thin with more butter or a good vegetable oil. Do not thin with water. That will almost guarantee lumps.

What you are looking for is browning. Unlike wheat flour, much of the GF flour isn't going to brown as you think it will, and this is never going to get as dark as it would if you were using wheat flour, but it will brown.

When it's brown, add a cup of turkey juice all at once, stirring like mad. It will get thick fast, and if you've been careful there will be no lumps. Have more juice ready to throw in as it will thicken fast. Keep stirring. Gluten-free flour thickens a lot more than wheat flour, and you'll want more turkey juice than you are used to if you're accustomed to doing this with wheat flour. If you run out of turkey juice and it's still too thick—you shouldn't, but it happens—you can add ordinary water, or coffee creamer, which will change the color of the gravy, but some think the coffee creamer improves the flavor. As you stir, you should be tasting, and adding small amounts of spices. Allspice, poultry seasoning, salt if you must, even less than a teaspoon of blackstrap molasses. If you don't trust your tastes, be careful or have someone else taste it. Couples often work well together at this phase, but if you're doing a big turkey, there's a lot going on out there and you're full-time keeping the gravy from lumping or burning, so there may be no one who has time to play with you here.

The resulting gravy isn't superior to wheat-flour-based gravy, and it's not as versatile in adjusting thickness and quantities, but it's every bit as tasty, and it doesn't take all that much more time and trouble. This may become a family tradition.

GRANDMA'S GOETTA
P. Andrew Miller

Goetta's origins lie somewhere in Germany. It is fairly common in Cincinnati and just about no where else in the states.

- 1 lean boneless pork loin, about 4-5 lb, plus 1 or 2 bone-in pork chops
- 5 c pinhead oatmeal
- 10 c broth
- 1 1/2 t ground allspice.
- 1 1/2 t salt or salt to taste
- Handful whole allspice and bay leaves

Trim the fat off the pork loin and chops to desired leanness. (More fat means more flavor). Cut up the pork into squares but leave some on the bones of the chops. Cover with water and boil the meat and bones along with whole allspice and bay leaves until done. Remove meat and let cool. Save the broth. When meat cools, grind in food processor. (You can now discard the bones after removing the meat.)

Put the ground meat into a six-quart crockpot and add the oatmeal. Add salt and ground allspice. Mix together. Add the ten cups of broth and stir again. Cook for eight hours in crockpot.

When done, remove goetta and put into bread pans to shape. Empty bread pans onto silver foil. Slice goetta and fry in olive oil until crispy. I like to use an iron griddle. You may want to salt to taste again.

Can be eaten for breakfast, lunch or dinner. The recipe can also be cut in half for a three-quart crockpot. The key is to make sure there is twice as much water as oats.

GRILLADES AND GRITS
James L. Cambias

(Pronounced "gree-yod.")
- 1 lb beef or veal (see below)
- 1 T oil or bacon fat
- 1/4 c flour
- 1 large onion, chopped
- 2 cloves garlic, minced
- 1 or 2 medium bell peppers (red or green), seeded and chopped
- 3 tomatoes, peeled and diced (or 1 can of canned tomatoes, chopped)
- 1 T tomato paste
- 1/2 c beef stock
- 1 t thyme
- 2 bay leaves
- Dash Tabasco
- Salt and pepper to taste (be heavy-handed)
- 1/2 c grits

The Meat: One pound beef, either thick beef round slices (half-inch thick) or cheap 4 ounce boneless steaks. Don't use the good stuff. For real authenticity, track down some boneless veal chops. Pound the meat with a meat mallet to tenderize and flatten it.

Heat the oil in a Dutch oven or deep skillet. Dust the meat with flour, brown the slices in the hot oil on both sides, then remove.

Sauté the onions and garlic for about five minutes. Add the tomato paste. Then the peppers, tomatoes, stock, and spices. Cook for a few minutes, then return the meat to the pan and cover with the sauce. Cook, covered, at a very low simmer, or put the pot in the oven at 350°F for 1-2 hours, or until the meat is very tender and the sauce has thickened.

While the meat is cooking, prepare the grits. Bring two cups of water to boil with one teaspoon salt. Add grits. Reduce the heat to simmer, and cook for 20 minutes (or whatever the manufacturer's recommended cooking time is), then turn off the heat and let it stand for another five minutes.

If you really don't like grits, substitute rice.

GUINNESS STEW
Talia Gryphon

Serves 6-10 people, depending on portion size

- 2 T extra-virgin olive oil
- 1 lb bacon, diced
- 2 tbsp extra virgin olive oil
- 2 lb chuck (or small chuck roast) (Cut into bite-sized pieces and set on paper towels to "dry." This will cause the meat to brown rather than to "gray.")
- 1 lb onions, diced
- 1 package baby Portabella or white button mushrooms, rinsed and diced*
- 1 can or two bottles Guinness Stout (approx 20-32 oz)
- 1 32 oz box of Swanson's Beef Broth
- 5 lb russet potatoes (about 6 medium-sized for mashing)
- 1 32 oz box Swanson's Beef Broth (or beef broth of your preference)
- 1 stick butter (8 T) (or Smart Balance—do not use margarine)
- 1/2 c whole milk (or half and half)

Spices:
- 1 t black pepper
- 1 t salt
- 1 T dried thyme
- 1 T dried marjoram
- 1 T dried savory
- Balsamic vinegar

Cut bacon into approximately one-inch pieces and cook in heated skillet. Do not skip this step; you want the bacon to be crispy. Using a slotted spoon, remove bacon from skillet and drain on paper towels; set aside.

Pour off all but two to three tablespoons of the bacon fat. Pour the remaining two to three tablespoons of bacon fat into a soup pot. Add the two tablespoons olive oil to the bacon fat and heat to medium. Add the cut-up chuck to the fat/oil. While the meat is browning, dice onions and rinse mushrooms. Add onions, mushrooms, and spices to the pot. Stir as it cooks. When the meat is browned, the onions start to become clear, and the mushrooms are becoming darker, add the beef broth and finally the Guinness. Cover, reduce heat to med-low, and allow to simmer, stirring occasionally, for about an hour.

While the stew is cooking, make the mashed potatoes. Peel and cut your potatoes and add them to a pot of well-salted water. Bring to a boil and set timer for 20 minutes. When the potato pieces can be pierced easily with a knife or sharp fork, take them off the heat and drain into a colander. In the same pot that you boiled the potatoes, add eight tablespoons butter, set back on the stove, and allow to melt. After the butter is melted, add the potatoes and half cup whole milk (or half and half). Using a hand potato masher, mash the potatoes into the melted butter and milk. You do not want overly smooth potatoes for this stew, so do not use a mixer but mash potatoes thoroughly.

When the stew is fully cooked through (it will reduce a little as it simmers), taste it to see if it needs more salt or pepper. Add the balsamic vinegar to the stew at this time and stir well.

To serve: Using a large spoon, place a quarter to half cup mashed potatoes into a bowl, then ladle the finished stew over it. Crumble some reserved bacon over the top of the stew. Place a bottle of balsamic vinegar on the table in case anyone wants to add a few more shakes to their dinner. The vinegar effectively "cuts the fat" from the bacon and makes it a delicious, savory dish.

Serve with Irish soda bread, a French loaf, or a ciabatta.

It is a rustic, peasant dish and should be enjoyed with simple accompaniments. Enjoy!

There is ongoing argument about washing or not washing mushrooms. On Good Eats, Alton Brown proved that there is no difference in texture, flavor, or quality of mushrooms which are washed right before use or mushrooms which are simply wiped off with a towel. For myself, even though mushrooms are grown in sterilized compost, someone has had their hands on them, so I prefer to rinse them before I use them.

HUNGARIAN-STYLE FRA DIAVOLO SAUCE
Steven Brust

The parallels between food and writing are so obvious and clear. It's hard to talk about them because they're inherent.

In writing, as you know, it's all about the details. You're making the fra diavolo; if you go to the really good butcher shop and get some really good Italian sausage, as opposed to going to the grocery and grabbing the package of Johnsonville, a lot of people won't notice the difference. If you are using fresh oregano instead of the dried stuff, ditto. If you're really careful selecting your peppers, or using fresh minced garlic instead of powder, a lot of people won't notice the difference. But if you do all of those things together, people will notice the difference. It's the cumulative effect of all those little decisions. Just like writing.

Traditionally, a fra diavolo is a marinara sauce with cayenne. I messed around with it—finally got it to the place where I like it. But the key, like I mention in the recipe, is using the Hungarian method of cooking onions, which is not the same as the Italian. Mixing that in really worked well.—Excerpt from Cooking the Books

I call it Hungarian-style because of how you cook the onion, which is the way you prepare onion for a paprikás or a pörkölt; everything else is fairly standard Italian. But it's amazing how much difference it makes if you do the onion this way.

- 1 cube chicken bouillon
- 1 Anaheim pepper, diced
- 2 jalapeño peppers, diced
- 1 can tomato sauce (I use Cantadina because I like it.)
- 2 cans diced tomatoes (You know, the usual can-size.)
- 2 packages fresh mini-bella mushrooms
- 2 packages fresh assorted or white mushrooms. (You know, the usual size packages fresh mushrooms come in.)
- 2 green peppers, diced
- 2 red peppers, diced
- 3 lb spicy Italian sausage (bulk, or chopped if you get links)
- 2 really fucking big yellow onions, diced
- 1 1/2 heaping soupspoons fresh minced garlic
- A bunch of oregano (fresh, if possible, dried if necessary)
- Basil
- Cayenne pepper
- Crushed and dried red pepper
- Marjoram
- Salt
- Black pepper
- 1 1/2 glugs red wine (pinot noir, burgundy, or Chianti)
- Olive oil

Make a mug of bouillon (you know, cube and boiling water in a mug?).

If you are using fresh oregano, finely mince half of it and set it aside.

Heat up a large stainless steel skillet over high heat. (Cast iron is not your first choice this time, because you need quick response. God help you if you're using an electric stove.)

When it's hot, pour in enough olive oil to barely cover the bottom.

When the oil is hot: If you had fresh oregano, take the half you didn't dice and put it in the oil. Let it season the oil for a couple of minutes, then remove, shake the oil back into the pan, and discard. Or, if you're crazy, set it aside, dice it, and add it when you add the rest of the oregano.

Throw in your Anaheim and jalapeño peppers. Sauté them for a moment, then add the onion. Swirl and stir the onion until it starts to stick a little, then immediately turn the heat down to medium or maybe a bit less, and add a couple tablespoons chicken bouillon. (You can also skip the bouillon and just use water. I tried wine once, but didn't like it.)

Continue stirring until the bouillon is evaporated, then add another couple of tablespoons, and stir some more.

Keep doing this until the onions are pulpy—that is, right before they turn translucent. It isn't easy. If it makes you feel better, I can only hit it about 50% of the time. It generally takes about 45 minutes.

While this is happening, get a large saucepan and pour in the cans of tomato-y stuff. Add the minced garlic, the mushrooms, the oregano, the basil (about a third as much basil as you used oregano), the marjoram (even less marjoram), cayenne to taste, crushed red pepper to taste, salt, and black pepper. For this, I tend to use ordinary table salt instead of kosher salt or sea salt, I guess because the sausage is salty enough to bring the flavors in the other stuff out. Freshly ground black pepper works best, *vide* Alton Brown.

Add in the wine and water or the bouillon you didn't use; I tend to use about half a can of liquid (wine plus bouillon). Heat medium low.

When the onions are perfect (or you've given up), add them to the sauce.

Turn the frying pan up to high, fry the sausage, then add it to the sauce.

Add the peppers to the sauce. Add more water if necessary to cover.

Cook down until the consistency is right. Makes 0.8 fucktons (English measure) on account of it's better the second day. Keep adding water when you reheat it to keep the consistency right. You eat it over noodles, of course.

JACK'S BOLOGNESE SAUCE
Jack Dann

When the Queen Mary was actually an ocean liner, I spent some time in Italy and France, where I developed a taste for pasta Bolognese. Oddly enough, in those days, I could get a cheap Bolognese pasta in cafés all over France, and I developed a taste for "French Bolognese". Unfortunately, I couldn't find it in the States (or Australia, where I now reside). I can get good pasta Bolognese, but not the Bolognese I love and remember from my misplaced youth. However, I found a recipe in the sturdy and ever-handy Joy of Cooking that was close, and which I've adapted to get that taste I remember. In fact, I just made a pot-full yesterday! This is how I make it:

Serves 4-6 (unless you eat like me!)

You'll need a large, heavy pan with a lid for this recipe (or a pot).

- 1 carrot, peeled and minced
- 1 medium onion, minced
- 1 to 1-1/2 lb lean mince
- 4 rashers of Canadian bacon or pancetta, chopped
- 2 stalks celery, minced
- 1/2 c chicken stock (You might need to add more stock as you cook.)
- 2/3 cup sherry (I use sherry; you can also use white wine.)
- 2 to 3 big T tomato paste
- 1 1/2 c whole milk (You can use skim, but whole is much better for taste.)
- 1 to 3 T olive oil, as needed
- 1 big pinch of nutmeg
- 1/2 t grated lemon zest (or a strip or two of zest)
- Salt and pepper to taste

Mince carrot, celery, and onion.

Heat oil in heavy skillet over medium heat. Add minced onions, carrot, and celery and cook until the onions just begin to soften. Add bacon (or pancetta) and cook until bacon is cooked through and vegetables are soft, but not brown.

Add the mince and, using a spatula to separate the meat (to make sure mince is . . . Minced), cook until mince is brown. While cooking, push mince and vegetables to the side, tilt pan, and using tongs and a bunched-up paper towel, soak up any grease that runs into the side of the pan. You'll probably only need to do this once or twice if you're using very lean mince.

Add tomato paste, stir through, and add wine (or sherry), stock, a pinch of nutmeg, and lemon zest. You can also add a good pinch of salt and a good grating of pepper. Stir and add some of the milk—easiest just to keep milk in its measuring cup and add as you go. The sauce should have a soupy consistency . . . if it's too dry, just add more chicken stock.

Let simmer, covered, over low heat for an hour and a half or so. Every once in a while add a quarter cup or so of milk and stir through. If looking too meaty (i.e., dry), add more stock. Conversely, if too wet, partially uncover pan to evaporate some of the liquid.

Correct spices (salt and pepper), if necessary.

Boil pasta and serve with sauce and plenty of fresh parmesan. Leftover sauce (hah!) can be frozen and then microwaved for a fast meal.

KICHAREE
(Food of the Gods)
Jeffe Kennedy

- 1/2 c mung beans
- 1/2 c brown rice
- 1 T salted butter
- Pinch cumin seed
- 1/3 t turmeric
- 1 t ground cinnamon

(Spices may be tripled, depending on personal taste.) Put in crockpot or other slow cooker with 5 c water. Longer simmer is better.

LOU'S LASAGNA & GARLIC BREAD
Lou Antonelli

(This recipe makes one large roaster pan of lasagna.)

- 2 lb sweet Italian sausage
- 2 lb ground beef (chili ground texture is best)
- 1 whole bulb of garlic
- 5 jars Ragu sauce, 45 oz. each
- 3 T standard Italian seasoning
- 30 lasagna noodles (Barilla Oven Ready is best)
- 32 oz ricotta cheese
- 4 lb mozzarella cheese, shredded
- 2 lb provolone, sliced
- Large shaker of Parmesan/Romano/Asiago cheese blend
- 1 stick butter
- Extra-virgin olive oil
- Salt

Melt stick of butter in medium low heat.

Break apart the bulb of garlic and peel the cloves. Get all the skin off. Mince well. Toss in skillet with melted stick of butter. Watch carefully. When the garlic starts to turn brown and caramelize, strain it. I've used a tea strainer. Put aside. It's not necessary to blot dry; some butter on the garlic is good. Save the melted butter.

Peel the Italian pork sausage (if you can get Italian sausage meat without the skins, so much the better). *Never use hot sausage—the combination of spice and garlic will be overpowering.* Mix the pork sausage meat thoroughly with the ground beef. Add three tablespoons of Italian seasoning. Mix well. Brown beef, sausage meat and Italian spices mixture.

Put all the Ragu sauce in a very large pot and slowly warm as meat is browning. Do not throw out Ragu jars yet.

Mix a little of the Ragu sauce and olive oil together on the bottom of the roasting pan. Swirl and coat thoroughly. Sprinkle a little salt on the bottom. This is to keep the bottom layer of noodles from sticking.

When the meat and spices mixture is just about done, stir in the garlic and mix well. Finish browning, and then drain.

Layer bottom of roasting pan with a double layer of lasagna noodles. Ladle in one third of Ragu sauce. Sprinkle one quarter of mozzarella cheese, then drop in evenly spaced dollops of one quarter of the ricotta. Use the back of a large spoon to swirl and flatten the mixture so it's flat.

Add single layer of lasagna noodles. It's okay to overlap to close up gaps, but don't go crazy with the noodles. Authentic Italian lasagna is considered a baked casserole, not a noodle dish.

Now, pour in one third of Ragu, spread one half of mozzarella and one half of ricotta. The middle layer is the crucial part. Again, use the back of a large spoon to swirl and flatten the mixture.

Top with a layer of noodles again; pour out the last of the mozzarella and ricotta. Swirl again. Don't pour out all your Ragu sauce, maybe leave a half cup.

Finally, top with double layer of lasagna noodles. Pour last of the Ragu sauce on top. The lasagna should fill out to the edges. If you see any space at the corners and sides, pour in Ragu sauce and/or press out filling mixture. If there are gaps, they will fill up with oil that comes out of the cheese, which doesn't taste good.

Preheat oven to 375°F. Cover top of roasting pan with tin foil. Remember to properly support the pan so you can take it out; it will be dense and heavy.

Put in oven; check at 45 minute mark. If any parts of the top layer of lasagna noodles are dry and crisping, try puncturing with a large fork. Hopefully juices will bubble up. If the top is too dry, try this: Put a half cup of water in empty Ragu jar. Shake and pour into second jar. Repeat until the fifth jar has a weak strength sauce you use to baste the top. Don't let the noodles on the top dry out and crisp. If the whole top layer gets overdone, peel off the noodles and throw them away. That's why you double layer the top. If you strip the top layer of noodles, you definitely need to baste with the dilute Ragu sauce.

No matter whether you keep the top layer of noodles or not, turn oven down top 350°F, and layer down all the provolone. It's to seal the top of the lasagna.

Puncture each piece once so juices can bubble up. Don't replace the tin foil. Put lasagna back in the oven.

After another 15 minutes (one hour mark) generously sprinkle Parmesan/Romano/Asiago blend of top. Provolone should be melting so cheese mixture sticks.

When it's finished, take out and let cool a few minutes. Serve with a ladle, not a spatula; remember, this is a casserole. If you use a spatula, the serving will slide apart. (Spatula is fine after it's cooled down and become leftovers, but piping hot from the oven you need a ladle.)

Garlic Bread
Take a loaf of unsliced Italian bread and slice open lengthwise. Put open sides up on cookie sheet. Brush with all the butter you had left from browning the garlic on both sides, and all the rest of the Parmesan/Romano/Asiago blend. Put both the lasagna and garlic bread back in the oven for another 15 minutes.

Monitor carefully. Don't let the provolone turn brown; bubbling is fine. Once the cheese mixture has melted all across the top of the bread, the garlic bread is done.

Eat; enjoy; go into a carb coma.

LEMON GARLIC CHICKEN
Marta Randall

The Chicken of the Gods, maybe. Easy to make, delicious to eat, and the leftovers are good, too. It may be impossible to make too much of this dish.

Preheat oven to 350°F.

Place:
Any number of chicken breasts in baking dish.
Add:
1 T vegetable oil.
Chop:
1 cube butter or margarine over the chicken.
Pour:
Juice of two or more lemons (depends on quantity of chicken) (or 1/4 c dry white wine) over the chicken.
Scatter:
Lots of garlic (at least one head), minced, over everything. (You can also add a sprinkle of pepper and garlic powder.)

Cover the baking dish with aluminum foil and bake for about one hour or until chicken is done. If you wish, you can uncover the dish for the last ten minutes of cooking, to brown the chicken slightly. If you do this, baste the chicken in the broth at least once.

Serve with sliced French bread to dip into the sauce.

METAPHYSICALLY AREFERENTIAL CHICKEN
Marianne Porter & Michael Swanwick

Marianne: *The first Philford Writers' Workshop (named in honor of the Milford and the Gilford Workshops) was held at our house in 1979. David Hartwell, Samuel R. Delaney, Gardner Dozois, Jack Dann, and several others attended. It was a very intense workshop. During a critique, one writer said that another's work was "metaphysically areferential." The author of the work being criticized didn't think much of the term, as he couldn't tell what it was supposed to mean. Also, he prided himself on his knowledge of metaphysics. Six months later, that writer visited again and, as a way of turning the pain into humor, I served him the Metaphsically Areferential Chicken dish that I invented for him.*

Michael: *A year later, Marianne submitted the recipe to* Gourmet Magazine. *They accepted it for publication, but changed the name to "Chicken Marianne."*

Marianne: *Even recipes get their titles changed.*

(Excerpted from *Cooking the Books*)

Bone a chicken. All you need is patience, big shears, and a small, sharp knife. There are lots of descriptions online and in Julia Child. Leave the lower leg bones in place and turn the wing skin inside out.

- 1 large eggplant
- 1 onion
- 2 cloves garlic
- 1 sweet red pepper
- 1/2 T basalmic vinegar (reduced is nice)
- Salt
- Pepper
- Olive oil

Cube the eggplant into 1/2 inch dice. Salt, and drain in a colander for half an hour. Rinse lightly.

Chop onion, mince garlic, chop red pepper. Mix vegetables, and sauté gently until softened. Moisten with vinegar, and stuff the chicken.

Lay the chicken spread out and open, skin side down on your work surface. Mound up the stuffing in place, draw up the skin and fasten with twine or toothpicks or skewers. Place in a shallow pan, seam side down. Pat it into chicken shape.

Roast at 350°F for about an hour, basting occasionally with a little oil. When roasted, bring to the table on a platter that has a bit of space (fill in gaps with parsley) and slice like a loaf of bread.

THE MEATY MESS
Mark L. Van Name

When I've wanted something hearty and satisfying but had to contend with whatever I could find in my pantry and refrigerator, this has been my go-to dish. The instructions are necessarily imprecise, but they're easy to adapt to whatever you have on hand.

There's nothing low-cal or healthy about it, so don't blame me if an artery hardens as you're eating it.

This version will serve two insanely hungry people, four normal people, or even more people trying to be healthy while still eating something full of meat and cheese.

- 4 c diced meat
- 2-4 c shredded cheese
- As much pasta as your crew needs
- Whatever spices and sauces you can find

Start the pasta water boiling. Put a little salt in it, as usual.

Take all the leftover or otherwise available meat in your refrigerator and dice it into half-inch cubes. If some of it is luncheon meat, no worries; you can cut it into half-inch squares and be fine. Keep it up until you have about four cups of meat. Mixing meats is just fine. In fact, that's the next step: mix all the meat chunks in a big bowl.

Grab all the cheese you can find. You can use grated Parmesan in a can for some of it, but it's better if you take other cheeses and grate them yourselves. If you've been wondering what to do with those little squares and odd wedges of cheese hanging out in your cheese drawer, wonder no more; this is their time. Grate up to four cups of cheese. Mix it all together in a big bowl.

Put on a large burner the largest sauté or frying pan you have. If your meat is juicy, you're set. If not, spread a little cheap olive oil on the bottom of the pan. Bring the pan up to medium, give or take; this recipe is very tolerant.

Spread the meat evenly in the pan. Heat it until all the chunks are warm. Sample regularly to be sure. Stir often, even constantly if you see meat starting to stick to the pan. While you're at it, add any sauces you like, a tablespoon at a time, and season to your taste. Apply spices with care, a pinch or two at a time. Soy sauce can work, as can a Thai chili sauce, Worcestershire sauce, or even barbecue sauce. Your goal is for the meat to have a strong flavor you like. As long as you never add more than a tablespoon of sauce at a time, you should be good.

Somewhere in here, the pasta water should have started boiling. When it does, add however much pasta your crew is likely to eat.

When all the meat is warm, pour the cheese on top of the meat. (I told you to get a big pan.) Spread it evenly over the meat and then stir it into the meaty mess. Stir until the cheese has completely melted and is covering the meat. At this point, you should have a pan full of meaty, cheesy mess. Turn the heat to low while you tend to your pasta.

With luck, your pasta is now al dente, which basically means firm to the bite. If you like your pasta a bit undercooked, feel free to do that; it's your pasta.

Drain the pasta in a colander.

Now, we come to a decision point. If you've been cooking your meat in a really big pan and so have lots of free space in that pan, add the pasta and stir it and the meat/cheese combo together. If not, put the pasta back in its pot and add the meat/cheese combo. Stir until all the pasta is shiny with meat and cheese and every big serving spoon you dip into the pan or pot will yield pasta, meat, and melted cheese.

You know how much you can eat, so serve appropriately, but know that this stuff has the density of a dwarf star.

Plan on a nap after you eat, though what you'll really need is a brisk two-mile walk.

Come to think of it, take the walk, so I won't have totally ruined your health for the day.

MULTITUDINOUS VEGETABLE SOUP
Ellen Klages

Ingredients (one each, unless noted)

- Potato
- Parsnip
- Onion
- Ear of corn (or small can of corn)
- Can of Blue Lake green beans (or equiv. amount of fresh)
- Zucchini
- Red pepper

- Head of cabbage (small)
- Tomato
- 3 Stalks of celery
- 2 Carrots (or 8 baby carrots)
- 1/2 T butter
- 1 T brown sugar
- 2 t salt (or to taste)
- 1 t black pepper
- 2 t herbs de provence (or other herb blend of choice)
- Olive oil
- Balsamic vinegar
- Seasonal vegetable of choice (optional)
- Rotisserie Chicken (from the grocery deli department—optional)

1) Pull as much of the meat as you can off the rotisserie chicken. Chop up and set meat aside.

2) Put chicken carcass and skin into a large stockpot. Coarsely chop 1/2 of the onion, 2 stalks of celery, and 1 (unpeeled) carrot (or half the baby carrots). Add to stockpot. Add 1 t salt and 1 t herb mixture. Fill pot with water. Simmer for 2-3 hours.

3) Peel parsnip and potato and other carrot. Coarsely chop, toss with olive oil and vinegar, and put into a 250°F oven to roast for about 45 minutes, stirring once or twice.

4) Chop or shred head of cabbage. Dice the other half of the onion. Melt butter in a very large skillet, then add cabbage and onion and turn flame to low-medium. Cook, stirring, until everything softens and gets translucent and the cabbage reduces down to about a handful. Add brown sugar, stir, and cook for another 10-15 minutes.

5) Strain chicken stock, discarding bones and limp vegetables. Return liquid to stockpot. Add chicken meat, roasted root vegetables, sautéed cabbage.

6) Cut kernels off corncob (or open can of corn) and add to stock.

7) Trim green beans (or open can) and add to stock.

8) Chop tomato, zucchini, red pepper, remaining stalk of celery. Add to stock.

9) Add pepper and remaining salt and herbs.

10) Simmer everything for 1-2 hours, or until it smells so delicious you can't stand it anymore. Taste. Adjust seasonings. (It probably needs more salt . . .)

11) Serve in big soup bowls with lots of crusty bread and butter.

(It is even better the next day, and the day after, and will freeze for up to six months.)

MYSTERY MEATLOAF
Brent Weeks

The Backstory:

Mystery Meatloaf is most famous for being served at the Vanity Fair Post-Party for the 2020 Oscars. George Martin was in attendance for his movie adaptation of the Game of Thrones (They All Die at the End). Joe Abercrombie (writer of Disney's Snow White reboot: She's Embalmed, Dude, Yuck) challenged him to a dance-off after his inflammatory comments over what was worse: Earl Grey Tea after the Great Tea Embargo of '15-'18, or Santa Fe tap water. Mary Robinette Kowal resolved the dispute without bloodshed or back spasms by performing a jeté assemblé so impressive, it shocked both men into silence. She then glamoured Mystery Meatloaf into a vegetarian dish before taking two of her dates onto the dance floor (said dates being statuette Oscar and Hugh Jackman, lead actor in her Oscar-winning NASCAR's Honour).

- 2 eggs
- 2 lb ground beef
- 2 T Worcestershire sauce
- 2/3 c any salsa
- 1-2 t salt
- 1/2 t ground pepper
- 1/3 c + 1/3 c brown sugar
- 3/4 onion, chopped fine
- 2 slices whole wheat bread, cut into 1/2" squares

Preheat oven to 350°F (175°C). Combine all ingredients (minus half the brown sugar) in a large bowl; your washed hands are the best tools for mixing. Pat onto a broiler pan, leaving slots unobstructed for drainage. Cook for 45 minutes. Coat with remaining brown sugar. Cook for an additional 15 minutes, or until meat has reached at least 160°F (72°C).

Brent's Tips:
- Ground Beef: I use 80% lean ground beef. The fat drains off with this method, but you may prefer a leaner ratio.
- Eggs: Add the eggs to the bowl first, in case you screw up and get some shell in.
- Bread: I like to use Dave's Killer Bread, but any hearty bread will do.
- Onion: If you don't dice the onion finely enough, it may not cook fully, which you may prefer. But if you want the larger chunks of onion well-cooked, sauté them in butter separately before mixing the onion into the meatloaf.

• Broiler Pan: Use a broiler pan—this will allow excess moisture and grease to drain. And with salsa and 20% fat ground beef, there will be plenty that needs draining! For easier cleanup afterwards, I line the bottom of the broiler pan with aluminum foil (that's aluminium foil for our spelling-challenged brethren across the pond).

• Shape: A flat rectangle works best to cook evenly. Think of the monolith in *2001: A Space Odyssey*.

PINEAPPLE FRIED RICE
via Leslie Howle, for Octavia E. Butler

Over the course of the 20-plus years I knew Octavia, she was vegetarian. The last year or so of her life she was talked into adding fish to her diet by her heart doctor. After that, whenever I picked her up for a day hike, Octavia would make herself a tuna salad sandwich to put in the cooler. She seemed to enjoy it, but it wasn't first on her list of great things to eat.

The dish that most delighted Octavia is Thai pineapple fried rice. Her favorite restaurant was the Royal Palm in Seattle's Roosevelt district. Sometimes when we went to dinner there, she would open her menu, look it over, and then say with a laugh that this time she should try something new. Inevitably, when the waitress took her order, she would shoot me an embarrassed look and ask for the pineapple fried rice. It became kind of a running joke. When she really liked something I would ask her, "like the pineapple fried rice?" and be rewarded by her rumbly laugh.

The Royal Palm served Octavia her pineapple fried rice in half of a freshly hollowed-out pineapple, and it was as attractive to look at as it was tasty. The first time she ordered it, she discovered it came with tiny deveined shrimp, but she loved it so much she simply picked out the shrimp. The next time she ordered it, she asked them to please not add shrimp. She would eat as much as she could of it, and if no one else wanted any, take the leftovers home. I remember once we had dinner there with Ursula LeGuin and China Miéville, among others, and Octavia recommended her favorite rice dish to them with high praise, so I think I can say with confidence that this was one of her favorite meals.

You can serve this as a main dish or a side dish to take to a potluck. The Royal Palm's version comes with shrimp, egg, raisins, onions, pineapple, snow peas, carrots, tomato, and yellow curry powder. This recipe is an approximate of their version. Using leftover rice makes sure that the rice stays firm and doesn't become soggy. If you don't have any leftover rice, you can cook rice and refrigerate, uncovered, for an hour or so to help it dry out before adding it to the stir fry. You can change the recipe by adding shrimp, chicken, or tofu. There are a number of similar recipes on the Internet, so find the one that most appeals and enjoy. I found a vegan version that has illustrations and tips on cutting the pineapple here: 86lemons.com/vegan-pineapple-fried-rice.)

- 2 c cooked jasmine or basmati rice, preferably a day old
- 1 c fresh pineapple, cut into bite-size chunks
- 1/4 c cashews
- 1 medium tomato, diced
- 1/2 c fresh cilantro, finely chopped
- 1/2 red bell pepper, cut into bite-size pieces
- 2 carrots, diced
- 1 red onion, roughly chopped
- 2 cloves garlic, diced
- 1 T sesame oil
- 1 T yellow curry powder
- 1 T soy sauce
- 1/4 to 1/3 c raisins or currants
- 1 t sugar
- Salt to taste

Cut a ripe pineapple lengthways in half. Cut out the center core, then cut out the pineapple in chunks. As you hollow out the pineapple, try to leave a thin layer of pineapple inside the skin.

In a wok, heat oil on medium high. Add cashews and stir until they turn golden brown. Remove with slotted spoon to a paper towel to drain (or buy already-roasted cashews).

Add onion and garlic and cook until fragrant.

Add vegetables (except for tomato) and continue to cook until the carrots are tender and can be pierced by a fork.

Sprinkle curry powder over the vegetables; continue to cook for about 30 seconds.

Add soy sauce, sugar, pineapple, and tomato, and stir fry on high for another 60 seconds.

Add rice and cilantro and stir until everything is mixed well and the grains of rice are coated evenly with the spice and sauce.

Taste to adjust the seasoning, then pile the mixture into each of the hollowed out pineapple shells.

Serve immediately with some fresh cilantro garnish.

RATATOUILLE Á LA MME. FOURNIER
Lynne M. Thomas & Michael Damian Thomas

Lynne: *I ate ratatouille for the first time during my junior year of college, while I was an exchange student in France. We spent our first month taking classes in Aix-en-Provence before we moved up to Paris for la Sorbonne's start of the university year in October. Another student from my program and I lived with a widow named Mme. Fournier, who made an enormous batch of ratatouille from in-season summer vegetables. I grew up eating mostly canned vegetables, so this was a revelation. She kindly provided the recipe, and noted that the proportions of all of the vegetables and seasonings could be altered, since the point of the dish was basically to use up whatever was left from your garden. This is the dish that I used to impress my husband Michael the first time I cooked for him.*

Michael: *I was impressed! I thought Lynne was super fancy! Later, I completely understood how the movie* Ratatouille *could use it as a magical food that channels warmth, family, and love. Though thankfully, Lynne has never cooked it with a rat in her hair.*

It's also an excellent potluck dish as it's completely vegan. For several years our ratatouille was a hit at an annual Bastille Day party thrown by a local colleague. We find that it gets better each time it's reheated. Ratatouille can be served at room temperature or warm, is easily frozen for later use, is delicious with any type of protein, and can be served on rice, pasta, or inside a savory crepe. Lynne deeply enjoys it under fried eggs (over easy or sunny side up) with a nice crusty French bread and some sharp cheese on the side.

- 2 diced zucchini
- 1 diced yellow squash
- 5 diced tomatoes
- 1 diced green bell pepper
- 1 diced red bell pepper
- 2 medium diced, peeled eggplants
- 1 diced onion
- 2 T minced garlic
- 1 T fresh basil leaves
- 1 t fresh thyme
- Salt and pepper
- 1/4 c olive oil

Add oil to enameled cast-iron Dutch oven on medium heat. Add garlic and onions and cook until lightly caramelized, stirring periodically. Add eggplant and cook until soft, stirring periodically. Add peppers, zucchini, squash, and cook until soft, stirring periodically. Finally, add the rest of the ingredients. Stir, cover, and simmer on low for a minimum of 30-45 minutes, stirring occasionally.

REAL MARYLAND CRABCAKES
Ann Crispin

- 1 lb REAL crabmeat, the kind that hasn't been frozen or canned. Backfin, of course, is best.
- 1 package Old Bay crabcake mix. It's the best!
- 1/2 to 1 c mayonnaise, depending on how much other liquid you'll be adding.
- 1 small onion
- 1 rib or so of fresh celery
- Fresh parsley
- Fresh lemon juice
- Ground mustard
- Tabasco sauce
- Old Bay Seasoning
- Butter
- Oil

First of all, THOROUGHLY pick over that crabmeat. It will take you a while. I do it front of the television, surrounded by big-eyed four-footed creatures who, fortunately, don't drool.

Second, mince up about one third cup onion, and one third cup celery, and finely snip about four to five tablespoons fresh parsley.

Mix up the Old Bay Crabcake mix, according to package directions. Add a bit of extra mayo if you like your crabcakes extra moist. Be careful mixing the crabmeat in; you want to keep the hunks of crabmeat pretty intact. Using your hands is best to kind of "toss" the mixture together. You want to mix most everything in at once, so you have to mix as little as possible.

While I'm making up the recipe using the Old Bay mix, I also add the following:
- 1/3 c minced onion, 1/3 c minced celery, and several T snipped parsley
- A splash of Tabasco and extra Old Bay seasoning, because Marylanders like their crab fairly highly seasoned.
- About 1 t ground mustard
- A few T fresh-squeezed lemon juice, if desired

(If you want to stretch the recipe a bit, you can add in an extra half cup to one cup finely ground breadcrumbs, without harming the recipe much, but you'll need to add that extra mayo. I use the reduced fat Hellman's and it works fine.)

Now, shape the crabmeat mixture into patties.

Here's the $64,000 question: broil or fry?

I like my crabcakes broiled. My husband prefers his fried, or, most accurately, sautéed. Either works great.

If you broil them, stay in the kitchen! They'll burn in a trice! Brush the crabcakes with a bit of melted butter, and turn a couple times to get them a lovely golden color on both sides.

If you fry them, press the crabcakes into extra bread crumbs, then sauté them in a mixture of butter and veggie oil; or you could use that really light-flavored olive oil, I suppose.

Serve with tartar sauce, or cocktail sauce, if you like. Or just a squeeze from a fresh lemon wedge. Of course you can put them in buns and have crabcake sandwiches, but I like to just serve rolls on the side, and let the crabcakes take center stage. They deserve it.

Enjoy!

SAIMEN & JAMAICAN JERK RUB
Ru Emerson

When I was taking classes at L.A. City College, there was a tiny Hawaiian café around the corner, and this was all they sold. I got a craving for it a year or so ago, realized I could never find a place around here that would sell it (or that I could eat: garlic and onion allergies). So I came up with this.

Chicken broth (make or buy, or in my case—allergies—I use the broth from a can of soup that I know I can eat, and dump the noodles and meat). Add your own noodles—I buy Saimen noodles at a Chinese grocer's, there are excellent noodles in the produce section of Safeway (after dumping the nasty little packet), or you could use soba (buckwheat noodles) or any others.

Let this simmer while you chop veggies: I use thin-sliced carrots, celery, snap peas, green beans, and absolutely spinach. My husband also likes kale, broccolini, and mushrooms. So just whatever.

Spinach last of course, and once it's cooked, the saimen's done. To top, you can add a little sliced barbecued pork, a sliced hard-cooked egg, or a bit of ham. Most important, drizzle with soy sauce; this takes the flavor right out of "just chicken soup" and makes it wonderful. It's my go-to after kick-boxing or a hard workout.

Jamaican Jerk Rub

It's those allergies again; thought I'd never get to try jerk until I found this recipe. I make it by the pint jar and it keeps in the cabinet for a very long time.

Combine 1/4 cup brown sugar, 1/2 teaspoon salt, 1 or more tablespoon allspice powder and as much cayenne as you like but at least 1/4 teaspoon (I ramp this to at least 1 1/2 teaspoon). It's pure bliss rubbed into pork, baby back ribs or chicken (I hear it's good on fish, but I'll never know).

SHRIMP ÉTOUFFÉE
Gregory Frost

- 2 T plus 1 t Creole Seasoning (I've a recipe for this, but you can buy it in stores)
- 4 T unsalted butter
- 1/2 c onion, finely chopped
- 1/4 c celery, finely chopped
- 1/4 c bell pepper, finely chopped
- 1/4 c flour
- 3/4 c fresh tomatoes, diced
- 1 1/2 c shrimp stock (made by simmering the tails and shells)
- 2 T minced garlic
- 1 bundle fresh thyme
- 2 t homemade Worcestershire sauce (SEE: nolacuisine.com/2005/07/21/worcestershire-sauce-recipe)
- 1 t hot sauce (like Crystal or Louisiana Gold)
- 1/2 c green onions, thinly sliced
- 3 T minced Italian parsley
- 2 lb good quality shrimp, peeled and deveined
- 3 T unsalted butter plus 2 more T
- Salt and freshly-ground black pepper to taste
- 1 recipe Creole Boiled Rice (SEE: nolacuisine.com/2005/07/18/creole-boiled-rice-recipe)

While the shrimp stock is simmering, melt butter (or bacon grease if you want the more authentic flavor of a roux) in a large cast-iron skillet, add flour, and stir to make a red brown roux, which takes about ten minutes. Remove the pan from heat and stir in a tablespoon of the seasoning, and the "Holy Trinity" (onions, bell pepper, and celery) and then the garlic and tomatoes. Set aside. (You can make it up to this point in advance if need be.)

When the stock is ready (and strained), bring one cup of it to a boil and whisk in the roux and vegetable mixture, reducing the heat to a simmer. Add a tablespoon of seasoning, Worcestershire, and hot sauce. Simmer for five minutes.

Have your Creole Boiled Rice ready and your serving dishes warm before starting the final step.

In a cast-iron frying pan, melt three tablespoons butter over medium heat, add green onions, shrimp, and remaining one teaspoon of creole seasoning. Sauté until the shrimp just start to turn pink. Pour in the gravy sauce. Add one half cup of the shrimp stock and the rest of the butter until it's melted and incorporated, about three to five minutes, constantly shaking the pan back and forth (versus stirring). If the sauce starts to separate, splash in a little more stock. You should have a rich brown sauce.

Serve it over a mound of the rice.

─

SHRIMP DE JONGUE
Mike Resnick

- 1 1/2 c unsalted butter (no substitute), softened to room temperature
- 3 cloves garlic (peeled and crushed)
- 1 shallot, peeled and minced (or 1 scallion, minced)
- 1 T minced parsley
- 1 T minced chives
- 1/4 t tarragon
- 1/4 t marjoram
- 1/8 t nutmeg (or a few scrapings of whole nutmeg)
- 1/8 t of ground cayenne red pepper (or more, to taste)
- 3 c panko breadcrumbs
- 2 T lemon juice
- 1/3 c dry sherry
- 3 lb shelled and de-veined boiled shrimp

Pre-heat oven to 375°F. Cream butter with garlic, shallot, herbs, cayenne red pepper, and nutmeg until well-blended. Mix in crumbs, lemon juice, and sherry. Butter a shallow 10x7-inch oven-proof casserole or something of similar size. Generously sprinkle bottom and sides with panko bread crumbs. Layer shrimp and top with bread crumb mixture, then sprinkle sparingly with paprika. Bake, uncovered, for 20 minutes or until topping is lightly browned and you see the butter bubble.

─

SONORAN CHOPPED SALAD
Catherine Wells

Like the desert Southwest, this salad blends many flavors and ingredients. Never eaten uncooked corn-off-the-cob? You've missed a treat. Never seen a jicama (pronounced hih-ka-ma)? It's a root vegetable vaguely resembling a large, fat turnip, with tan skin and a sweet, potato-like flesh. I generally cut the jicama in half, place the cut side down on a board, and pare with the same large knife. (Yes, you could use a potato peeler, but the flesh right next to the skin tastes a little woody and is better cut away.) Cilantro is a broad-leafed parsley used in Asian and Mexican cooking. You can add or subtract ingredients to suit your taste. I love taking it to potlucks—that way, I know there will be vegetables for me to eat! (Just took off the weight from that last cruise . . .)

Salad

- 3 c chopped romaine lettuce (may substitute mixed greens)
- 1 can (15.5 oz) black beans, rinsed and well-drained
- 3 roma tomatoes, seeded and diced (may substitute 3/4 c grape tomatoes)
- 3/4 c diced, peeled jicama
- 1 cob fresh corn kernels, uncooked (may substitute 3/4 cup frozen corn, but why?)
- 1/2 ripe avocado, diced
- 1 red bell pepper, diced
- 1/4 c crumbled feta cheese (I use reduced-fat variety)

Honey-Lime Dressing

- 1/4 c fresh-squeezed lime juice
- 1/4 c olive oil
- 2 T honey
- 2 T finely-chopped fresh cilantro
- 1 garlic clove, minced
- 1 t chopped jalapeño pepper (optional)

Rinse and drain black beans, then prepare the rest of the salad ingredients. Toss together in a large bowl. In a small bowl, mix dressing ingredients, then pour over salad and toss. Add salt and pepper to taste. To make a meal of this salad, add diced cooked chicken or imitation crab flakes.

SOPA ANASAZI
Dean Ing

I tried variations of Anasazi stew, while writing Anasazi about 1977, having done my M.A. thesis years before on Amerind studies. I know the region and most of the foods available to Four-Corners folk but I'm lazy, so I combined canned versions of the viands available to the Anasazi and added those items that don't come in cans. It made a stew/chowder/soup that was close to what a family ate at Mesa Verde, and works for my family. Stan Schmidt, who bought the story for Analog, *and is a trencherman of no little repute, wanted a dose of the stuff when he visited in Ashland. I honestly don't recall if he liked it; but come onnn, what was he gonna say?*

- 12 oz cooked, shredded turkey dark meat
- 12 oz diced, cooked squash
- 12 oz diced tomatoes in can with juice
- 12 oz corn kernels

- 12 oz cooked pinto beans in can
- 2 oz jalapeño peppers, diced
- 1 heaping T sage, coarse ground
- Sea salt, to taste

Toss it all together and stir, while heating to a simmer. Proportions aren't salient but enough juice from cans should be available for a few minutes of simmering. Purists can find speckled Anasazi beans and cook them endlessly. They'll turn color anyhow. The Anasazi traded for salt (coral and parrot feathers too, for other purposes). Turkey, venison, and puppy meat were local and more common than bison, but so were grasshoppers. You judge . . .

TIMELESS BEER BREAD
Eugie Foster

Beer is one of the oldest prepared beverages, with its origins dating from the early Neolithic period, with written records of it appearing in Ancient Egypt. Likewise, the origins of bread parallel the development of beer during the Neolithic period, as hunter-gather societies shifted to an agricultural way of life, and bread became a staple food. Beer bread is the best of both—a fast and easy bread recipe with a sophisticated and robust flavor that requires no additional yeast, no laborious kneading, and no waiting for the dough to rise.

For this recipe, I've used pilsners, wheat beers, India Pale Ales, lagers, brown ales, and even Guinness stout; cheap beers from the grocery store, expensive microbrews, and everything in between. I tend to toss in a little more sugar (an extra tablespoon or so) with the darker brews such as stouts and porters to offset the bitterness of the beer. Whatever type of beer used changes in subtle or dramatic ways the flavor of the resultant bread, but it's always delicious.

This recipe is great for the hungry writer looking for something hearty and quick for brunch, to serve to guests as a delicious counterpart to a warm bowl of soup or chili, and is fabulous to share at a potluck. The simplicity of the recipe is totally out of proportion to the enthusiastic "ooh's" and appreciative "yum!'s received when you offer up your home-made beer bread (but you don't have to tell folks how easy it was to make).

- 3 c all-purpose flour
- 3 1/2 t baking powder
- 2 t salt
- 4 T sugar
- 12 oz beer

Preheat oven to 350°F. Grease 9x5x3-inch loaf pan.

Combine flour, baking powder, salt, and sugar in a large bowl. Add beer gradually, stirring it into dry mixture until dough is mixed well.

Spread dough in prepared loaf pan.

Bake at 350°F for 45-50 minutes. Bread is done when a toothpick inserted into the center comes out clean. Turn out on rack to cool.

TURKEY TURKEY TURKEY
Charles N. Brown

Charles would throw a big Thanksgiving dinner every year for the staff and friends, about a week before the holiday. He made a great turkey, and was asked for the recipe a few years ago by an editor friend, so he finally had to write down what he had always done just from memory.

Always buy the biggest turkey you can. A 20-pound turkey cooks better than a 14-pound turkey; 22 pounds or so is perfect. Ignore most cooking instructions. Cook 11 to 12 minutes per pound (smaller turkeys take 12-14 minutes per pound). Cook at 400°F the first hour, then 375°F for two hours, and 350°F the last hour or so. Do not baste until the second hour, then every 30 minutes. Do not marinate.

Always cook breast side down to keep white meat from drying out. If you must, turn it over for 30 minutes or so and baste twice, but always end up breast-side down so the cooking juices keep white meat moist. Remember, the turkey will keep cooking when you take it out (wait 25 minutes before carving), so don't worry if it's slightly pink when you cut into it at the thigh junction. The secret of turkey is not to overcook!

Stuffing

I use 24 ounces Pepperidge Farm Herb Stuffing and add mushrooms, cooked spicy chicken or turkey sausage (meat sausage is too fatty), green onions, water chestnuts, sometimes pine nuts, etc. (The etc. means it's different each time depending on what sounds good or what's in the house.) Stuff both cavities fairly tightly (ignoring official directions) and close with skewers and string.

Baste with

Soy-Ginger Glaze
- 6 T sesame oil
- 9 T soy sauce (Regular is best; if using lower salt, try half and half.)
- 4 t sugar
- 6 T ground ginger (Dried is good; if using fresh, increase by 50% at least.)

- 3 T crushed garlic [The garlic can be skipped if you're doing a side dish (like garlic mashed yams) with garlic.]
- 2 t chile paste (I use Hunan Red Chile with Garlic.)

Mix sauce at least an hour before basting and let sit at room temperature. If it seems too thick, add a little chicken stock. (If it's too thick, it will burn at 375°F, but not at 350°F). I usually adjust it with pan juice during basting.

Any leftover basting sauce becomes gravy. Add pan drippings, put in the freezer for the time between taking the turkey out of oven and cutting. The fat should separate, and can be discarded. If there isn't enough left, add chicken stock and thicken again with a little corn starch.

WELSH RAREBIT
Cat Rambo

Serves 4-6, depending on serving size
Preparation time: 15 minutes

- 3 T butter
- 3 T white flour
- 1 12-oz beer (A strong tasting beer will make for more flavorful rarebit, but too dark and it will look unappetizing.)
- 1 T Worcestershire sauce
- 16 oz Cheddar cheese (The sharper the better.)
- 1 t mustard
- 1/4 to 1/2 t cayenne pepper (More for spicier rarebit.)
- Pepper to taste (I suggest at least 1/2 t)

Melt the butter over medium heat in a two quart sauce pan. While butter is melting, grate the cheese. When the butter is melted, add the flour and cook, stirring frequently, until it is golden brown.

Add the beer and Worcestershire sauce. Bring to a boil.

Mix the cheese and mustard together, then gradually mix, adding a half cup at a time, into the beer, stirring constantly in order to keep it smooth. Heat, stirring constantly, until it's thickened somewhat but is still pourable.

Serve ladled generously over slices of bread. I prefer a thick, crusty homemade bread; it's worth splurging on a nice bread to enjoy with this over it.

JACK'S JEWISH CHINESE CHICKEN SOUP
Jack Dann

This is a quick recipe for those times when you don't have time to cook. I've adapted this one from Ian Hewitson, one of my favorite Australian chefs. It's good for sick spouses or Wednesday nights in front of the television. Easy-peasy.

This is one of those recipes that you can easily make your own (as I've done). Try adding noodles, maybe sprinkle with some chopped parsley, add cecci beans . . . or frozen peas. Just don't forget the egg and corn!

You should live and be well!

You'll need a large, heavy pan (or a pot) with a lid for this recipe.
- 1 chicken breast, skinned
- 2 t light soy sauce
- 2 t cornstarch
- 1-2 scallions, depending on size
- 2 T (or more) peanut or vegetable oil
- 2 c chicken stock, homemade or bought (but not canned)
- 1 can cream corn
- 1 egg, beaten lightly
- salt and pepper to taste

Chop scallion(s) and set aside. Mince chicken. Mix soy sauce and cornstarch in a medium bowl and add chicken. Combine.

Heat oil in heavy-bottomed cooking pot over medium heat. When oil is hot, add the chicken and stir-fry until it's white; watch it, though, as you don't want the chicken to brown. It will taste all right, but there will be brown flecks in your finished soup, which spoil the presentation. When chicken is almost cooked, add scallions. Cook a little more, then add two cups of chicken stock and a can of cream corn. (I know, corn in a can, but it makes it taste right.)

Add lots of pepper and, if needed, salt. (Taste before salting, as the corn and stock might already be salty enough.)

Simmer, covered, on low heat for ten minutes.

Whisk egg in a small bowl while soup cooks.

After ten minutes, take the pot off heat. While stirring, drizzle the egg into the soup. Keep stirring: the color and texture of the soup will now change.

Ladle into bowls (or bowl).

LENTIL SOUP
Russ Galen

I think it would be too much to call it a recipe, but I have a food process that I indulge in at every possible opportunity.

Basically, it's lentil soup. You sauté onions and garlic, then into the pot goes chicken or vegetable broth, a cup of French Green lentils, and stewed tomatoes. After that it's different every time. I throw in whatever strikes me. You just can not go wrong. Mushrooms, peppers, carrots, celery, potatoes, farro or any other kind of whole grain, oregano, dried parsley, basil, etc., and if you want, any kind of meat. It is always the same because of the broth/tomato/lentil base, and always different because exact ingredients and measurements are never the same.

I've been poor and I could be poor again if necessary. I can spend $500 taking a client out to dinner in Manhattan and I enjoy it, but this soup, which only costs a few dollars for half a dozen portions, tastes better than anything I've ever had in a restaurant, bursts with flavor, prevents cancer, and takes almost no time to make. I could live on this. (Excerpted from *Cooking the Books*.)

THE PERFECT LUNCH
Michaela Roessner

As a writer and a mostly online teacher, my life is far too sedentary. Every year that I age, my body and my doctor demand that I find simpler, cleaner and healthier ways to eat in order to compensate for my work lifestyle.

But I come from a line of writer-epicureans (both my father and grandfather were journalists, and Grandpa Elmer Roessner not only wrote pulp short stories as well, he was the author of the original drinking man's diet, "The Delirious Diet," which ran in the September 1953 issue of Esquire Magazine.*) So it's been a challenge to satisfy body, doctor, and my taste buds. Here is one of my solutions. Although it's a daily meal for me, I've snuck it in as a party appetizer many a time with nobody the wiser as to its near-Puritan virtues. The recipe is lunch for one; just make more of the dip and slice more apples to serve as appetizer.*

- 1 crumbled wedge of Gorgonzola
- 32 oz. tub nonfat cottage cheese
- Nonfat milk
- Pinch of kosher salt to taste.
- One refrigerator-chilled Fuji apple
- Stick cinnamon fresh ground to taste

Blend Gorgonzola, nonfat cottage cheese, salt, and a bit of milk until as thick and velvety as whipped clotted cream The amount of nonfat milk added depends on how thick or thin you like your dips. Experiment.

Fix this up a couple of days before beginning to use it, leaving it to set in the refrigerator so that all the Gorgonzola goodness infiltrates the creamed cottage cheese.

Take the single cold, juicy Fuji apple, well-washed with the skin left on, thin-slice it, and place in a circle on a plate. (Only Fujis possess the necessary combination of rich meatiness, satisfying snap, and a perfumed taste equal to the scent of apple blossoms.) Grace the apples with a dusting of fresh-ground cinnamon, deepening their über-apple flavor.

Last, in the middle, dollop a soft, cool, virginal mound of the Gorgonzola mixture.

Glide a slice of apple into the dip, raising it enrobed like an emperor in ermine. Bite in, the sweet chilled crispness of the apple exploding against your teeth in perfect harmony with the fulsome salty unctuousness of the Gorgonzola infusion laving your palate. Life is good.

REAL FAST 10-MINUTE MEALS FOR DEADLINES
C.J. Cherryh

Fast Mac

- Boil 1/2 cup elbow macacroni according to package instructions.
- Drain.
- Add black pepper.
- Add 1 cup sharp cheddar or Mexican cheese mix, pre-grated.
- Stir violently until cheese melts.
- If you really want posh, toast it under broil.
- Serve with side salad.

Fast Spaghetti

- Boil serving of spaghetti according to instructions.
- In skillet, while that cooks (about 10 minutes), heat: dose of salt, dose of black pepper, dose of dry basil and oregano, or Italian spice in olive oil (or whatever you have).
- Add pepperoni to skillet. Warm, do not burn (setting: 7/medium).
- When spaghetti is cooked, drain it well, toss it in skillet with pepperoni, cook for 1 minute, serve with side salad.

Fast Parmesan Chicken Caesar Salad

- Bag of pre-washed Romaine or regular salad, your preference.
- Serving of pre-done chicken bits—Tyson, Foster Farms, your choice.
- Parmesan cheese, usually Kraft, powdered.
- Heat saucepan with olive oil, add chicken bits, cover, cook till thawed and hot.
- Add salt, add pepper.
- Turn off heat.
- Add as much as a cup of parmesan to pan; stir fast, until all chicken is coated.
- Add parmesan-ed chicken to salad; add Cardini Caesar dressing.
- Serve with garlic toast.

SHORTCUT DINNER
P. Andrew Miller

- 1 package ready-to-use chicken (I prefer using Southwest flavor.)
- 1 can Crescent Roll Creations Seamless Dough
- Peppers, onions, mushrooms, cheese
- Cooking spray
- Sesame seeds

Roll out the dough on a cookie sheet. Put meat and whatever peppers, onions, mushrooms, etc., you want on it. (I like to use pepperjack shredded cheese). Fold the sides over the mixture in the middle. Spray with cooking spray and sprinkle sesame seeds on it. Bake according to directions for dough. Remove from oven. Can be cut into serving sizes for meals or snacks. Can also easily be doubled and cooked together.

BARBEQUED ELF RIBS
Golaka, Goblin Chef (Translated by Jim C. Hines)

Golaka has been cooking for goblins (and cooking goblins) for longer than anyone can remember. She's the author of Twelve Recipes for Human Warriors Who Got Lost in the Tunnels and Wandered Into an Ambush and Stewed Garbage: Because Those Ungrateful Wretches Aren't Worth the Effort. *She's best known for her role in the goblin trilogy by Jim C. Hines, and for her ability to slay a fully armored warrior with one blow from her enormous soup spoon.*

Warning: This recipe was designed for goblin digestive systems, and may not be compatible with delicate human sensibilities.

Serves: 4-5 goblins per elf

- At least 1 elf
- 1 pouch of fire-spider eggs
- 1 dwarven breastplate and backplate
- Salt
- At least 30 brown mushrooms (NOTE: Do not use the red-speckled mushrooms. Except maybe for Jurok. It would serve him right for trying to use my best saucepan as a chamber pot.)
- 2 handfuls of dried mustard grass
- 2 jugs of Klak beer (One for the meal, one for the chef.)

Kill an elf. Better yet, send a hunting party out to kill the elf for you. Elves are sneaky bastards, and they'll generally kill at least four goblins before you bring them down. Stupid elves. Use one of the goblin bodies for a bacon garnish, and save the rest for next week's stew.

Start your cook fire.

Butcher the elf. There should be very little fat to trim away. Stupid, skinny elves. Make sure to save the blood.

Fill a bowl with Klak beer. Add half of the fire-spider eggs and mustard grass. Grind it all together with a rock, and rub the mixture onto both sides of the ribs.

Lay the ribs out on the dwarven breastplate. Don't try to use elven armor for this. Elves craft their armor out of leather, or worse yet, wood. Stupid elves.

Cover with the backplate and set the whole thing directly onto the fire.

Wait at least four hours. Elf meat is tough. Pour elf blood over the ribs once an hour to keep the meat from drying out.

Using one freshly-sharpened cleaver, fend off any goblins trying to sneak into your kitchen to steal a bite of half-cooked elf.

Ribs are ready when they no longer smell like trees. Stupid, smelly elves.

Spread mushrooms over the meat and cook for another half hour.

Lay fresh goblin bacon around the ribs (optional).

Remove from heat. Drain elf grease into a pot. Throw hot grease into the face of the next goblin to ask if it's ready yet. Club goblin with empty pot for good measure.

Brush elf ribs generously with a mixture of Klak beer, onion juice, fire-spider eggs, crushed apple, and tunnel-cat milk. Important: Don't try to milk the tunnel-cat yourself. Send the survivors from the elf-hunting party.

Carve while hot. Set the best cut aside for yourself. Serve the rest to those vulgar, greedy savages, who'll just scarf down all of your hard work and complain.

Pick the loudest of the whiners and send them out to hunt more elves.

―

HOW TO STEW AN ALIEN
Mari Ness

1) Choose your alien species carefully.

While human children have frequently been observed to consume vast amounts of silica in the form of sand, we advise adult humans to avoid the consumption of silica-based lifeforms, as these species types frequently have an adverse effect on human digestion. Also, entities with a strong fondness for sulfur are best avoided as the major meat component of stew, as their aftertaste is generally disdained by even the most discriminating or adventurous gourmands.

Also, note that some species, such as the C'rag!A of the Dogskatch system, may have a sweet delicate flavor when eaten raw, but gain a turpentine flavor when cooked in stew.

Persons on the Adkins or South Beach diets are advised to avoid the F'karthucks of the Dogskatch system, since their flesh is unusually high in carbohydrates.

Chefs unsure of which meat to use should consult Ralph Erickson's *The Joy of Aliens: 150 Ways to Consume the Natural Enemies of Humanity*. Erickson's book has a helpful listing of alien races and their meats on page 84. True gourmands, however, are advised to avoid his recipes, which unwisely blend French Provincial style with recipes for Mexican fajitas. Also, Erickson has no recipe for stew.

2) Choose your vegetables.

Carrots and potatoes generally go well with most alien meats, although a chemical found in the muscles of the Drykar race tends to turn carrots purple. Should your guests ask, advise them that this change is harmless and has been done purely for aesthetic purposes. Be sure to have large supplies of your preferred antacid treatment on hand. Do not, under any consideration, use broccoli. Although tender pieces of broccoli cooked with a Béarnaise sauce can form a delightful accompaniment to grilled alien, broccoli is just awful in stew.

3) Braise the meat and tenderize carefully before placing it in the stew.

While some alien meats, including the liver of the Verterx race, will remain moist under virtually any conditions, most alien meats must be carefully prepared to retain their moisture and flavour during stew cooking. Olive oil often works well; remember, use only extra-virgin olive oil, and for the sake of your guest's health, use olive oils enriched with Vitamin E.

Cook the stew for at least six hours. Slow cooking enhances the alien flavour, and makes even the Flygrout race a gourmand's delight.

4) Consider your guest list.

Some of your guests may be tantalized and charmed by the presence of Quatar claws in their stews, feeling (correctly) that the claws give an exotic glamour to the meal. Less sophisticated guests, however, will want all of the meat to look like chicken. Cut your alien meats accordingly.

5) Choose your wine.

Forgo the temptation to serve a light Chardonnay out of respect for your guests' delicate palates. This is stew. Your only option is a full-bodied Burgundy. And for after-dinner drinks, avoid any alcohol with even the hint of green coloring. It's simply disrespectful.

THE HORDES PLEASURE
Bud Sparhawk

Into the helmet of your vanquished enemy or any suitable bowl, crush the souls from a ton of Graham crackers. Then, using your sacred silver sword of Athena dice an equal amount of gum or spice drops and have your priests sprinkle them over the cracker crumbs. From the forbidden forest have our brave warriors gather and smash three tons of various tasty nuts with their war hammers of Righteousness and add them to the mix. From the captured groves have the camp maidens chop a ton of dates and an equal measure of sweet raisins to be added to the mix.

Sacrifice a ton of marshmallows and dash of magic vanilla to the heat in a sacred vessel or a LARGE pot until liquid, quickly remove from heat and stir in all the other ingredients until everything is thoroughly confused. Have your captives roll double handfuls of the mix in waxed paper and refrigerate until cool. Using a sacred sword slice the rolls into thin slices and serve.

NOTE: If you do not have a horde this recipe may be scaled down to smaller amounts.

KLINGON TOASTS
Lawrence Schoen, with David Peterson

Traditional Klingon Toasts:
- 'IwlIj jachjaj — May your blood scream!
- bISuvtaHvIS bIHeghjaj — May you die in battle!
- 'oy' DaSIQjaj — May you endure the pain!

Klingon Phrases Typically Heard During the QI'lop Holiday:
- Hoch DaSopbe'chugh batlh bIHeghbe' — Eat everything or you will die without honor.
- reH 'uQvam vIqawtaH — I will remember this dinner forever.
- Ho'Du'lIjDaq to'baj 'uSHom lughoDlu'bogh tu'lu' — You have some stuffed to'baj leg in your teeth.

All of the previous are "official" Klingon phrases. However, you might want something simple, that plays on the familiar Klingon expression "Today is a good day to die," but aimed more for a cooking. Thus, I offer you the following:
- vutlu'meH QaQ jajvam — Today is a good day to cook.
- Soplu'meH QaQ jajvam — Today is a good day to eat.

ABOUT THE CONTRIBUTORS

Rachael Acks is a writer, geologist, and dapper sir. She's written for *Six to Start,* has a steampunk mystery series from Musa Publishing, and been in *Strange Horizons, Lightspeed*, and more. Rachael lives in Houston with her two furry little bastards.

Cie Adams writes paranormal and historic novels with co-author Cathy Clamp, sometimes as Cat Adams. The two have collaborated on 18 novels, including *To Dance with the Devil*, *The Eldritch Conspiracy, Serpent Moon*, and *Cold Moon Rising*.

Kyle Aisteach is a short storyist who lives with his husband in granola-crunchy Central California. When he's not looking for cool hacks to get around his diet . . . well, let's be honest, he spends most of his spare time coming up with cool hacks to get around his diet.

Anna D. Allen lives deep in the woods with too many books and not enough dogs. She spends most winters snowed-in and trying to remember what "warm" was. When not writing or reading, she can be found in the kitchen.

Lou Antonelli has had 91 short stories and three collections published in the past eleven years. His collections include *Fantastic Texas, Texas & Other Planets, The Clock Struck None*, and *Letters from Gardner.*

Liz Argall's stories can be found in venues like *Apex Magazine, Strange Horizons*, and *This is How You Die*. Liz writes love letters, songs and poems to inanimate objects, and two of her short stories have become plays. She creates the webcomic *Things Without Arms and Without Legs*. Website: lizargall.com.

Elizabeth Bear is the Hugo, Sturgeon, Locus, and John W. Campbell Award-winning author of 27 novels—the most recent is *Karen Memory*, a Weird West adventure from Tor—and over a hundred short stories. Her dog lives in Massachusetts; her partner, writer Scott Lynch, lives in Wisconsin. She spends a lot of time on planes.

Greg and **Astrid Bear** share their home with artwork, yarn, and 20,000 books. Greg has served SFWA as Grievance Committee Chair and President, and—with Astrid—edited the *SFWA Forum*. They both eat often and well, and look forward to trying the other recipes in this volume.

David Brin is an astrophysicist whose bestselling novels include *The Postman, Earth*, and most recently, *Existence*. His nonfiction book about the information age—The Transparent Society—won the Freedom of Speech Award of the ALA. Website: davidbrin.com.

Maurice Broaddus' fiction has been published in numerous venues, including *Asimov's, Cemetery Dance, Apex Magazine*, and *Weird Tales*. He co-edited *Streets of Shadows* and the Dark Faith anthology series. Broaddus authored the urban fantasy trilogy Knights of Breton Court. His website is: MauriceBroaddus.com

Charles N. Brown was the co-founder and editor of *Locus*, the long-running trade publication covering the speculative fiction genre, which has won 29 Hugo Awards and administers the yearly Locus Awards. One of the most respected and loved figures of the field, Charles left a legacy that lives on to this day. Thanks to the staff of Locus for providing us with his recipe.

Steven Brust is an American fantasy and science fiction author of Hungarian descent. He is best known for his series of novels set on a world called Dragaera. His recent novels also include *The Incrementalists*, with co-author Skyler White. His theory of cooking is that you start with onions and garlic and that a whole chicken had better be sold with giblets and a neck.

The first science fiction writer to receive a MacArthur Fellowship, **Octavia E. Butler** received multiple Hugo and Nebula awards for her writing. In 2012 she received the SFWA Solstice Award, given to individuals who have had "a significant impact on the science fiction or fantasy landscape, and is particularly intended for those who have consistently made a major, positive difference within the speculative fiction field."

Pat Cadigan is always cooking something up in North London.

James L. Cambias is a New Orleans native, educated in Chicago, who lives in Massachusetts. He writes science fiction and designs games. Tor Books published his novels *A Darkling Sea* (2014) and *Corsair* (2015). He blogs at jamescambias.com.

John F. Carr is a science fiction author and editor who has edited over 20 anthologies. He is also an authority on the life and works of H. Beam Piper and the author of *H. Beam Piper: A Biography.*

New York Times bestselling author **Gail Carriger** writes comedic steampunk mixed with urbane fantasy. Her debut novel, *Soulless*, won the ALA's Alex Award; its sequels were all bestsellers. Once an archaeologist, she is currently working on her YA Finishing School series, and her adult Custard Protocol series. She is overly fond of tea. More: gailcarriger.com.

Beth Cato is the author of The Clockwork Dagger series of steampunk fantasy novels. She's a California native transplanted to the Arizona desert, where she lives with her husband, son, and requisite cat. Her *Bready or Not* food blog runs every Wednesday on BethCato.com.

Jeanne Cavelos (jeannecavelos.com) is director of the Odyssey Writing Workshops Charitable Trust, which offers in-person workshops, online classes, and free resources for writers of SF/F/H (odysseyworkshop.org). As senior editor at Bantam Doubleday Dell, Jeanne won the World Fantasy Award. She is also a bestselling author.

C.J. Cherryh says: "We both write full-time . . . in between herding cats, managing a website, blog, and online business and keeping a house with a front and back garden and koi pond, besides our slight fondness for online gaming. Just now and again I go full-blown cook, but often enough I hit the kitchen with a mission and a deadline."

Wesley Chu is the bestselling author of the Tao series. In 2014, he was nominated for the Campbell Award for Best New Writer. His debut novel, *The Lives of Tao*, won the Young Adult Library Services Association Alex Award and was a finalist for the Goodreads Choice Awards. His next series begins with *Time Salvager*, which will be published July 2015.

Brenda W. Clough has been a SFWA member and publishing fantasy and science fiction since 1984. A Hugo and Nebula Awards finalist, she has published eight novels and dozens of shorter works. Her web page is sff.net/people/Brenda; she also blogs regularly at bookviewcafe.com/blog.

Tina Connolly is the Nebula-nominated author of the Ironskin trilogy and the Seriously Wicked YA series. Her stories have appeared in *Lightspeed*, *Tor.com*, and more. She has narrated for *Podcastle*, *Beneath Ceaseless Skies*, and more. She runs the Parsec-winning flash fiction podcast *Toasted Cake*.

Larry Constantine is an award-winning author with eight novels and a collection of short stories written under his pen name of Lior Samson.

A.C. (Ann) Crispin wrote *New York Times*-bestselling tie-in novels for the *Star Trek*, *Star Wars*, and *V* franchises, as well as her StarBridge Series of original SF novels. She was named a Grand Master by the International Association of Tie-In Writers in 2013. Co-founder of *Writer Beware,* she received the Service to SFWA Award in 2004.

Canadian **Julie Czerneda** has authored novels and short stories, and edited several anthologies. She won the Prix Aurora for *In the Company of Others*.

Jack Dann is a multiple award-winning author who has written or edited over 75 books, including the international bestseller *The Memory Cathedral* and *The Silent*, which *Library Journal* chose as one of their "Hot Picks."

Russell Davis has written numerous novels and short stories in virtually every genre of fiction, under many pseudonyms. He has also worked as an editor and book packager. A past president of SFWA, he teaches in the Genre Fiction MFA program at Western State Colorado University.

Aliette de Bodard is an engineer, writer, and keen amateur cook. Winner of two Nebulas and a Locus Award, her novel of a post-apocalyptic Paris ruled by fallen angels, *The House of Shattered Wings*, is due out in August 2015. She blogs at aliettedebodard.com.

Ef Deal is a high school English teacher in South Jersey. Her SF/F/H fiction has appeared in *Eternity Online, Flashshots: Daily Genre Fiction, The Fortean Bureau,* and T*he Magazine of Fantasy & Science Fiction.*

Carole Nelson Douglas' 60 published novels include *Good Night, Mr. Holmes*—the first Holmes spinoff to feature a woman protagonist and a *New York Times* Notable Book of the Year. Her bestselling works include the Irissa/Kendric high fantasies. Midnight Louie's feline noir mysteries, and Delilah Street's noir urban fantasies (featuring original cocktail recipes).

Scott Edelman has published more than 85 short stories in various magazines and anthologies. His complete zombie stories were gathered in *What Will Come After;* his science fiction stories can be found in *What We Still Talk About.* He has been a Stoker Award finalist five times.

Ru Emerson still lives in rural Western Oregon with the Phantom Husband (I asked in 2008), three cats and lots and lots of garden. She really is working on a new novel (follow-up to *Spell Bound*) in between seven cardio, boot camp, and kick-boxing classes a week.

JG Faherty is a Bram Stoker and ITW Thriller nominee, and the author of five novels, seven novellas, and more than 50 short stories. He writes adult and YA SF/F/H ranging from quiet, dark suspense to over-the-top comic gruesomeness. Website: jgfaherty.com.

Eugie Foster shared a mildly haunted, fey-infested house in metro Atlanta with her husband, Matthew, and a pet skunk. After earning a MA in Developmental Psychology, she began penning flights of fancy—over a hundred of her stories have been published and she received a 2009 Nebula. Eugie was a dedicated SFWA volunteer; we miss her very much.

Nebula Award winner **Esther Friesner** is the author of 40 novels, nearly two hundred short stories, and was a multi-time finalist in a local cooking contest. She lives in Connecticut where she bakes a lot. Her family motto is: *Aut OM NOM NOM, Aut Bellum.* Look it up.

Gregory Frost is the author of novels, including *Shadowbridge, Lord Tophet,* and *Fitcher's Brides,* and short fiction. A Clarion graduate and instructor, he serves as Fiction Workshop Director at Swarthmore College. See gregoryfrost.com for more.

Russell Galen can be found at SGG Literary.

Jaym Gates is an editor, author, public relations specialist, and the Communications Director for SFWA. More about her can be found at jaymgates.com.

William Gibson is the Hugo, Nebula, Philip K. Dick, Seiun, and Prix Aurora winning author of short stories and novels including *Neuromancer, Pattern Recognition,* and *The Peripheral.*

Laura Anne Gilman is the author of the Vineart War trilogy, the Cosa Nostradamus urban fantasy series (including the forthcoming *Work of Hunters*), and *Silver on the Road.* She also writes mysteries under the name L.A. Kornetsky. Website: lauraannegilman.net

Sarah Goslee loves to research food, but is exceedingly bad at planning for potlucks. She works in agriculture, teaches fiber arts, and loves to feed both her short story characters and her guests. She can be found online at sarahgoslee.com.

Chet Gottfried lives with his wife Sue, and three ex-feral cats, in State College, PA. His *Einar and the Cursed City* won first place in the 2015 Editors & Preditors poll's YA novel category. His website is lookoutnow.com.

Talia Gryphon is the author of the Gillian Key, ParaDoc series, published by Ace/Rock a division of Penguin Publishing. She lives in the Green Country area of Oklahoma with her family, her menagerie, and her many books.

Rebecca Gomez Farrell blogs about food, travel, and writing at rebeccagomezfarrell.com.

Eric J. Guignard is a writer and editor of dark and speculative fiction, operating from the shadowy outskirts of L.A. Winner of a Bram Stoker Award, he was a finalist for the International Thriller Writers Award. Visit Eric at: ericjguignard.com.

Joe Haldeman is the author of more than 20 novels, including the Marsbound Trilogy and T*he*

Forever War. He is the recipient of five Hugo Awards, the Campbell Award, five Nebula Awards, the Damon Knight Grand Master Award, the Locus Award, the Rhysling Award, the World Fantasy Award, and the James Tiptree, Jr. Award. **Gay Haldeman** received the Big Heart Award at the 2011 World SF Convention. She's been going to SF conventions since 1963 (so has Joe) and loves to meet new people. They've been happily married for 47 years.

Lee Hallison writes fiction, mostly SF/F, mostly short, in the beautiful Pacific Northwest. She's held many jobs including being a bartender, a pastry chef, a tropical plant-waterer, a small town librarian, a CPA, and a university lecturer. She awaits her next adventure.

Barbara Hambly is a prolific American novelist and screenwriter who works in multiple genres, including mystery, fantasy, and science fiction. She has written for the *Star Trek* and *Star Wars* universes as well as for TV series *Beauty and the Beast*. She served as president of SFWA from 1994-1996 and is a multiple Nebula Award nominee.

A native of the Mississippi Delta, **Charlaine Harris** has lived her whole life in various southern states. Her first book, a mystery, was published in 1981. After that promising debut, her career meandered along until the success of the Sookie Stackhouse novels. All her books are in print, so she is a very happy camper. She is married with three children and two grandchildren.

A desert native, **Erin M. Hartshorn** now lives in Pennsylvania. Her fiction has been published by *Clarkesworld* and *Daily Science Fiction* as well as in various anthologies. She blogs at erinmhartshorn.com/blog and is on Twitter @ErinMHartshorn.

Jim C. Hines (jimchines.com) is the author of 11 fantasy novels, including the Magic ex Libris series, the Princess series of fairy tale retellings, the humorous Goblin Quest trilogy, and the Fable Legends tie-in *Blood of Heroes*. An active blogger, he's won a Hugo Award for Best Fan Writer. He lives in mid-Michigan with his family.

Daughter of two Cuban political exiles, **M.C.A. Hogarth** was born a foreigner in the American melting pot and has had a fascination for the gaps in cultures and the bridges that span them ever since. She has been a web database architect, product manager, technical writer, and massage therapist, but is currently a parent, artist, writer, and anthropologist.

Nalo Hopkinson is a Jamaican-Canadian whose tap roots extend to Trinidad and Guyana. She has published numerous books and short stories and occasionally edits anthologies. Her writing has received the Campbell Award, the Locus Award, the World Fantasy Award, the Sunburst Award, and the Norton Award. She is a professor of Creative Writing at the University of California, Riverside. Collection *Falling in Love with Hominids* will appear in 2015.

Dean Ing is the author of over 30 novels and a *New York Times* bestseller. A Hugo and Nebula nominee, Robert A. Heinlein's novel *The Cat Who Walks Through Walls* was dedicated to Ing and the eight other members of the Citizens' Advisory Council on National Space Policy.

Elaine Isaak is the author of *The Singer's Crown* and its sequels. As E.C. Ambrose, she also writes The Dark Apostle historical fantasy series about medieval surgery, which began with *Elisha Barber* in 2013. For more, see: TheDarkApostle.com

Julie Jansen writes science fiction and horror, usually with a comic twist. She lives in the Northwest where she spends rainy days writing, painting, and teaching Italian. You can visit her website, juliejansen.blogspot.com, for information about her stories and art.

Author of the Sunburst-nominated *Blackdog* and its sequels—*The Leopard* and *The Lady*—**K.V. Johansen** has also written two works on the history of children's fantasy and many books for children and teens. Her websites are at kvj.ca and pippin.ca.

Alaya Dawn Johnson is the author of six novels for adults and young adults. Her novel *The Summer Prince* was longlisted for the National Book Award for Young People's Literature. Her most recent, *Love Is the Drug*, was nominated for the Norton Award. Short stories have appeared in many venues including *Asimov's*, *The Magazine of Fantasy & Science Fiction*, and *Zombies vs. Unicorns*.

Rosemary Jones has written three novels set in the Forgotten Realms—*Cold Steel and Secrets*, *City of the Dead*, and *Crypt of the Moaning Diamond*—as well as several short stories about this Dungeons & Dragons shared world. She is the co-author of the *Encyclopedia of Collectible Childrens Books*.

Vylar Kaftan has published about 50 short stories in various markets such as *Asimov's*, *Lightspeed*, and *Clarkesworld*. She won a Nebula for her alternate history novella "The Weight of the Sunrise." She's online atvylarkaftan.net.

Jeffe Kennedy is a scientist and an award-winning author of fantasy, fantasy romance, and erotic romance. She lives in Santa Fe, NM, with two Maine coon cats, plentiful free-range lizards. and a handsome Doctor of Oriental Medicine.

Kay Kenyon's SF/F novels include *A Thousand Perfect Things*, *Tropic of Creation*, and the Philip K. Dick-shortlisted *Maximum Ice*. Her latest work, *Queen of the Deep*, blends Renaissance intrigue with the magic of an enchanted ocean liner. Website: kaykenyon.com.

Ellen Klages wrote two award-winning YA historical novels: T*he Green Glass Sea* and *White Sands, Red Menace*. She has won a Nebula Award, and her novella "Wakulla Springs," co-authored with Andy Duncan—nominated for the Nebula, Hugo, and Locus awards—won the World Fantasy Award. She lives in a small house full of strange and wondrous things.

Alethea Kontis (aletheakontis.com) is the award-winning *New York Times* and *USA Today* bestselling author of the Woodcutter Sisters fairy tale novels, *The Dark-Hunter Companion* (with Sherrilyn Kenyon), and the AlphaOops series and other acclaimed picture books. She hosts the popular YouTube series *Princess Alethea's Fairy Tale Rants*.

Mary Robinette Kowal is the author of The Glamourist Histories series of fantasy novels and a three-time Hugo Award winner. She served two terms as SFWA's vice president. Mary, a professional puppeteer, lives in Chicago. Visit her online at maryrobinettekowal.com.

Nancy Kress' fiction has won four Nebulas, two Hugos, a Sturgeon, and a John W. Campbell Memorial Award. She teaches regularly at summer conferences such as Clarion West and Taos Toolbox and has written three books about writing.

Jay Lake (jlake.com) received the Campbell Award and was a multiple nominee for the Hugo, Nebula, and World Fantasy Awards. He lived in Portland, OR and lost a six-year battle with colon cancer on June 1, 2014. Best known for his novels featuring the character Green (*Green*, *Endurance*, and *Kalimpura*), he also authored nine other novels and many short stories. His final collection, *The Last Plane to Heaven*, was released in 2014.

David Glen Larson is a California-based poet, writer, and screenwriter. His work has appeared in such places as *Daily Science Fiction*, *Escape Pod*, and *Flash Fiction Online*.

Nicole J. LeBoeuf (nicolejleboeuf.com) writes fantasy and horror briefly and at length. She also skates roller derby, spins yarn, knits socks, and occasionally pilots fixed-wing aircraft. Originally from New Orleans, Nicole lives with her husband in Boulder, CO.

Yoon Ha Lee's short stories have appeared in *The Magazine of Fantasy & Science Fiction*, *Clarkesworld*, *Lightspeed*, *Tor.com*, and elsewhere. Collection *Conservation of Shadows* was published in 2013. She lives in Louisiana with her family and has not yet been eaten by gators.

Ann Leckie (annleckie.com) is the author of the Hugo, Nebula, and Arthur C. Clarke Award-winning novel *Ancillary Justice*. She has also published short stories in *Subterranean*, S*trange Horizons*, *Beneath Ceaseless Skies*, and *Realms of Fantasy* among others.

SF/F writer **Stina Leicht** lives in central Texas. Short-listed for the Crawford Award for debut novel *Of Blood and Honey*, her sequel *And Blue Skies from Pain* was on the Locus Recommended List. A two-time Campbell Award, she is currently working on the second book of The Malorum Gates series, *Blackthorn*. She may be found online at csleicht.com.

David D. Levine is the author of novel *Arabella of Mars* (forthcoming 2016) and over 50 SF/F stories. His story "Tk'Tk'Tk" won the Hugo, and he has been shortlisted for awards including the Nebula, Campbell, and Sturgeon. Stories have appeared in *Asimov's*, *Analog*, *The Magazine of Fantasy & Science Fiction*, five year's best anthologies, and his award-winning collection *Space Magic*. His website is daviddlevine.com.

Maria Lima is a writing geek with one foot in the real world and the other in the make-believe. Her Blood Lines series is set in the Texas Hill Country, a great place for things that go bump in the night. Her non-fiction work appears in various anthologies and collections.

Mary E. Lowd has had more than 50 short stories published, as well as two novels, *Otters In Space* and *Otters In Space 2: Jupiter, Deadly*. She lives in Oregon with her husband, children, cats, dogs, and many imaginary creatures. Learn more at marylowd.com.

Natalie Luhrs reviewed SF/F for *RT Book Reviews* for eight years before launching out on her own. Now she can be found on podcasts including *Rocket Talk*, *Skiffy & Fanty*, and her own blog, pretty-terrible.com. She considers herself a free-range reviewer and opiner.

Catherine Lundoff is an award-winning author and editor from Minneapolis, MN, where she lives with her fabulous wife and cats. She works in IT by day and writes things by night, including columns for *SF Signal* on LGBT SF/F. Website: catherinelundoff.com

Scott Lynch was born under the Sign of the Frosted Donut at the height of the Year of Fresh Coffee. In his short life he has eaten many irresponsible things, most of which he does not regret. In between bites of pizza and naan, he occasionally writes books, such as the internationally bestselling Gentleman Bastard sequence, which commenced in with *The Lies of Locke Lamora*. Scott lives in Wisconsin, ancestral home of the cheese curd, and frequently visits Massachusetts, proud bastion of fried seafood.

Sometime Naval officer, sometime EMT, occasional magician, full-time writer—**James D. Macdonald** knows how to tie a lot of knots, and cook some, too. Born in White Plains, NY, the son of a commercial artist and a chemical engineer went to Catholic school. It shows.

Ricia Mainhardt has run her own agency for 30 years, specializing in the field of SF/F. She has taken unpublished writers and groomed them into authors with successful careers and still looks for new talent as well as continuing career development of established writers.

Michael J. Martinez is the author of the Daedalus trilogy from Night Shade Books, along with other bits of fantastical prose. He's also an avid homebrewer, barbecuer, and cook. He lives with his wife and daughter in New Jersey.

Mary Mason has run several Nebula Award banquets for SFWA as well as science fiction conventions, and founded the 1993 San Francisco WorldCon bid. She co-authored *Throwing Lead: A Writer's Guide to Firearms (and the People Who Use Them)* with J. Daniel Sawyer and has co-authored multiple works of fiction with her spouse, Stephen Goldin.

Vonda N. McIntyre writes science fiction.

Victoria McManus was born in Louisiana and she's lived in Center City Philadelphia, PA, since 1992. She graduated from Bryn Mawr College with a degree in Classical and Near Eastern Archaeology. Aside from her fiction writing, she reviews for *Publishers Weekly* and other venues.

Jennifer Melchert does an assortment of freelance work while dividing her time between New York, Minnesota, and Boston. She can cook excellent meals but only for prime numbers of people; dinner parties of four are right out.

P. Andrew Miller's short story collection *In Love, In Water and Other Stories* was published in 2014. He teaches creative writing at Northern Kentucky University and is also a member of the Science Fiction Poetry Association. Website: pandrewmiller.com

Jaime Lee Moyer writes novels about murder, betrayal, the occasional ghost, friendship, magic, and love. Her cats approve this message. Learn more about her at jaimeleemoyer.com.

John P. Murphy is an engineer and writer living in New England. He has a PhD in robotics, and his writing includes speculative mysteries set in the greater Boston area. Links to his work and his blog can be found at johnpmurphy.net.

Mari Ness prefers not to disclose exactly what extraterrestrial ingredients she might be using in her kitchen. Her work has appeared in multiple publications, including *Tor.com*, *Clarkesworld*, *Daily Science Fiction*, and *Apex Magazine*; for a list, see mariкness.wordpress.com. She lives in central Florida.

Teresa Nielsen Hayden is a consulting editor for Tor Books, a Hugo-nominated essayist, and the founder of *Making Light* (nielsenhayden.com/makinglight). At various points in her career she has also edited comic books, literary criticism, and utopian literature; she teaches science fiction and fantasy writing every year at Viable Paradise.

Larry Niven has written fiction at every length, and speculative articles, speeches for high schools and colleges and conventions, television scripts, political action in support of the conquest of space, graphic novels, and a couple of comic book universes. Among his many awards are Hugos, Nebulas, and, in 2015, SFWA's Grand Master Award.

Sharyn November is senior editor for Viking Children's Books. As editorial director for Firebird Books, she was nominated twice for the World Fantasy Award, and once for *Firebirds Rising*, an anthology she edited. Her website is sharyn.org; Twitter: @sn0vember.

Stephanie Osborn is a veteran of 20+ years in the space program, with graduate/undergraduate degrees in astronomy, physics, chemistry, and mathematics, is "fluent" in several more, including geology and anatomy. She has authored, co-authored, or contributed to some two dozen books, including the celebrated *Burnout* and the Displaced Detective series.

When **Andrew Penn Romine** isn't writing, he's an animator, a foodie, and a booze nerd. Whether scouring old tomes for forgotten recipes or just mixing the classics, he loves to craft cocktails at home for his friends and family.

Author **Aly Parsons** has written in the Darkover universe. She is a longtime writer and leader of the same writing group for over 30 years.

Sarah Pinsker's fiction has appeared in *Asimov's*, *Strange Horizons*, *The Magazine of Fantasy & Science Fiction*, and *Lightspeed*, among others, and numerous anthologies. She is a Sturgeon Award winner and Nebula finalist. Her wife is a chef but Sarah swears she didn't help with this particular recipe. Find at sarahpinsker.com and @sarahpinsker.

Marianne Porter is the editor and publisher of Dragonstairs Press, and is retired from a career in public health.

Jerry Pournelle is a longtime science fiction writer. With his partner Larry Niven he has been responsible for five *New York Times* bestselling SF novels. He lives in Chaos Manor, an older house in Studio City, CA.

Tim Powers is the author of 14 novels, including *The Anubis Gates*, *Hide Me Among the Graves*, and *On Stranger Tides*, which was adapted for the fourth Pirates of the Caribbean movie. His books have twice won the Philip K. Dick Award, three World Fantasy Awards, and three Locus Poll Awards. Powers lives with his wife, Serena, in San Bernardino, CA.

Marta Randall was born in Mexico City, raised in Berkeley, was a longtime resident of Sonoma County, and now lives on the side of an active volcano on the Big Island of Hawai'i. She is an ex-president of SFWA.

Cat Rambo lives, writes, and cooks beside an eagle-haunted lake in the Pacific Northwest. Her most recent book is *Beasts of Tabat*. She is a frequent SFWA volunteer. Find more information and links to her fiction at kittywumpus.net

Mike Resnick is, according to *Locus*, the all-time leading award winner, living or dead, for short fiction. He is the author of 75 novels, almost 300 stories, three screenplays, and currently edits *Galaxy's Edge*. He chairs SFWA's Anthology Committee.

Tansy Rayner Roberts is an award-winning Australian fantasy writer and one of the founding members of *Andromeda Spaceways Inflight Magazine*. She has served as the overseas director for SFWA since 2013.

Spider Robinson has published over 35 books, including a collaboration with Robert A. Heinlein, and won three Hugos, a Nebula, the Campbell Award, the Robert A. Heinlein Award, and numerous other honors. His wife of 35 years, Jeanne Robinson—with whom he co-authored the award-winning *Star Dance Trilogy*—died in May 2010. Since her death, Spider has lived on an island in Howe Sound, BC.

Michaela Roessner has published four novels, and short fiction and nonfiction in publications that include *Asimov's*, *The Magazine of Fantasy & Science Fiction*, *OMNI*, *Room Magazine*, and various anthologies. Her novel *Walkabout Woman* won the Crawford and Campbell awards. She teaches creative writing at WSCU's low-residency MFA program and online at Gotham Writers' Workshop. Website: brazenhussies.net/roessner/

Mary Rosenblum has been writing SF and mystery for 25 years and never had the sense to get a real job. She ended up a nominee for the Hugo, Nebula, and even won a couple of very nice awards. She now helps aspiring writers publish and promote successfully without getting scammed: newwritersinterface.com.

Patrice Sarath is the author of the Gordath Wood series and *The Unexpected Miss Bennet*. Her short stories have appeared in *Weird Tales*, *Alfred Hitchcock Mystery Magazine*, *Realms of Fantasy*, and *Year's Best Fantasy*. She lives in Austin, TX and blogs at patricesarath.com.

Steven Saus injects people with radioactivity as his day job, but only to serve the forces of good. His work has appeared in multiple anthologies and magazines. He also publishes speculative fiction as Alliteration Ink. Find him at stevensaus.com and alliterationink.com.

John Scalzi is a former president of SFWA. He enjoys pie.

Ken Schneyer and **Janice Okoomian** have been giving their annual Prancing Pony Party for over five years. A Nebula nominee and Sturgeon Award finalist, Ken's first collection, *The Law & The Heart*, was released in 2014. See writertopia.com/profiles/KennethSchneyer for more.

Lawrence M. Schoen is a Campbell, Hugo, and Nebula Award nominated author, a small press publisher, research psychologist, hypnotherapist, and one of Earth's preeminent authorities on the Klingon language. His recipe here actually comes from his wife, Valerie. They live outside of Philadelphia, PA.

Nisi Shawl is co-author of *Writing the Other: A Practical Approach*, a founder of the Carl Brandon Society, and a longtime member of Clarion West's Board of Directors. Her 2008 story collection *Filter House* won the Tiptree Award. She edits book reviews for *Cascadia Subduction Zone*. Her Belgian Congo steampunk novel *Everfair* is due out spring 2016.

Hugo and Nebula Award-winning **Charles Sheffield** was an English-born mathematician, physicist, and science fiction writer. A longtime SFWA member, he served as its president from 1984-1986.

Fraser Sherman writes historical fantasy in periods including post-revolutionary Boston, 1600s France and Victorian England. He's also the author of three film reference books, most recently *Screen Enemies of the American Way*. He lives with his amazing wife in North Carolina.

Hugo nominee **Steven H Silver** has published a handful of short stories, edited books for DAW and NESFA Press, and was the publisher and editor of ISFiC Press for eight years.

Rosemary Claire Smith (rosemaryclairesmith.com) draws on her background as a trowel-wielding archaeologist and reformed lawyer to write stories appearing in *Analog*, *Fantastic Stories*, *Bastion*, and elsewhere. Her fiction showcases her interests in dinosaurs, folklore, genetic engineering, aliens, abstract photography, foil fencing, and astronomy.

Cat Sparks (catsparks.net) was born in Sydney, Australia. Before settling down to do a PhD in YA climate change fiction, she worked as a graphic designer, photographer, and media monitor amongst other things. She's currently fiction editor of *Cosmos Magazine*.

Bud Sparhawk has published two novels, *Vixen* and *Distant Seas*, and two collections: *Sam Boone: Front to Back* and *Dancing with Dragons*. Short stories have appeared in *Analog*, *Asimov's*, and several anthologies. Website: budsparhawk.blogspot.com.

Nancy Springer has passed the 50-book milestone, having written that many novels for adults, young adults, and children. In 2007 she moved to an isolated area of the Florida panhandle, where the birdwatching is spectacular and where, when fishing, she occasionally catches an alligator.

Jennifer Stevenson (jenniferstevenson.com) lives in the Chicago area with her husband and two unmanageable kittens, She commits excesses with bacon, roasted whole pigs, chocolate, blender drinks, and sexy fantasy novels.

Bonnie Jo Stufflebeam's fiction has appeared in magazines such as *Clarkesworld*, *Lightspeed*, *Beneath Ceaseless Skies*, and *Interzone*. She lives in Texas and holds an MFA in Creative Writing from the University of Southern Maine's Stonecoast program. She curates the annual Art & Words Show in Fort Worth. Website: bonniejostufflebeam.com.

David Lee Summers (davidleesummers.com) is the author of eight novels and numerous short stories. His most recent novel is western steampunk adventure *Lightning Wolves*. When he's not writing, David operates telescopes at Kitt Peak National Observatory.

James L. Sutter is a co-creator of the *Pathfinder Roleplaying Game* and the managing editor for Paizo Publishing. He's the author of novels *Death's Heretic* and *The Redemption Engine*, plus numerous short stories and game products. Online: jameslsutter.com and @jameslsutter.

Michael Swanwick writes science fiction and fantasy stories and novels, as well as the occasional nonfiction essay or book.

Mary Vigliante Szydlowski began her professional writing career in 1977 when her first feature story appeared in the *South Middlesex Sunday News*. She's the author of six adult novels and two children's books as well as numerous short stories, magazine articles, and poems.

Lynne and **Michael Thomas** are publishers/editors-in-chief of *Uncanny Magazine*. Lynne was the editor of *Apex Magazine* with Michael Damian Thomas as her managing editor. Lynne co-edited the Hugo Award-winning *Chicks Dig Time Lords*, and Michael co-edited the Hugo-nominated *Queers Dig Time Lords*. Together, they solve mysteries.

Kathy Tyers went gluten-free and low-FODMAP (a diet developed in Australia) in 2011. She has been blogging about the experience and modifying recipes since 2013 at *Comfortable Comfort Foods*, aiming for recipes that her free-eating friends will also enjoy.

Mark L. Van Name is a writer, technologist, and spoken-word performer. He is the author of five novels and many short stories, articles, and essays. He has created and performed four spoken-word shows. He's also a foodie who still loves hot dogs and macaroni and cheese.

Carrie Vaughn (carrievaughn.com) is the author of the *New York Times* bestselling series of novels about a werewolf named Kitty. She's written several other contemporary fantasy and young adult novels, as well as upwards of 80 short stories. An Air Force brat, she survived her nomadic childhood and managed to put down roots in Boulder, CO.

Ursula Vernon is the author and illustrator of the Hugo Award-winning comic *Digger*, as well as the Dragonbreath series for kids. She writes for adults under the name T. Kingfisher. She lives in North Carolina, where she draws honey badgers on all the things.

John Walters is a Clarion West graduate who recently returned to the U.S. after living abroad for 35 years in India, Bangladesh, Italy, and Greece. He writes SF/F, thrillers, mainstream fiction, and memoirs of his wanderings around the world. Website: johnwalterswriter.com.

Brent Weeks was born and raised in Montana. He wrote on bar napkins and lesson plans before landing his dream job years and thousands of pages later. Brent lives in Oregon with his wife, Kristi, and their daughter.

Miriam Weinberg is an editor at Tor/Forge, where she acquires adult and young adult speculative fiction. She can also be found haunting bookstores and museums across New York City, testing recipes in her Brooklyn kitchen, or on Twitter as @MiriamAnneW.

Chuck Wendig is a novelist, screenwriter, and game designer. Novels include *Blackbirds, Atlanta Burns, Zer0es,* and the YA Heartland series. He is co-writer of the short film *Pandemic* and the Emmy-nominated digital narrative *Collapsus.* He is also well known for his profane-yet-practical advice to writers, which he dispenses at his blog, terribleminds.com.

Longtime editor **Toni Weisskopf** is the publisher of Baen Books, established in 1983 by SF/F editor Jim Baen. She is a recipient of the Phoenix Award for Excellence in Science Fiction and the Rebel Award for lifetime achievement in Southern Science Fiction Fandom.

Fran Wilde's first novel, *Updraft,* debuts in 2015. Her short stories appear in publications including *Asimov's, Nature, Tor.com,* and *Beneath Ceaseless Skies.* Her interview series *Cooking the Books*—about the intersection between food and fiction—has appeared at *Strange Horizons, Tor.com,* and on her website, franwilde.wordpress.com.

Sean Williams is a #1 *New York Times* bestselling author of over 40 award-winning novels, one hundred short stories, and the odd poem. He lives in Adelaide, South Australia.

Walter Jon Williams is the author of *Hardwired, Metropolitan,* and *The Fourth Wall.* He's studying for his fifth degree black belt in Kenpo Cookery.

Connie Willis' work has garnered multiple awards, including the Hugo and the Nebula. In 2009, she was inducted into the Science Fiction Hall of Fame and awarded the title of Grand Master by SFWA. And she's a fantastic toastmaster.

Mercedes M. Yardley is a dark fantastic who wears red lipstick and poisonous flowers in her hair. Her latest novel is *Pretty Little Dead Girls.* Website: mercedesyardley.com.

Jane Yolen has published over 350 books and at age 76 is still moving forward. She's won two Nebulas, three Mythopoeic Awards, oodles of children's book awards, six honorary doctorates and is a World Fantasy Grand Master and a SFWA Grand Master. Her NESFA Skylark Award set her good coat on fire.

Kate Yule is a knitter, square dancer, and science fiction fan. She's been active in fandom since 1984, and co-edited the fanzine *Bento* (1989-2013) as well as helping to organize numerous Pacific Northwest conventions. She lives in Portland, OR, with her husband David Levine, and blogs at kateyule.livejournal.com.